MW00437364

ALEXANDRE SAFRAN

Wisdom of the
KABBALAH

ALEXANDRE SAFRAN

Wisdom of the
KABBALAH

FELDHEIM PUBLISHERS Jerusalem / New York

Originally published as
Sagesse de la Kabbale
Editions Stock, Paris, 1986
Published in German as
Die Weisheit der Kabbala
Francke Verlag, Bern und Stuttgart, 1988

Translated from the French by
E.M. Sandle

English edition published 1991
ISBN 0-87306-582-4

Copyright © 1991 by
Alexandre Safran

Philipp Feldheim Inc.
200 Airport Executive Park
Spring Valley, NY 10977

Feldheim Publishers Ltd.
POB 35002 Jerusalem, Israel

Printed in Israel

In blessed memory of
my mother and teacher
the saintly Rabbanit
Nurit Finkel Safran ע"ה

"Wisdom has built her house..."

Mishlei 9:1

Foreword

Wisdom of the Kabbalah is the title of this volume.

Readers will, I hope, acknowledge that, even from passages that necessarily deal with abstract, theosophical or ontological themes. illuminating beams of Wisdom, of ethics, can shine out. At the source of this Wisdom is a Revelation, which Tradition interprets and explores.

I would like to thank Rabbi Israel Cohen who edited the English manuscript with remarkable erudition and Ms. Ruth Bar-Ilan who prepared the final manuscript for publication.

I am happy to see this book, after the preceding one, coming out at Feldheim Publishers, a respected address for the dissemination of Torah.

Alexandre Safran

From the same author:

La Cabale. Paris: Payot, 1960, 1972, 1983, 1988.
    Die Kabbala. Bern und Munchen: Francke Verlag, 1966.
    The Kabbalah. New York and Jerusalem: Feldheim Publishers, 1975, 1977.
    La Cabala. Barcelona: Ediciones Martinez Roca, 1976.
    La Kabala. Roma: Carucci Editore, 1981.

Israel dans le Temps et dans l'Espace: Thèmes Fondamentaux de la
    Spiritualité juive. Paris: Payot, 1980.
    Israel in Zeit und Raum, Grundmotive des judischen Seins. Bern und
        Munchen: Francke Verlag, 1984.
    Israel in Time and Space: Basic Themes in Jewish Spiritual Thought.
        New York and Jerusalem: Feldheim Publishers, 1987.

Sagesse de la Kabbale. Paris: Editions Stock, Vol. I, 1986.

Sagesse de la Kabbale. Paris: Editions Stock, Vol. II, 1987.
    Die Weisheit der Kabbala. Bern und Stuttgart: Francke Verlag, 1988.

Resisting the Storm: Memoirs. Jerusalem: Yad Vashem, 1987.
    Un tison arraché aux flammes: Mémoires. Paris: Editions Stock, 1989.
    El Mul P'nei Hasa'ara: Zikhronot. Jerusalem: Yad Vashem, 1990.

Contents

INTRODUCTION

An Outline of the Doctrine and the History of the Kabbalah

Existence forms a unified whole within which the visible and the invisible merge and become one.
God gives man the gift of grace so that he can be profoundly aware of, and sense, the divine life-giving presence.

The Kabbalah is a doctrine of unity. Reality is a whole in which the visible and the invisible, the material and the spiritual, mingle and unite. This dynamic intermingling is the sign that reality is alive. Its life has its origin in the "Life of Life"; it derives from the "Cause of Causes"; it draws its strength from the "Root of Roots," which nourishes the whole tree of life. The "Life of Life," the "Cause of Causes," the "Root of Roots" is the Creator Himself. He is the Master, the Director of His creation, of life. He cannot be comprehended but is always intrinsically present in everything that lives.

In the midst of His creatures, God has placed one being, man, who in himself is no more than all the other beings He has created; like them, he is "nothing" in relation to Him; he is only "dust and ashes," as Abraham said of himself (Gen. 18:27) before his "creator whom he knew," his "God whom he made known." However, to man, God gives the boon of being able to become profoundly conscious of His life-giving Presence and to think of Him even though he cannot perceive Him. He gives man the faculty of consciously being aware of Him through His acts, so as to serve Him consciously through his own actions.

Invested with a unique mission by Him who is One, Unique, man strives to embrace with his spirit this total union of both spiritual and material reality, therein to discover visible evidence of His Presence. It is in the Torah and the universe that His Presence and His manifestations are most clearly to be perceived. The Torah (the divine teaching concentrated in the Hebrew Bible) expresses the purpose that the Creator had in creating the world, and the world represents His handiwork.

> God grants man the privilege of serving Him, because when he serves God, he acquires the ability to see himself in God's light.

Man is searching for Him, the Absolute. However, he cannot grasp Him in His *Ayin*, His "Unsubstantiality," in His *Ein-Sof*, His "Infinite." Against every attempt to demarcate Him, God sets a "No"; He is "Indefinable." The very terms *Ayin* and *Ein-Sof* are inadequate for defining Him. "It is impossible to define by a name or a word That which we cannot grasp," says the Kabbalah. He is He, without a name. But through the *Ma'aseh Bereshit*, the "Primal Works," which He formed as Creator of the world, and through the *Ma'aseh Merkavah*, the "Description of the Divine Chariot," which He communicates to the world, of which He is the Master, there are revealed Names — His Names — that are One with Him. He has "created the world" and "granted it the Torah" "to do good to His creatures." To enable man, chosen out of all creation to be His communicant, to address Him, God permits him to call Him by the Names which He "reveals" to him, by His Names, through which He "makes Himself known."

In forming the *Ma'aseh Bereshit* and the *Ma'aseh Merkavah*, God was thinking particularly of man. Through the *Ma'aseh Bereshit* He placed man in overall charge of the world so that he might take care of it, reveal His Presence within it and lead mankind back to Him, the Source. Through the *Ma'aseh Merkavah*, He offers man the opportunity to associate with Him in unfolding History in Time, linking it to meta-History and placing it within Eternity.

The one God thus offers man a dual way of approaching Him — by way of the *Ma'aseh Bereshit* and by way of the *Ma'aseh Merkavah*. If man takes this dual way, he will be able to "serve" Him, that is, "act" to reveal Him in *this* world. But does God need man's "service," "work," and homage? Indeed, "If thou art righteous, what givest thou Him?" (Job 35:7). Nevertheless, God grants man the privilege of serving Him, for it is in serving Him that man becomes capable of seeing Him and seeing himself in God's light; of acting for His glory and judging his own deeds by His light. God will thus honour and overwhelm man with His acts of kindness, not indeed as giving "alms," but as a reward earned by his own labour. It is from this angle that the Kabbalah interprets the verse of the Book of Isaiah (43:7), in which the prophet transmits to us these words of God: "Every one that is called by My name: whom I have created *for My glory*; I have formed him; yea, I have made him."

> There is an interaction between the world and
> the Torah.
> The world must execute "in deeds" what the
> Torah — God's plan for creation — lays down for
> it.

In revelation, and so too in benevolence, the initiative has come from God: the Creator, the Master, reveals Himself throughout the world; the Lawgiver, the King, reveals Himself through the Torah. Between the world and the Torah there is an interaction; the world must crystallize "in deeds" that which the Torah, the Plan of its creation, ordains for it. The first revelation took place "in the beginning" of the world's existence; it is renewed "daily" in the sight of man. The second revelation took place at the time of the "promulgation of the Torah," contained in the Decalogue, on Mount Sinai, in the desert, a place not belonging to any people. This second revelation was to Israel as the intermediary of mankind. The "echo" of this revelation reverberates "daily from Mount Horeb," from Mount Sinai.

> In order for the Torah to open itself up to a Jew,
> he must first observe its *mitzvot.*

The *Ma'aseh Bereshit* and *Ma'aseh Merkavah*, the "Primal Works" and the "Description of the Divine Chariot," are the two axis of the Kabbalah, of Jewish mysticism. All Jewish mystical thought gravitates around them; it unfolds from the Book of Genesis (which contains the *Ma'aseh Bereshit*), continuing through the Books of the prophets Isaiah and Ezekiel (containing the *Ma'aseh Merkavah*), to the Talmud (in particular the H̲aggigah Tractate), and thence in the Kabbalah, down to our own time.

These two foundations of Jewish mysticism are written in the Torah. It is therefore the Torah, in which these foundations of Jewish mysticism appear, that the Sages were to elaborate in universal terms. The mystics would attempt to penetrate to its "very core," there to discover the essence of things.

The Torah and its commentaries become the subject of profound research by all those who "occupy themselves therein," who study it, who consecrate themselves to it. However, in order that the Torah may open up to them, they must first scrupulously observe its *mitzvot,* its "religious commandments." In studying it they must "*count* its letters"; in observing the rules it ordains they must "*count* its mitzvot." An *arithmetical* precision is required of them: precision in the "calculation" of the numerical values represented by the letters and words; precision in the "calculation" of the mitzvot, in the "calculation" of their relation to man — body and soul, and to time — hours, days, weeks, months, and years.

> **The Torah is a revelation of the Word of God. The written Torah is preceded by an oral Torah that heralds the former; but it is also followed by an oral Torah that explains the written Torah. Accordingly, the Torah is a *kabbalah,* a Torah "received" and "transmitted."**

As a Person-to-person revelation, the Torah through its Author in Person addressed itself to Man: to Israel as a community, to the Israelite as an individual. It is thus a revelation through the Word of God, the instrument of spiritual communication between two individuals.

The *written* Torah, as holy *Scripture,* is in origin a revelation of the Word of God (cf. Ex. 20:1), an oral revelation (though we cannot limit the scope of the attributive *oral*). That is why the Torah revealed by God to Moses on Mount Sinai, which Moses "*received* and *transmitted* to Joshua....," is looked upon by the Sages as a *kabbalah,* a "receiving."

The *written* Torah was preceded by an *oral* Torah that

heralded and prefigured it, but it is also followed by an *oral* Torah that completes and explains it and sets out, in a detailed manner, the methods by which its principles and ordinances are to be applied. From within the written Torah, the Sages discovered precise indications concerning Jewish daily life; they unveiled them, "revealed" them, thanks to the illumination of their reason by the Holy Spirit; thus they developed the oral Torah. The two Torot, written and oral, meet again in their original unity; they form a single Torah: the Torah.

So the Torah is a *kabbalah*, a Torah "received" and "transmitted." *Kabbalah* is *Tradition*, for it derives from a divine revelation, unique and paramount, "received" by man and "transmitted" by him *orally*, "man to man": "*kabbalah ish mi-pi ish, ad le-Moshe mi-pi ha-Gevurah.*" This transmission takes place "by word of mouth from man to man in an unbroken sequence from Moses, who received it from the *mouth* of the Almighty." This is how the RaMBaM, Maimonides (1135-1204), the master codifier of religious law, defined the *Kabbalah*, which he regarded above all as a *Torah she-be-al-peh*, an oral Torah.*

> *Kabbalah* is Transmission.
> Even in written form it retains its eminently oral, living character because it was created for life, for the development and fulfilment of life according to the "Word of God."
> Consequently, "the Word of God is *Halakhah*," it is Law.

The Kabbalah is thus both divine revelation and human acceptance and transmission; it is Tradition. Even when written, it retains its eminently *oral* character; it is alive because it is made

---

* Cf. Alexandre Safran, *The Kabbalah*, Feldheim Publishers, New York/ Jerusalem, 1977, pp.33-65.

for *life,* for the development and fulfilment of life according to the "Word of God." Consequently, "the Word of God is *Halakhah"*: it is Law. That is why the term *kabbalah* in halakhic literature has an essentially juridical meaning. It has this sense not only when it concerns religious ordinances of a juridical nature, which are for the most part contained in the Pentateuch, but also when it relates to the inspired words of the prophets and the sober historical accounts of the hagiographers. It is precisely when the Kabbalah refers to these two nonjuridical sources that it is designated *Divrei Kabbalah,* "Words of the Kabbalah." This designation is an interpretation of the intrinsic unity of the TaNaKH, the written Torah, in which Law, Poetry, and Narrative are intertwined; it equally reveals all the unity of the oral Torah in which, especially in the Talmud, are intertwined the *Halakhah,* the "Law," and the *Aggadah,* "Poetry and Narrative." (The *Aggadah* is a favourite source of inspiration for the kabbalists, who nevertheless also reveal the mystical content of the *Halakhah.*)

The oral Torah is imparted mainly in the Talmud. This teaching (beginning with, and based upon, the *Mishnah,* the "lesson") was composed over several centuries, from the 2nd to the 6th century C.E.

> In the 13th century, the term *kabbalah* acquired a special mystical connotation without, however, losing its halakhic significance.
> The Kabbalah is profoundly related to the Halakhah, which it illuminates from within.

The three master works of Judaism are, in order of importance, the Bible, followed by the Talmud, and then the *Sefer ha-Zohar,* the "Book of Splendour," which comprises the fundamental teachings of Jewish mysticism. This latter magnum opus is a key work presenting the mystical doctrine of Rabbi Simeon bar Yoḥai, the *tanna* who lived in Galilee during the 2nd century.

It was disseminated in Spain during the 13th century.

It was in the 13th century that the term *kabbalah* began to have a particular connotation with mysticism, without, however, losing its halakhic import. On the contrary, the Kabbalah is closely linked with the Halakhah, which it illuminates "from within."

Since that time, the term *kabbalah* has been used in the current Hebrew language to mean Jewish mysticism.

However, the Kabbalah continues to be an oral Tradition. The kabbalists, the Sages of the Truth (that is, those who wish to know the Truth), those who know the hidden wisdom (that is, those who wish to know it), pass on their teaching *orally* to their friends and colleagues, and to those disciples who are worthy of it. Nevertheless, these Sages, who transmit their teaching orally to their companions and even give them practical counselling on how to "cleave to God" and "serve Him," can hardly impart to them their own mystical experiences, since such experiences occur in the depths of a rare human being and cannot be communicated.

"The *Kabbalah* is transmitted by the *mekubbal* (i.e., the kabbalist, who having already received the Kabbalah, is thoroughly steeped in it) to the *mekabbel* (the recipient), who grasps it (also) by his own intelligence." Thus, the RaMBaN, Nachmanides (13th century) defined the conditions for the "transmission" of the Kabbalah from master to disciple. Only those who live a pure and holy life can transmit the Kabbalah, and only those who have attained great "spiritual" maturity can receive it.* Down the centuries, these restrictions have

---

* The Sages state that it is "only at the age of 40 that the disciple is fit to understand properly the thought of his master," for "forty years is the age of wisdom." That is why, in general, the kabbalists prefer to "transmit" their teaching to disciples who are at least forty years old. In their opinion, at that age the human "soul" becomes spiritually mature. The Hebrew word *neshamah*, "soul," confirms this; the letters which compose it also make up the words *mem shanah*, "forty years."

been respected when the Kabbalah has been taught and practised. They are still observed today, even though certain masters of the Kabbalah, such as Rav Kook (20th century) and Rav Ashlag (20th century) in the Holy Land, encourage kabbalists to make the "mysteries of the Torah" known to those who wish to know them, although indeed, on condition that they are *conscious* withal of the religious and moral duties that are incumbent upon them when they enter into the "paradise" of the Kabbalah.

> **Jewish mystical thought has never failed to take account of Jewish philosophical thought.**
> **The development of Jewish religious, philosophical thinking is just as much subject to the Halakhah, the Law, as is Jewish mystical thinking.**

Historically and geographically, the Kabbalah movement is rich and varied. It has appeared at different periods and in different countries. Nevertheless, it exhibits a perfect and impressive continuity not only in its external features, but above all, through its inward unity. Indeed, it is identified with the very continuity of Jewish history, with the very unity of Judaism. Both are alive because they constantly renew themselves, building on an immutable foundation.

Jewish mystical thought has never ignored Jewish philosophical thought. Quite the contrary, it has made use of it, as is the case specifically with the rationalist thinking of Maimonides. At times the fundamental constituents of mystical thought were overlaid with speculative philosophical elements. These two thought forms have influenced each other at various times. However, Jewish mystical thought has a more permanent, and above all a more purely Jewish, character than Jewish philosophical thinking. From the origins of Judaism to our own times, Jewish mysticism has crossed the vast plain of Jewish history like a mighty river, nourishing it with its fresh waters and penetrating the deep regions of the Jewish soul, while at the same time setting it ablaze with its fire. Thus, Jewish mysticism, even as the Torah, acts in every respect "like water and fire."

Kabbalistic thought evolved — in the religious, spiritual, and intellectual fields — by a small elite. Nevertheless, the Kabbalah exerts a psychological, moral, and practical influence over the whole of Jewish existence and it does so directly and indirectly, tangibly and daily; thus, it gives substantial nourishment to Jewish faith and strongly fashions the Jewish soul. It confirms the consciousness of the Jew, helps him to assert his identity, prepares him to meet the vicissitudes of his existence and enables him to go even so far as sacrificing his life to protect, and live according to, the tenets of his faith, "sanctifying the Name of God."

Jewish philosophical, rationalist religious thinking was also developed by a small elite. At the same time, its influence only reaches that section of the Jewish people which has access to the garden of philosophical thought. In addition, neither in time nor in space is Jewish philosophical thought as extensive as Jewish mystical thought. The latter is drawn from Jewish sources, whereas the former uses elements foreign to Judaism to enrich its works. It seeks to emphasize the values of Judaism for the benefit of those Jews who desire a philosophical justification for these values, intending to defend them against non-Jews who attack Judaism.

However, notwithstanding their universal scope, both Jewish religious philosophical thinking and Jewish mystical thinking develop under the authority of the Halakhah — the Law, the Torah. It is the Law that animates both, giving harmonious life to the Jew as an individual and providing the Jewish people with the assurance of an especial perpetuation. Generally speaking, Jewish religious rationalist philosophy seeks to give Jews a closer comprehension of the Law; and yet, being human, they cannot attain a complete comprehension of the Law through their own reasoning. The real *raison d'être* of the Law is above every utilitarian notion. In contrast, the Kabbalah does reach the goal it pursues; thanks to it, Jews can fully live out the Law, in a selfless manner. Philosophical thought makes possible a sincere, sound application of the Law; the Kabbalah seeks to inspire observing Jews with a resoluteness and comprehension that go beyond all rational justification. However, for both schools of thought, the Law is not a rigid, detached reality, and the proof is in the very manner in which it addresses the Jews. The Law is a *mitzvah*, a "commandment" of God, of that personal God who communicates with man. This divine mitzvah transcends man's reason. The Kabbalah endeavours to penetrate its meaning by sounding the depths of its spirit; far from disregarding the rationale of the Law, it rather seeks to reach its supra-rational dimensions.

On the other hand, though religious rationalist philosophy has certainly and vastly enriched the Jewish spiritual heritage, it is by no means indispensable to it. In fact, having its source in the divine Revelation expressed in the Torah and its mitzvot, Judaism hardly needs support from philosophy. In essence, Judaism is not a theology but a *torah*, a "teaching," *Torat Hayyim*, a "Torah of Life," which Tradition bears through the ages.

Jewish philosophy endeavours to direct the course of the mighty floodtide of Jewish thought, albeit without genuine success. The Kabbalah succeeds in fertilizing this vast field and strengthening the Jew's faith, for it demonstrates that faith, without being in conflict with reason, transcends reason. The Kabbalah links man intimately with his God; holding him all the while in a continual creative tension, it binds the Jew firmly to his origin, to the Torah, so that he may understand it and live up to its teachings.

By the relationship it hopes to establish between man and God, religion is of a mystical nature. Mysticism, which is directed toward establishing an intimate affinity between man and God, is thus the heart of religion: it is mysticism that breathes life into religion.

> **The Kabbalah has never ceased to strive for the ideal of a profound communion between God and mankind.**
> **This ideal is expressed by the term *Devekut*.**
> **This noun defines how human beings seek an ever-closer relationship with God.**
> **The experience of *Devekut* leads human beings to ethical action.**

"Throughout its history — through the visions of the prophets of Israel, the reflections of the Sages of Israel, and the doctrines of the masters of the kabbalist schools — Jewish mysticism has not ceased to pursue the ideal of a deep, personal communion between God and man. This ideal, which is at the heart of Jewish mysticism, is expressed by the word *Devekut*. This noun has its root in the verb *davok*, which means "to bind oneself to," "to unite oneself with."

Around this central ideal of *Devekut* are ranged all the other fundamental ideas that the Kabbalah seeks to fathom: God and the Creation; Man and the Universe; the Torah and Israel; Sin and Repentance; Exile and Redemption.

Through *Devekut* man reaches a clearer vision and a deeper, though yet only partial, comprehension of these essential ideas.

The Creator himself has engraved in man's nature the desire for *Devekut*. Man becomes conscious of it when he contemplates the "image of God" engraved within him and arouses the divine spark, "portion of God above" (Job 31:2), which is inherent in his "divine soul."

In this moment of awakened consciousness, of "enlightenment," man finds himself in quest of God; he aspires to come close to Him, to reach Him.... At the same time, he finds that God too is seeking him, is coming towards him; he feels that his "desire" is real, for the "Will" of God responds to it. Man's aspirations here below evoke the "Will on high."

God and man meet. Man feels himself to be face to face with God; he experiences the "Presence of God"; "he sees the face of the *Shekhinah*," if one dare so express it.

But *Devekut* is not confined to this meeting.

The Hebrew Bible, the Talmud, the Midrashim, and the different schools of Kabbalah agree in their overall teaching that *Devekut* does not entail the dematerialization of man, that is to say, the dissolution of the human soul in God. So it is not what non-Jewish mysticism terms the *unio mystica*, but rather a sign of man's coming to a standstill before God — a status caused by the very great closeness of the Divinity.

Moreover, when a man has entered into *Devekut*, he must not remain in this state of suspension; he must distance himself from his personal, immanent God, who is also the transcendent God, and this calls for action, especially an ethically inspired action. Thus, the experience of *Devekut* impels man to act, to forge ahead in the world, carrying God within himself, within his soul. In fact, it is by *seeking within* himself, by *descending* into the very depths of his being, that man recognizes the divine nature of his soul, coming face to face with the Divinity within himself; it is then that he fully experiences the "illuminated moment" of *Devekut*.

At each of these "moments," man rises and then turns again towards this world, so as to *"enlighten"* his fellowmen. He cannot share with them his experience of *Devekut*, but he can and will communicate the teaching he has received in the course of this experience and which concerns his relations with his fellowmen, with the world.

The Hebrew Bible, the Talmud, and the Kabbalah are unanimous in attributing this finality to *Devekut*.

In the Book of Deuteronomy (11:22) we read: "For if you shall diligently keep all these commandments which I command you, to do them, to *love* the Lord your God, to *walk* in all his ways and to *cleave* unto Him...." Therefore Man must continuously strive for an ever-new *Devekut*, leading on to ever-higher moral, religious behaviour: perseverance in the observance of the mitzvot is the sign of an *unfailing love* for God.

The Sages make the following comment on this verse from Deuteronomy: "The Torah says, 'to *cleave* to Him.' Is it possible to cleave to the *Shekhinah*? Is it not written (Deut. 4:24; 9:3) 'God is a consuming fire'? Yet man can cleave to Him in 'following all His ways.' He is gracious, be thou gracious; He is beneficent, be thou beneficent."

Man must therefore "follow all His ways." Thus it is written: "You shall follow the Lord your God," "You shall walk after the Lord your God" (Deut. 13:5), which means to say, according to the Talmud, "You shall emulate His ways and His attributes of goodness"; as the Zohar comments, "You shall walk in the ways of the Holy One, blessed be He."

King David himself exclaimed in his Psalms (63:9): "My soul *clings* to Thee to follow Thee" so that its love for God may continue and grow.

That is the *Devekut*, the embodiment of the supreme love of man for his God.

> **As a result of the *Devekut*, man can go beyond the limitation of being a "creature who receives." Ennobling this condition, man exploits it in order the better to give.**

Devekut, man's cleaving to God, his search of God in an attempt to be united with Him, is compared to the "cleaving" of man to his wife, leading to their union.* In its purity, loyalty, and "holiness," his conjugal devotion metaphorically mirrors the *Devekut* that binds man to God. In turn, man and wife should even draw inspiration from this *Devekut* as a basis for their relationship. Indeed, in the Book of Genesis (2:24) it is said: "a man...shall cleave — *ve-davak* — unto his wife, and they shall become one flesh." The "moment" of their union as "one flesh" blossoms into the loving kindness that each demonstrates for the other. Yet both partners, enriched by their union, keep and respect their respective identities.

Nonetheless, it is patently clear that the *Devekut* that exists between man and his God is of quite another kind.

The *ve-davak* that binds a man to his wife is a physical union which has a moral, spiritual objective and takes *place* in the confines of space.

The *Devekut* between man and God, between the human soul and the "Soul of Souls," has no location, for it is a *Devekut* that binds man, who is within the world, to God, who is "the Place of the world, though the world is not His place." The *Devekut* that binds the spirit to the Spirit cannot be located in a confined space. Even when man comes near to God and God comes towards him, man remains the prisoner of his human status whilst God remains God! Each retains his own, disparate identity.

By *Devekut* man gives his Creator a *nahat ru'ah,* a "spiritual joy," and God, as it were, enriches and invigorates man's soul. His soul is now able to induce the body that it inhabits to act — that is to say, to emulate the acts of God, in particular those that testify to His beneficence. The entire Jewish religious literature presents the *Imitatio Dei* as emulation of His works

---

* There is another example of this bond between man and God, namely, the bond between *Keneset Yisrael,* the "Community of Israel," and the *Shekhinah,* the "Divine Presence," which in turn seeks to identify itself with *Keneset Yisrael.*

of goodness alone (and not of justice!). Such emulation makes man a creature *akin to* his Creator, one who *gives* without any need to *receive*. Through the *Devekut*, man goes beyond his status of "a creature who receives" without wholly freeing himself from it. Ennobling his status, he exploits it the better to be able *to give*. He becomes a being that *gives*, doing good to others unselfishly, "in His Name," "for the Name of Heaven," as a mitzvah of the Torah.

"The human soul is a *He'arah*," writes Rav Ashlag, "an illumination coming from the Divine Presence. God has clothed this illumination with the craving to *receive* and to rejoice in what it receives; thus, He has made the soul a *separate* being. At the same time, He inscribed in it the yearning to return to its Divine Essence. To enable it to return to its origin of beneficence, God has granted man the Torah and the mitzvot, through whose observance the soul will crave to *give*, to do good to others."*

Devekut thus teaches man to *give*; when the spirit of man is "dedicated" to the Divine Spirit, he will act in the spirit of God.

Spanning the development of Jewish mystical thought, we distinguish five distinct eras.

In the course of this study, we will return to this important question of *Devekut*: it is the pivotal point, the magnetic pole,

---

* It should be emphasized that — according to Rabbi Moses Cordovero (1522-1570), Rabbi Shneur Zalman of Lyady (1745-1813), and Rabbi Hayyim of Volozhin (1749-1821), who base their thinking on Maimonides — this *"separation"* from the Being is real only from our point of view. From God's "side," *everything* is divine. "Everything is filled with the Essence of His Unity alone." "He is everything, but not everything is God." Being One, He alone Is. In reality nothing is separate from Him, for nothing can exist apart from Him; so nothing has its own existence. Only He alone exists. (footnote continued on next page)

for all kabbalistic thought. For every student of the Kabbalah it is the summit he is striving to reach, the goal of his mystical experience. On this essential point, the masters of the Kabbalah are unanimous. However, in the method they use to build the *ensemble* of their mystical thinking, and in the style they present it to us, here they differ from each other. Method and style vary from one period to another, from one region to another, from one school to another. Despite this, Jewish mystical thought, having its roots in the Torah itself, has unfolded in a coherent fashion throughout the two millenia, from the destruction of the Second Temple to our own day.

Spanning this era of the development of Jewish mystical thought, we can distinguish five periods. The first period, embracing the first millenium, is marked by ecstatic mysticism, with its centre in the Near and Middle East. The second period, spanning the 12th and 13th centuries and extending into the 16th century, is marked by Hasidic mysticism, pietistic and ascetic, with its centre in Germany. The third period, from the 13th through the 15th century, is marked by meditative mysticism and by the "Zohar" mysticism, with its centre in Spain. The fourth period, covering the 16th and 17th centuries and extending into the eighteenth, is marked by messianic mysticism, with its centre in the Holy Land. The

---

"Know therefore this day and consider it within thy heart that the Lord He is God in heaven above, and upon the earth beneath: there is no other" (Deut. 4:39). The Shelah ha-Kadosh (1565-1690) makes the following comment on the last part of this verse: " *'there is no other'* does not mean (only) that there is no other God but He: this has already appeared simply and clearly in the verse, 'The Lord (is) our God; the Lord is One' (Deut. 6:4). Above all, *'there is no other'* means that nothing exists but His Existence, for He, blessed be He, creates everything, gives life to everything, and He is the Existence of everything that exists." The dialectic of separation or nonseparation from the Divinity leads us to think that as far as we humans are concerned, divine transcendence and immanence unite to give us a certain liberty of action, the exercise of our free will.

fifth period, covering the 18th, 19th, and 20th centuries, is marked by Hasidic mysticism that is personalistic and fellowship-based, having its centre in Eastern Europe. (After the destruction of Jewish life in Eastern Europe by the Nazis, its centre moved to Israel and the United States.)

The great schools of mysticism that spread the radiance of the Kabbalah throughout the world included the School of Provence in the 12th century, the School of Gerona in Spain in the 13th century, and the School of Safed in the Holy Land in the 16th century.

The great luminaries that lit up the sky of the Kabbalah were, in particular, Rabbi Isaac the Blind and Rabbi Moses ben Nahman, Nachmanides, both in the 13th century; Rabbi Isaac Luria, the Ari ha-Kadosh, in the 16th century, and Rabbi Israel Ba'al Shem Tov in the 18th century.

> **The Mysticism of the *Merkavah*, of the "Chariot." *Sefer Yezirah*, the "Book of Creation." The Mystical Interpretation of the Letters of the Hebrew Alphabet.**
> **The Ten *Sefirot*.**

The first period is known as that of the "mystics of the *Merkavah*," and is a development of Ezekiel's vision of the Chariot (Chap. 1) and his description of the heavenly Throne. This school of mysticism gives a moral interpretation of the vision.

Through the ascension of their souls in ecstasy, the *Merkavah* mystics in the Holy Land and Babylon strove to reach the *Heikhalot*, the "Palaces," the heavenly dwellings described in the Books of the *Heikhalot*, in the Talmud itself. Their desire was to sing their hymns of *Kavod*, of the "Glory" of God, the King, in those "palaces."

These same mystics, inspired by the *Ma'aseh Merkavah*, the "Description of the Divine Chariot," gave careful study to the

Ma'aseh Bereshit, the "Primal Works." They studied an important cosmological theory contained in the *Sefer Yezirah*, the "Book of Creation."

This brief, very old, kabbalistic text, written in Hebrew and known since the 3rd century, presents a mystical interpretation of the letters of the Hebrew alphabet: a true "science of the Holy Language." These letters are looked upon not only as the bearers of the world's creative powers, but also as the revealed forces of the Creator. It was by contemplating the Hebrew letters that the patriarch Abraham (to whom the *Sefer Yezirah* is attributed) penetrated the meaning of Divine Revelation.

The Hebrew letters and, *ipso facto*, their numerical values had an essential function in the creation of the world and they play a normative function in the spiritual and moral life of man here below. Just as the Creation constitutes a linguistic and numerological process, so man must be *attentive* to the words he pronounces, the letters he reads, and the numbers he *counts*. Letters and numbers make up the *sefer*, the "Book" on the life of the universe; letters and numbers form the *sippur*, the "recital" of the life of man.

Sefer Yezirah begins with the words, "By thirty-two ways of the mysterious wisdom God created His world." These "thirty-two ways" embrace the ten *Sefirot* and the twenty-two letters of the Hebrew alphabet. The term *Sefirot* comes from the Hebrew verb *safor*, which means "to count"; the number *ten* represents, according to the Sages of the Talmud and the Zohar, the wholeness of every "holy thing."

The ten *Sefirot* are the channels through which flows the creative emanation that comes from the *Ein-Sof*, the Infinite. They control the ethereal, spiritual elements, which they set in motion and bring into contact with one another; these elements, becoming condensed, are transformed into the material elements that constitute the universe.

The ten *Sefirot* also correspond to the moral, divine attributes (which give them their names), which man is called upon to emulate in his everyday religious and moral conduct.

The twenty-two letters made up the Torah before the creation of the world, and their permutations served to create the heavens and the earth. One who wishes to meditate upon the creation of the world and its religious and moral destiny is invited to investigate these letters, which form the Torah with all its religious and moral Teachings.

Corresponding to the ten *Sefirot* — to the point of being identified with them — are the "Ten Utterances by which God created the world" so that man should consider His works, and the "Ten Utterances by which God revealed Himself" to man, making known what He expects of him in this world.

Thus, the Creation, a munificent act reflecting the Wisdom and Goodness of God, serves as a standard for man, a creative, wise, and benevolent way of exercising his freedom.

> **Hasidic Mysticism in Germany.**
> **Asceticism.**
> **Mystical Ascension.**
> **Love of God.**

Hasidic mysticism in Germany in the 12th and 13th centuries is represented by Rabbi Judah he-Hasid (d. 1217). His *Sefer Hasidim*, the "Book of the Devout," written for his family, was greeted with veneration by his co-religionists. It occupies a high place in the literature of mysticism, but equally it has a great influence in the world of the Law, due to the halakhic regulations it contains.

This book is also a mirror of its time, for it gives us information about the religious ideas and practices of the German Jewish Hasidim in that era. Their ideal was that of mystical ascension to God. It is accomplished through prayer, in particular through the *kavvanah*, the sincere "devotion" of the one who prays and who humbly "directs" his prayer to God in His Honour. Every word of the traditional prayers, especially those which have their origin in the Hebrew Bible and the Talmud, is pronounced with an intense spiritual concentration, and its numerical value is at the same time present in the mind of the one who prays. The number of words that a prayer contains reveals to us its particular meaning. Thus, for example, Rabbi Eliezer of Worms (1160-1230), author of the *Sefer ha-Roke'ah*, a disciple of Rabbi Yehudah he-Hasid, teaches us that the two Blessings of the Torah, those prayers recited respectively before and after the public reading of the Torah, contain forty words (each has twenty words) to remind us of the forty days that Moses spent on Mount Sinai so that the Torah might be bestowed on Israel (cf. Deut. 9:18).

To be capable and worthy of accomplishing this mystical ascension, the Hasid must "purify" his body by strict asceticism, that is, he must not give way to temptations but hallow "what is permitted him" in his physical and material existence, which means he must sanctify *all* the functions of his physical life, without exception; and if he transgresses a commandment of the Torah, he must submit to a harsh penance in order to "return" purified to his God.

By this mystical ascension, the Hasid attains the love of God. But for this love to be genuine, the Hasid must have opened his heart to his fellowmen, to every creature, to all the elements of creation; he must have drawn near to men irrespective of their religious status; he must have respected them and aided them with an unselfish love.

Therefore, this ascension is not reserved solely for privileged persons, for scholars. The possibility of achieving it is offered to every man.

Mystical ascension leads the Hasid to the Divinity, to the

Shekhinah itself, to the "Presence of God," which "dwells" in us, with us, and around us. It is of course impossible for man to attain God in His Essence, in His Transcendence, to have an intellectual conception of Him through thinking. But it is given to man to be able to experience Him in His Immanence, to feel Him in his soul, to perceive Him in the world, by conforming to His will, that is, by studying His Torah and observing His mitzvot. Only then is man worthy of singing His *Kavod*, His "Glory"; he can "contribute his own *kavod* to God's *Kavod*," to the Shekhinah, in which He clothes Himself so that man may approach Him and prostrate himself before the *Kisse ha-Kavod*, before His "Throne of Glory."

Rabbi Yehudah he-Hasid sang His Glory in a hymn that he composed, called *Shir ha-Kavod*, "Song of Glory," which closes the liturgy on Sabbath and Festivals in numerous synagogues.

Kabbalistic Activity in Southern France.
Mysticism, Halakhah, and Philosophy.
The Homiletic Kabbalistic School of Gerona.
The Meditative Kabbalistic School in Spain.
The Science of the Permutation of Numbers and of Letters.

Parallel to the pietistic kabbalistic movement in Germany, and connected with it, there developed in Provence a remarkable period of kabbalistic activity, the influence of which spread into Spain, in particular into Catalonia.

It was in Provence, in the 12th century, that the Jewish mystics first examined with interest the *Sefer ha-Bahir*, attributed to the *tanna* Rabbi Nehunya ben ha-Kanah. This book, written in Hebrew and Aramaic and related to the literature of the Midrash and Aggadah, takes up the principal themes of the *Sefer Yezirah*. Subsequently, in Spain, the contents of the *Sefer ha-Bahir*, whose importance stems from its antiquity, was even more highly valued.

Both in the South of France and in Catalonia there was fruitful co-operation between the rabbis, the halakhic scholars, and the philosophers on the one hand, and the mystics on the other. Sometimes the Halakhah, philosophy, and the Kabbalah were all represented in one person.

In the South of France, Rabbi Isaac the Blind, in the 13th century, made famous the kabbalistic school near Narbonne. He devoted himself entirely to the Kabbalah.

In Catalonia it was Rabbi Moses ben Nahman, the RaMbaN (1195-1270), who brought fame to the School of Gerona. In his own person he combined vast knowledge of the Kabbalah, the Torah, the Talmud, the Halakhah, homiletics, and ethics.

Representative of the new meditative kabbalistic school founded in Spain in the 13th century is Rabbi Abraham Abulafia (1240-1290). His ambition was to raise the Kabbalah, by his teaching and his mystical experiences, to the rank of prophecy.

To accomplish this, he lived in a state of *devekut* arising from profound contemplation of His Names. Concentrating on them mentally and spiritually in the solitude and silence of the night and purified by an ascetic life, he entered into intimate communion with God. He thus attained moments of ecstasy, in the manner of the masters of the mystical doctrine of the *Merkavah*. During these moments of illumination, he believed himself to be in possession of prophetic gifts.

This kabbalist, who was versed in philosophy, logic, and mathematics, meditated not only on the letters of the Names of God, but also on all the letters of the Torah, which like the former, though to a lesser degree, contain hidden within them the powers at work in the world. Through this meditation, the kabbalist is led to a deepening knowledge of God and a comprehension of the world. Thus, the science of the combination of letters and that of the combination of the numbers corresponding to the letters (the creation of the world was the result of these combinations) allows the kabbalist to grasp the whole of reality, to capture the "music of the cosmos." This music is created by the vibrations of the letters moving or "flying" in space. It is a hymn in honour of God the Creator, who manifests Himself in the Tetragrammaton, in the *Shem HaVaYaH*, in His Name, which is composed of four principal letters.

The numerical value of these Four Letters is twenty-six. According to his own testimony, Rabbi Abraham Abulafia wrote twenty-six kabbalistic works corresponding to the numerical value of the *Shem HaVaYaH*, the Name of God, Creator of the world, and twenty-two "prophetic works," corresponding to the twenty-two letters of the Hebrew alphabet, which God used to create the world.

Sefer ha-Zohar, "The Book of Splendour," is a mystical interpretation of the Torah; it is the most significant work of the Kabbalah.

An event of outstanding importance in the history of the Kabbalah occurred in Spain at the end of the 13th century, producing a deep and decisive effect on the evolution of Jewish mysticism. This was the discovery of *Sefer ha-Zohar*, "The Book of Splendour." According to tradition, the author was the *tanna* Rabbi Simeon bar Yohai, who lived in Galilee in the 2nd century. To Rabbi Moses de Leon (1250-1305) fell the credit of making it known within the Iberian Peninsula.

The Zohar is a *midrash*, a commentary on the Five Books of Moses (which form the Torah in the strict sense of the term), the Song of Songs, and the Book of Ruth. This great work, written in Aramaic with additions in Hebrew, provides a mystical interpretation of the Torah in the widest sense of the word, that is, embracing the whole of the traditions, laws, and religious writings belonging to the Revelation, to the "Torah from Heaven," to the written and the oral Torah. It is this Torah in the widest sense that governs the life of Jews and assures Judaism's perpetuation.

The Zohar is centred on the Torah. Everything proceeds from the Torah and everything leads back to it. Not only is it, in its origin, the work of God: it personifies Him. The Divine Presence is revealed in every letter, in every word, and in every accent of the written Torah. It justifies all the teaching that the Sages derive from it so as to make possible its faithful observance.

The letters, words, and accents of the Hebrew Bible, and particularly of the Pentateuch — *Oraita* — constitute the Names of God. "The Torah is filled with the Names of God." However, "the letters composing the Names of God, in particular those that form the *Shem HaVaYaH*, the Tetragrammaton, encompass all Existence," the whole of Reality. It is with the Torah that God created the world; it is with the Torah that the divine purpose of Creation is revealed. God's Names and His Attributes reveal this purpose. They express His acts, and His moral attributes, which man is called upon to contemplate. We know no Name that can be ascribed to God before the creation of the world, before He revealed Himself and drew near to us. Such as He is in Himself, he is above all thought, all perception, all intelligence: there is no Name suitable for him. We dare to say of Him only one thing: He is *Ein-Sof*, the "Infinite." We cannot even say of Him that He is *Ein-Reshit*, the "Non-Beginning," for "He is without beginning and without end," and the ideas of "beginning" and "end" cannot be applied to Him. We dare to say of God that He is the *In-finite*, for we are placed after the *Be-Reshit*, the "beginning" that He Himself established for us. He established a *reshit*, a "beginning," so that we should become aware of Him, as the Torah says: "*Be-Reshit* (in The Beginning) God created the heavens and the earth."

"Thinking," "wishing" to create, the *Ein-Sof*, the Infinite, leaves — if one may so express it — "His hidden state" of *Menuhah*, of "Rest," and creates without expecting anything for Himself in return, for He Himself lacks nothing. He creates for "others," whom he causes to leave Him and whom He summons to return to Him. When He creates, it is "to do good to those who will be called His creatures," and particularly to man. He desires man to draw near Him, to meet Him, to know Him, to "understand His love for him," and to be able to "glorify Him." God creates, He acts, He "shows Himself." His creative power, "emanating" from Him, will first form the *Adam Kadmon*, the "Original Man." Man will become the symbol of the Universe; he will be the Creator's interlocutor.

The Creator pours the light of His creative, purely spiritual, power into vessels created to receive it. He concentrates the light into channels to conduct it down to Earth; the nearer this light comes to the world, reducing its initial brilliance, the more the world assumes a material form. These vessels, which bring the original light, are called the *Sefirot*; they are as luminous as *sappir*, they shine like the "sapphire."

Within the *Sefirot* throb the motive powers that the Creator has given His work. God's actions, deriving from the original, unique act of creation, have their own order of rank in the metamorphosis from the immaterial to the material.

The *Sefirot* form a living unity; the breath of God passes over and animates them, collectively and individually; the Spirit of God, leaving the *Ein-Sof*, fills them.

In fact, the *Sefirot* are interlinked; each *Sefirah* is prefigured and virtually contained in the one that precedes it and influences the one that follows it.

The *Sefirot* are ten in number; emanating from the *One*,

who alone is *Unique*, they move into the "unity" of the number *ten*. In messianic times, man is called upon to bring them back, by his meritorious acts, to their original unity, to the *One*. The Jew in particular is charged with carrying out this task of universal, nay cosmic, significance through studying the Torah, the instrument of the world's creation, and by applying its mitzvot, due to both of which the world may enjoy the full richness of life.

The "Ten Sefirot" are the "Ten Utterances with which God created the world." He could have created it with only one "Utterance," but He chose to create it with ten, so that man, made of "flesh and blood," might welcome their light, the brilliance of which was "blinding" at its inception. When it is "subdued" and "cloaked," man can "bear" it, adapt to it and rejoice in it. Spiritually refined by this light, man will now be able to climb the ladder of the *Sefirot*, to reach the first stage of pure spirituality, and so to come close to their Source. He will be "associated with God in His work of creation."

The tenth *Sefirah*, "*Malkhut*," is in direct and continuous contact with man. By this *Sefirah*, man can be linked with God. Through this *Sefirah* the Shekhinah shines, revealing that this last *Sefirah* must become the *Malkhut*, the "Kingship" of God here below. Man must acknowledge the *Malkhut*. He must nurture it so that it may become this earthly kingship, for "there is no king without a people."

The *Malkhut*, the "Kingship" of God, the perfecting of the last *Sefirah* here below, reflects and completes the *Keter*, the royal "Crown" from on high, which adorns the first *Sefirah*. Thus man's mission consists of uniting the *Keter* and the *Malkhut*, the "Crown" and the "Kingship" of God.

It is through study of the Torah and observance of the mitzvot, through prayer and meritorious deeds, that the Jew establishes the *Malkhut*, unites it with the *Keter*, and here below "offers" to God the Crown from on high. It is through all this "labour" of the Jew that *Keneset Yisrael*, the "Community of Israel" on high, the spiritual archetype of the community of Israel here below, is identified with the Shekhinah.

If a Jew transgresses the commandments of the Torah, he commits a *het*, a "sin," he "fails" in his task, which is to bring together the *Malkhut* and the *Keter*; he commits a "fault" in not "directing" his actions as he should, but, instead, deflecting them elsewhere.

Sin "separates" man from God, the creature from his Creator. Having turned away from the one God and renounced "seeking Him," he is "in exile" in the "world of separation," of "division." He can no longer count on anything other than himself and locks himself into his own "exile," into his personal *Galut*. Inevitably, he provokes the *Galut ha-Shekhinah*, the "Exile of the Shekhinah." The Presence of God sought man, desiring his presence, but man turned away.

Adam himself, the First Man, "God's very own handiwork" (formed without the intermediacy of a mother and a father), "separated himself" from his Creator by his Sin. He wished to be his own god; "Adam was an atheist!"

In misusing his body, man corrupts it; and his nature too, though intrinsically good, becomes influenced to the bad. This magnificent work of God, this wonderful instrument He has given man to serve Him, is transformed by man into a source of evil and death. By doing so, man violates the last *Sefirah*.

The Zohar presents several ethical and ontological theses on the nature and function of evil; it is the moral theses which prevail. Without "subjectivizing" or "relativizing" evil, as did the Jewish philosophers of the Middle Ages, the Zohar adopts the ethical, biblical, and talmudic conception according to which, evil is not an autonomous reality but a "messenger" of the Creator.

God, who is Bountiful, who wishes man to be able to choose

and to do good, "sends" him "evil," that is, the "temptation" to act wrongly. Thus tested and provoked by this contradiction of evil, man may make good use of the very great privilege he has received from God: the exercise of liberty.

Man has an *inclination* to commit sin and thus to "separate himself" from God, to provoke a "division" in the world and even, if one dares express it so, a "division" in the Godhead. This "division" would describe the "separation" of the Holy One, blessed be He, from His Shekhinah, which, because of man's decadence, is forced into *Galut*, "Exile," together with him. When man, created free but now temporarily enslaved, regains his liberty, he undertakes a work of reconciliation: with God, with the world, and with himself. He labours to deliver the Shekhinah and himself from Galut. He is thus accomplishing a work of "unification": "unification" in himself and around himself; "unification of the worlds"; and again, if one may so express it, "unification" in the Divinity — "unification of the Holy One, blessed be He, and the Shekhinah."

This work of "unification" leads man to a renewed union with the one God.

Rabbi Isaac Luria, the Ari ha-Kadosh.
The Originality of His Teachings.
The Event of the Creation and Its Eschatological Effects.

The Zohar found its most eminent commentator in the person of Rabbi Isaac Luria (1534-1572), who under the title of Adoneinu Rabbi Isaac (A-R-I) became known as the Ari, the "Lion," and was to be revered down the centuries under the name of Ari ha-Kadosh, the "Sacred Lion." Through the strength of his personality and the originality of his doctrine, he was to exercise a determinative influence on the development of the Kabbalah.

In integrating his doctrine with the kabbalistic Tradition, the Ari ha-Kadosh gave the latter new depth, new enrichment, and a fresh orientation.

The influence of his doctrine on Jewish history was to prove considerable. The authenticity of his teaching lies in its messianic character. Rabbi Isaac Luria was born into an especially grave historical era. At that time, Jews were living in a traumatic state, caused by the expulsion of their co-religionists from Spain in 1492. The contemporaries of the Ari ha-Kadosh were themselves survivors of this disaster. The catastrophe profoundly disturbed the Jewish soul, which though inhabited by faith, was yet tormented with anxiety.

The generation that experienced this disaster needed to find religious explanation for it; they looked to receive comfort and light from their spiritual leaders.

Now, according to the Jewish eschatological conception, catastrophe must lead to salvation; alas that salvation is preceded by catastrophe. The MaHaRal of Prague, a contemporary of the Ari ha-Kadosh, also represented and vigorously upheld this idea. The Maharal (1525-1609) — the celebrated mystic, Grand Rabbi Loew ("Lion"!) — espoused the Jewish messianic idea contained in the Bible and the Talmud, according to which every joyful birth must be preceded by the pangs of childbirth.*

Rabbi Isaac Luria's kabbalistic approach follows the same line of thought. But it goes beyond Jewish national frontiers, beyond even the confines of humanity, and embraces the very cosmos itself.

From a biblical and talmudic standpoint, the Kabbalah examines the History of the people of Israel from its very

---

* Under foreign influence, one part of Judeo-Hellenistic literature transformed the Jewish messianic idea, which is essentially ethical, into a dramatic, apocalyptic conception in which fate is substituted for human liberty.

beginnings, in its relation to the History of the cosmos (the Hebrew Bible opens with the description of the creation of the world and ends with that of the return of the Jews to the Land of Israel and the rebuilding of the Temple in Jerusalem). To the life of the Jewish people, the Kabbalah gives a special significance and a scope which is universal and even cosmic. The salvation of Israel, and thus that of humanity and of the world, is the outcome of a powerful cosmic experience that must be brought to completion in a cosmic, eschatological event.

Now, according to Rabbi Isaac Luria, the creation of the world is intrinsically bound up with a primordial catastrophe, which he calls *Shevirat ha-Kelim*, "the breaking of the vessels." How did this come about? To create the world, the *Ein-Sof*, the Infinite, proceeded (if one may use the term) to make a *Zimzum*, a "contraction," a "concentration," into Himself; He "withdrew" from Himself into Himself, so as to make place for, and give boundaries to, the world He was about to create. These boundaries would prevent the world from dissolving into the *Ein-Sof*. Thus the world would have its own reality, and yet "God is the Place of the world, though the world is not His place."

The space made free to contain the world is, however, not "empty," for "there is no place empty of Him." Within it remain the traces of His original light, so that the world can be born and continue to exist there. Consequently, the *Ein-Sof* has caused to be present in this "empty" space His *creative* light emanating from Him. This light flows into the *kelim*, the "vessels" created to collect and store it. But they cannot contain it, being unable to withstand the force of its abundance. This is the moment when that violent "breaking of the vessels" occurs; the pieces scatter, taking with them the "holy sparks of divine light." These sparks will remain within the fragments, the "husks," far removed from their Source, imprisoned in Galut. And so the Shekhinah is thenceforward in the darkness of exile, separated from the Original Light.

But why did God not create vessels capable of withstanding the violence of the divine, creative light? Why did God not subdue the flood and force of that light?

The answer to this question is that God wishes to associate man with His work of Creation, which must culminate in His final work of Redemption. As the Book of Genesis teaches us, God created the world *la-asot*, so that it might be "developed" and "completed" by Him and by man united with Him. The eschatological completion of the Creation depends on man's "labour" and "industry." It is man who must accomplish the *Tikkun*, the "repair and restoration," of this troubled world, into which the "breaking of the vessels" has precipitated him. He must re-establish harmony within humanity, which has been thrown into disorder by a second disintegration. This second breaking up was brought about by the sin of Adam, who "confused good and evil." There is a fundamental relationship between that ontological catastrophe — the breaking of the vessels — and the ethical catastrophe of Adam's sin. It is man himself who represents this link, being the sum of all the elements, spiritual and material, which make up the world: he is the *olam katan*, the microcosm. That is why his evil actions have destructive repercussions and, conversely, his good actions exercise a beneficent influence on the whole world. So it is up to man to bring about the *Teshuvah*, the "Return" of humanity. With them, in their wandering into exile, men have drawn the Shekhinah, and the Shekhinah, in turn, yearns to be present in the world and close to man.

Ontological "Disintegration" and Messianic "Restoration."
The role of Israel is determinative for the historical process that leads to Redemption.

It is the Will of Divine Providence that human history take place between two poles: the ontological Breaking of the Vessels and the ethical Sin of Man on the one hand, and the *Tikkun*, "Restoration," on the other.

The *Tikkun*, the Salvation, will be acquired by man's merits and bestowed by God's grace, simultaneously. Redemption must inevitably take place, for this is the Will of God: He is the Redeemer, He is the Creator; He created the world with the intention of redeeming it. Creation and Redemption are interdependent; the span of time separating them may be abridged, depending on man: "If he has merits, God hastens the coming of the time of Redemption; if he has no merits, God will bring about Redemption in His own time." (If Adam had not sinned on the day he was created, a Friday (cf. Gen. 3), the sabbatical, definitive Redemption would have followed on the morrow, the Sabbath. Equally, if Israel had not committed the sin of "the golden calf" (cf. Ex. 32), the Redemption brought about during the Revelation on Mount Sinai, which wiped out the "stain" provoked by Adam's sin, would have been definitive.)

It is man's zeal that will hasten the coming of Redemption and bring closer together the Beginning and the End of Days.

Of what does this "zeal" of man consist?

It is here that Israel, personifying mankind, has a singular responsibility and a determinative role in the historical process that leads to Redemption.

In fact, it was Israel that was "present in the mind of the Creator even before He created the world." God destined Israel to receive the Torah, which was itself conceived before the creation of the world. And it is Israel whom God "constrained" on Sinai to receive the Torah and to promise to observe its mitzvot. In truth, "the whole world was only created for the Torah," and once it had been given spiritual life, the material world too was destined to become a Torah. Here is the world's *Tikkun*; here is man's *Tikkun*. Therefore, without Israel, the people of the Torah, the *Tikkun* cannot be accomplished.

By "studying the Torah for its own sake"; by observing the mitzvot with *kavvanah*, with a sincere "intention" that the world and humanity may attain their *Tikkun*; by "serving God with love and fear"; by loving Him with *Devekut*, which allows the closest relationship with Him; and by worshipping Him "from afar," with "reverential, elevating fear," Israel develops a spiritual, inner life. By its "inner life," its *penimiyyut*, it will attract those who are still "outside," in the *hizoniyyut*. They in turn will develop their own "inner life" and will unite in prayer, together with Israel, in honour of their Creator, who will have become their Redeemer. This prayer, itself transformed into a Torah and "directed" by a *kavvanah* that arises from the "inner life," raises the worlds up to God. Those who pray thus, like Abraham before them, restore the worlds to Him, pacified and returned to their Origin. Thus the *Tikkun* is accomplished, Israel is brought out of its Galut, man puts an end to his exile, Israel enters the Promised Land, and man re-enters the Garden of Eden.

When Israel subjects *all* of its activities to the Torah and its mitzvot, it delivers the imprisoned "holy sparks" scattered throughout the world. "The prisoner cannot free himself"!

The fragments of decaying matter produced by the breaking of the vessels and by Adam's sin fall away, releasing the sparks that enabled them to survive. The "mixtures of good and evil" are purified; the vestiges of evil clinging to the "broken vessels" and the "mixtures" disappear. All is well. Darkness is dissipated. All is light. And "God Himself is the light of the world" (cf. Isa. 60:19), of a world restored to harmony.

Returning from Its Galut, "the Shekhinah is united with the Holy One, blessed be He." "The Names of God are united." The Name of God, split asunder by Man's sin, again becomes One. The *Tikkun* is completed; the End of Days rejoins the Beginning of Days. Redemption and Creation are one again, in the unity of the one God, Creator and Redeemer.

The Hasidic Movement in Eastern Europe.
The Hasid tries to sanctify all of his deeds so that they may please God and men.

Rabbi Isaac Luria's messianic kabbalistic doctrine had a considerable influence on Jewish mystical *thought*, giving it a new direction. What is more, it influenced the *life* of Jewish communities in the Near East and Europe by way of religious practice. Rabbi Isaac Luria did not himself commit his doctrine to writing, but it penetrated kabbalistic circles, above all thanks to the work Ez Hayyim, written by his disciple, Rabbi Hayyim Vital (1543-1620). His doctrine also enriched the daily life of Jews by creating a new pietistic *movement*, a *Hasidic* movement which later spread to Eastern Europe, especially to Poland and the Ukraine. The Jewish populations of those countries had been severely afflicted. In 1648 the hordes of Chmelnitski, the terrible warrior chief of the Cossacks, massacred entire Jewish settlements in the Ukraine and Poland. Those Jews who survived, poverty-stricken, humiliated, torn with anxiety, looked for reassurance from their religious leaders. They found it in the Hasidic movement inspired by Rabbi Israel Ba'al Shem Tov, "Master of the Good Name" (1699-1760).

While the Ari ha-Kadosh was the Zohar's most eminent commentator, the Ba'al Shem Tov was the most fervent interpreter of the messianic doctrine of the Ari ha-Kadosh, a doctrine stamped with a particularly metaphysical character. He interpreted this doctrine in terms of ethical and practical mysticism.

Like the Ari ha-Kadosh, the Ba'al Shem Tov too did not put his teachings into writing; it was in particular his disciple, Rabbi Jacob Joseph ha-Kohen of Polonnoye (d. 1782), who disseminated his master's teachings, especially in his work entitled *Toledot Ya'akov Yosef*. It is indeed a matter of instruction and not of doctrine. It is an instruction intended to guide the Hasid in his daily life and introduced by the Ba'al Shem Tov by means of "parables," homilies, and commentaries on the Torah. His successors gathered them, enriched them and built up on them a rich, diverse Hasidic literature — purely mystical, mystical-intellectual, mystical-talmudic, and mystical-narrative. The Hasidic school of Habad deviates in its attempt to interpret Luria's kabbalism in a way that is coherent, rational, and psychological.

The teaching of Hasidism is a theoretical synthesis of all the preceding Jewish mystical thinking and its practical, personal, and social effects. The express purpose of Hasidism is to make of the Hasid an *oved ha-Shem*, a servant of God. This is also what the Torah demands of every Jew, but Hasidism makes a special demand on the Hasid, namely, to serve God with joy.

The Hasid tries to live up to that which the Creator had in mind when He gave man a soul; he attempts to sanctify all his actions so that they may gain the approval of God and men. Therefore, the Hasid undertakes nothing before he is certain that what he is about to perform really conforms with the will of the Creator. It is the Torah which gives him this certainty, being a "Torah of Life," which "tells" him what he should do and offers him the mitzvot to be able to perform it. The Hasid therefore bases each of the actions of his daily life on the corresponding mitzvah.

> Humility that is not genuine is worse than pride.
> To be honest means to be "whole" with oneself,
> with others, and with God.
> This implies taking one's stand fully in the truth.

According to Hasidic teaching, man is compared to the ladder in Jacob's dream, which was "set up on the earth, and the top of it reached to heaven" (Gen. 28:12). Even when he is dealing with earthly realities, the Hasid has to consider the corresponding spiritual realities in heaven. There on high are to be found the "roots" of the earthly realities upon which the Hasid's thoughts must dwell. "May all thy actions be done in the Name of Heaven." To this saying of the Sages, Rabbi Menahem Mendel of Kotsk (1787-1859) added with biting irony, "May all thy actions be done in the Name of Heaven, even the act of saying or thinking that you are doing them in the Name of Heaven!" May they be truly done in the Name of Heaven, and not in your own name, not to pride yourself with them, not even for the sake of your salvation in the world to come; do them simply because they respond to the will of the Creator....

The disciples of the Ba'al Shem Tov used to say that their master came into this world to teach them "true humility and true joy."

It is necessary to attain a genuine humility, for humility that is not genuine is worse than pride, and pride being the source of all envy is, therefore, the root of all sins.

True joy is that which is tested in the service of God. "Without it there is no real service of God, while joy experienced outside the service of God is worthless."

Truth must, therefore, be present in everything we think, say or do. We must be "the same within as without." "Words spoken must correspond to the thought within." When the Torah tells us, "Let none of you deceive his neighbour" (cf. Lev. 25:17), it asks us not to deceive the neighbour who is *within* us, that is, ourselves. In forbidding us to "steal the thoughts of another," the Law also prohibits us from stealing our *own* thought. We must speak the truth when we communicate with God in prayer. When we say, for example, these words of a daily prayer, "In *truth* we rely on your great goodness," we should ask ourselves, as Rabbi Menaḥem Mendel of Kotsk invites us to do, whether or not we are lying. Above all, our actions ought to be imbued with truth in the eyes of God and men. Rabbi Menaḥem Mendel of Kotsk would say to his followers, "It is better to disclose the *averot*, the transgressions we have committed, and conceal our good deeds, rather than display these and conceal our *averot*."*

"Thou shalt be whole (upright) with the Lord thy God" (Deut. 18:13) — be upright "*with*" Him, in your relations with Him. "I am the Almighty God; walk before Me — in the sight of men — and be whole (upright)" (Gen. 17:1), said the Lord to Abraham. Likewise he said to him (Gen. 12:1), "*lekh lekha*, go *to* yourself." (Rabbi Zussya used to say, "If God asked me to be like Abraham, I should answer Him I am not capable of that. But if He asks me to be Zussya, I must try!"). To be upright means therefore to be "whole" with oneself, with others, and with God — to stand wholly within the truth.

Certainly, it is not easy to live entirely within the truth. One of the masters of Hasidism, Rabbi Phineḥas of Koretz (1726-1791), admitted to his followers that he had struggled for twenty-one years to achieve it: "seven years to know what the truth is, seven years to banish lying, and seven years to make truth enter into my bones." From that moment on, truth

---

* Nevertheless, the Ba'al Shem Tov asked his followers to conduct themselves in such a way that simply by walking down the street, without any intention of "displaying" themselves, they would immediately be recognized as Hasidim. In doing this, the master was only repeating the recommendation of the Sages: "'And thou shalt love the Lord thy God': behave in such a way that thanks to you, the Name of Heaven is loved" by men. Furthermore, the Torah commands Jews as a mitzvah "to sanctify the Name of God" publicly, by their actions.

is no longer for man a simple negation of lying. It has become the link which binds him to the "Lord God, who is the essence of Truth" (cf. Jer. 10:10); it helps him to understand the Torah, which is the "Torah of Truth." It leads him to the ultimate Truth. Thereafter, man will have attained the ideal that is at the heart of Hasidism, namely *Devekut*, communion with God.

> **Man can cause the desire that comes from above to plunge down into the world of sin.**
> **He can also cause it to mount up again into the higher world of the mitzvot.**

It is written in the Book of Psalms (85:12), "Truth will spring out of the earth." In fact, truth ascends from the earth below to be elevated towards the ultimate Truth. Man's life on earth has not only a spiritual side, but also, and above all, a physical, material life; and although he has the right to live it to the full, he must do so in moderation, just like the Children of Israel who enjoyed the manna in the desert in moderation, although it was abundant. Man will thus be spared much sorrow and discontent.

Now, at the source of life there is the motivation of desire, physical desires having their roots in the vegetative "animal soul" of man, and spiritual desires radiating from man's "divine soul." The desire that induces man to sin and the desire that drives him to study the Torah or perform a mitzvah, both draw their strength from the higher worlds, from the world of desire, which opens up into the world of pleasure. Man can cause his desires to fall into the world of sin, but he can also infuse his physical desires with spirituality, thus causing them to rise up again into the higher world of mitzvot. Thanks to his free will, man can direct his desire, but since his power is limited, he prays to God to help him: "not to let him fall into sin," and equally "to make the words of the Torah sweet to him." The value of a mitzvah, a religious act, is that much greater when it is done with an ardent desire, with *hishtokekut*, with spiritual "yearning," and with *hitlahavut*, "enthusiasm." Conversely, an *averah*, "transgression," and the sin it entails, are the more serious when man commits them with zeal.

The man who is separated from God by his own wrongdoing can always return to God.

Hasidism recommends man not to let himself be thrown into despair by his sins, even when the latter grow more serious and are repeated. Man is never imprisoned by his sins, for he can always transform an "impure desire" into a "pure desire." The masters of Hasidism apprise us of the fact that the Hebrew word *het*, which means "sin," ends with the silent letter *Alef*, "A," which denotes *Alufo shel olam*, the "Master of the world." This teaches us, says the Ba'al Shem Tov, that the man who "has separated himself" from God by rejecting Him through his misdeeds can always return to Him. God is always near him, for He is everywhere, declared Rabbi Dov Baer, the Maggid of Mezhirich (1704-1772). Only it is vital that man should *want* to see Him; but, as Rabbi Menahem Mendel of Kotsk reminds us, "He who does not see the Place [God] in every place, will not see Him in any place."

God is present to man, the sinner, and offers him His grace so that he may consciously "return" to Him, by doing *Teshuvah*. Such is the paradox of sin, which the Sages had already revealed in the Talmud. Sin, caused, alas, by an *averah*, by a "transgression," can lead to the performance of a mitzvah, in particular the significant mitzvah of *Teshuvah*. And if a state of *Teshuvah*, a "Return" to God, is achieved by man out of sincere love for God, it is considered a privilege.

According to the masters of Hasidism, it is this privilege which is recalled in the exhortation of the prophet Hosea (14:2): "O Israel, return to the Lord thy God." The man who fully achieves *Teshuvah* finds in God his own personal God; and God, who has seen His son going astray, finds him once more very close to Him. (It is true, nonetheless, that man can achieve *Teshuvah* in its highest degree without being led to it by sin. Such an achievement will have raised him to the very origins of his being and eventually to the Fountainhead of Existence, to God.)

> **Man must also serve God with his physical activities.**
> **"The fear of God without joy is nothing more than melancholy."**

Thus "the evil caused by sin has, as it were, supported the good," observes the author of the *Toledot*. The evil has been dissolved in good and the good alone remains. The *ba'al teshuvah*, one who has achieved *Teshuvah*, releases the "sacred sparks" imprisoned by sin and scattered abroad; he liberates them and causes them to "rise" to the "divine lights" whence they came.

At the same time, man must also serve God through *gashmiyyut*, through the material world, through the "earthly" elements, through his physical functions. He must not fear them, for they do not necessarily lead to sin; on the contrary, it is in using them in the service of God that man gains considerable merit. This is a fundamental teaching of the masters of Hasidism. They trust in man. They encourage him to make a right and joyful use of all the means of serving that He has offered. It is thus that man can transform an "inclination" to do wrong into an "inclination" to do good. Even when the "bad inclination" "grows in strength" and becomes "unclean" in its reluctance to be transformed, the sinner should not lose hope, for by a meticulous observance of the mitzvot he can liberate the "sacred sparks" imprisoned by his sins. For God, who "created the bad inclination, also created the appropriate remedy, the Torah." The "sacred sparks" that man must liberate are present even in these places we call "impure," even in the impure "alien thoughts" which can invade our minds when we pray, even in the thoughts of atheists. It is the task of the Hasid to "raise" these sparks and to return them to their shining Source.

Innumerable ways of serving God are offered to man. "If a Jew sees his neighbour falling (spiritually), it is his duty to help him; let him not say, 'It is a judgment from heaven,' but let him make every effort to raise him," says Rabbi Jacob Isaac, the "Holy Jew" of Przysucha (1776-1813). For "in each man there is something precious which cannot be found in another man," states Rabbi Phinehas of Koretz. And Rabbi Levi Isaac of Berdichev (1740-1809) proclaims: "Every man is enveloped in a holy light that radiates particularly at the moment when he loves and wherever he loves God!" The Creator has presented man with the gift of love, He has "breathed" the power of loving into him, He has enabled man to respond to God's love for him, for "He loves him." ("If only I could love the greatest zaddik, the greatest 'just man' in Israel, as the Name, blessed be He, loves the greatest rasha, the greatest 'wicked man' in Israel!" exclaims Rabbi Solomon of Karlin (1738-1792). "To love one's neighbour is to love one's Creator," proclaims the Ba'al Shem Tov, "for when one loves the Father, one loves His children."

The love which is expressed in joy fills the life of the Hasid.

The desire which impels man towards physical, unspiritual love, a self-centered love, leads him also to the love of God, a self-denying love. It is this love of God which is the ultimate goal of desire.

And so the desires originating in the vegetative, "animal soul" of a human being join with the spiritual desires that flow from his "divine soul" and that lead toward the love of God. These two souls, the animal and the divine, are bound to each other and form a single soul, thus teaches the Habad movement. Together, they move towards unity, towards the One, Unique, Soul of Souls; united, they reach upwards towards their Source, towards that Love which is God.

> **The Hasid must reach the point of experiencing a profound and confident joy in the love and the fear of God.**

The Hasid's desire is expressed unceasingly in these words: "My soul longs, indeed, it pines for the courts of the Lord; my heart and my flesh sing for joy to the living God" (Ps. 84:3). He has adopted for himself these words in which the psalmist, King David, exalts the faith of the human hasid and celebrates "the works of the Divine Hasid" ("The Lord is ... *hasid* (gracious) in all his works" — Ps. 145:17.) It is in these hymns that the psalmist glorifies the *hesed*, the "Grace" which God lavishes upon man, and the *hesed*, the "loving-kindness," which man demonstrates towards his fellowman.

In truth, it is this Book of the *Tehillim*, of the "exalting Praises" composed by King David, which constantly feeds the soul of the Hasid. This book is *his* book; it accompanies him everywhere; it comforts him continually; through it, the Hasid speaks to God.* It is due to *Tehillim* that the Hasid *mithased im kono*, "enters into an ardent relationship with his Creator," and offers his love to God.

---

* A Hasid complained one day to his Rebbe that he felt alone and abandoned. The Rebbe said to him, "How can a Jew feel alone? He takes out his little book of *Tehillim*, reads it, pours out his heart before his Creator, and is no longer alone."

The Hasid's love for God culminates in *Devekut*, in communion with Him. As the teachers of Habad attest, at certain moments this *Devekut* can lead the believer to feel a temporary sensation of *hitpashtut ha-gashmiyyut*, the "casting off of one's materiality"; such a sensation can even arouse in him "the desire to no longer have his own existence, but rather to melt away within Him" — *bittul ha-mezi'ut*.

But it is at this precise moment when his love for God is most intense, when his joy is complete, that the believer is seized with dread, is assailed by fear of God!

It is love of God which allows man to live joyfully, in the "contentment" given him by God's direct *closeness*. This personal God, who inspires him very particularly when in *Devekut*, also reveals to him that an immeasurable distance *separates* him from Him, the *Ayin*, the Impersonal; that he is *as far as ever* from fathoming what one may call His Essence. At that very moment, having achieved *Devekut*, the Hasid shares the feeling of King David, "The Lord is near to all those who call upon Him" (Ps. 145:18); he also understands what the prophet Jeremiah was saying (31:2): "The Lord has appeared to me from *afar*." One Rebbe recalled this to his Hasid: "Know that even if you are far from God, He is close to you; but know also that even though He may be close to you, you are still far from Him." In truth, "He is far from man, further than anything that is far from him; yet He is close to man, closer than anything that is close to him," wrote Rabbi Judah Aryeh Leib of Gur (1847-1905) in *Sefat Emet*.

This ambiguous position of man in the presence of God is described by King David in the following verses: "I will rejoice in the Lord" (Ps. 104:34); "My flesh shudders for fear of Thee" (Ps. 119:120). The closeness of God fills the man of *Devekut* with joy, whereas the distance that separates him from God arouses in him the fear of God. Nevertheless, in this very fear, joy is not absent; King David memorialized it: "Serve the Lord with fear, and *rejoice* with *trembling*" (Ps. 2:11). According to the Ba'al Shem Tov, "The fear of God without joy is only melancholy"; it is not different from being afraid. Such a fear of God is "impure." He who is afraid flees, thus avoiding the being or the thing that he dreads; he is seized by *yir'ah ḥizonit*, a "fear that comes from without." In contrast, he who fears God with *yir'ah penimit*, that "fear that comes from within" and elicits a sense of the Divine Presence, feels a "holy" fear. God's nearness arouses this fear which, in turn, allows an even greater closeness. This "holy" fear suppresses dread, which is unworthy of a believer, and gives birth to joy. It is a "reverent fear," a "fear which uplifts" the spirit. It strengthens man's character, fortifies his virtues and impels him to *act* according to the Will of Him whom he fears (but not for fear of being punished if he does not carry out His Will). It is the "portal" enabling the believer to attain the love of God. This love must take concrete form in the joyful observance of the mitzvot, which brings man nearer to God. For a mitzvah not observed with joy, one uninspired by the love of God, is worthless. "The Shekhinah is present only in joy," the joy born of fear, the joy of *Devekut*. The Torah itself stresses this in the Book of Deuteronomy (10:20): "Thou shalt *fear* the Lord thy God: Him shalt thou serve and to Him (only) shalt thou *cleave* — *u-vo tidbak*."

So the Hasid must arrive at a point of feeling a deep and trusting joy in the love and fear of God.

This love and this fear must complement each other in a relationship which unites man to God. The love of man for God responds to the love of God for man. Yet love is a gift of God, while fear comes from man alone and, unlike the love of God, it is not part of the *Imitatio Dei*.

The believer experiences the love of God gladly, thanking Him for this precious gift. Of the fear of God, too, the believer is joyfully aware, again thanking Him for the gift He has made him, namely, the wisdom to fear Him. Indeed, "The fear of the Lord is the beginning of wisdom" (Ps. 111:10; Prov. 9:10); thus it is "fear of God" that is the foundation of the entire life of the believer.

> The deeds and the thoughts of man should daily renew his *Emunah*, his faith.
> Time and again as he observes the mitzvot, he demonstrates a new *Emunah*.

Emunah, "Faith," rests on the love and the fear of God. The observance of the mitzvot "with fear and love" is the foundation of *avodat ha-Shem*, "the service of God." "But the keystone of this foundation is *Emunah*, 'Faith,' " says the Ba'al Shem Tov. Why has the Torah not, therefore, explicitly ordained *Emunah*? Because "without *Emunah* there is nothing," replies a *zaddik*. "All thy commandments are (but) *Emunah*," proclaims King David (Ps. 119:86). Without *Emunah* there are no mitzvot, and the mitzvot "appear new to us every day."

"Faith," *Emunah*, should daily put new life into man. He who believes in God and serves Him today, must regard himself as if he had never yet begun to believe and must "imagine"* that he has never served Him until this very day — whether it be in physical, material actions or in spiritual acts such as prayer, which is "service of the heart." He who expresses his *Emunah* in prayer (and *Emunah* itself is *tefillah*, "prayer," says Rabbi Nahman of Bratslav) must think of himself as having just been born. If he prays today, it is not because he prayed yesterday; today he is learning to pray....

---

* Rabbi Nahman of Bratslav (1772-1810) wrote, "*Emunah* is founded on the existential power of the imagination. For *Emunah* is not applied to that which reason comprehends; it intervenes where reason stops. When reason can no longer help man to comprehend, he must appeal to *Emunah*." At that point, says Rabbi Menahem Mendel of Kotsk, *Emunah* is for man clearer than the clearest vision.

He believes that "this very day" God created the world, for he sees that "every day God in His goodness renews the work of Creation." The believer is part of this world, so he participates in the renewal of the world. He manifests an ever-new *Emunah* in observing the mitzvot, which they too seem to him always new, "as if they had been revealed this very day." "This very day" the Creator grants anew the gift of *Emunah* to him who is ready to receive this gift, which He inscribed into man's nature in the beginning. At the same time, He asks man to discover this gift within himself and to direct it so as to meet up with the "light of *Emunah*," which descends afresh upon him.

Thus, *Emunah* proceeds both from God and from man, thanks to their mutual "trust": God bestows it on man and man makes it re-ascend to God. Man is a *ma'amin*, a "believer," who daily renews his *will* to receive *Emunah*; God is the *Ne'eman*, the "Faithful," who daily bestows upon man the grace to be *able* to receive *Emunah* and who augments the latter in proportion to man's desires.

Both the human *ma'amin* and the divine *Ne'eman* participate in the "merits" of *Emunah*. In praising Abraham's supreme virtue, his *Emunah*,* the Torah says of him (Gen. 15:6), "And he believed in the Lord; and he counted it to him for righteousness." In Hebrew the phrase "and he counted it to him" is elliptical; it is not clear *who* "counted it for righteousness." Abraham and God are equal syntactic subjects. Abraham "counted it for righteousness," thanking God for the "grace" of *Emunah*, for the *ability* to believe in Him (an ability which he found, whole and renewed, during the "vision" in which God showed Himself to "Abraham who loved Him"); and God "counted it for righteousness" in recognizing Abraham's

---

* Rabbi Na<u>h</u>man of Bratslav sees in Abraham, who is *rosh ha-ma'aminim*, "chief of believers," the personification of *Emunah*, Abraham being the personification of *<u>h</u>esed*, of human "goodness" responding to the divine *<u>H</u>esed*."

virtue of faith. These two "merits" meet, identify with each other and, as the Torah tells us, form "one single merit."

Well before he became the "father of believers," Abraham had "recognized" God. He had "recognized" Him with his intellect; he had "recognized" that God exists, that He created the world, that He is the "Master of the City." Nevertheless, this "knowledge of God" could not make of him a believer, could not of itself have given him *Emunah*. Tending towards the Infinite, *Emunah* goes far beyond the limits of intellect. To attain it, man must dedicate all of his being, not excluding his intellect. Having reached the Infinite and experienced His Presence, man has no further need for his intellect, for he now believes in God as does a simpleton or a child. The *Emunah* which he possesses henceforth is for him *Emet*, "Truth," for it is pure and simple, whole and absolute.

> **The Hasid does not observe the mitzvot in order to profit from them, but rather in order to be "with" Him, with the Giver of the mitzvot.**

The Ba'al Shem Tov praises the believer, *ha-adam ha-pashut*, "the simple man," who possesses *emunah peshutah*, "simple faith" in Him who is the essence of *Pashtut*, "Simplicity." The father of Hasidism gives honour to the *am ha-arez*, the "common man," the "ignorant person," who, when he believes, does so with an unshakeable faith. Such a man does not seek to found his faith on philosophical speculations or scientific proofs, which come from uncertainty and lead to scepticism. The Ba'al Shem Tov encourages the *am ha-arez* to study God's Torah, which is a *Torat Emet* (cf. Mal. 2:6), a "Torah of Truth," but he charges him to study "for the sake of the Torah," without taking pride in his study as certain erudite rabbis tend to do. He further encourages him to observe God's commandments, *mitzvotekha Emunah* (cf. Ps. 119:86), "Your mitzvot are Faith," without looking for rational or utilitarian justifications for them. He encourages him to pray even if he does not understand the meaning of the Hebrew words he is mouthing. Let him bathe his sight in the "letters" of these words that smile on him; let him pray with *kavvanah*, with simple devotion, without seeking some sort of advantage. Let him thank his God with gladness for permitting him to approach Him whose "greatness is unfathomable" (cf. Ps. 145:3) and whose "Nearness is closer to him than anything else that is close to him," nearer than he is to himself. Let him "give Him thanks with uprightness of heart" (Ps. 119:7), as did King David, acknowledging himself to be a "simple" Hasid, "humble" though "upright" before Him. Adds Rabbi Naḥman of Bratslav, the great-grandson of the Ba'al Shem Tov, the *Yosher Levav*, the "uprightness of heart," is *Emunah*, "faith," and *Emunah* is *tefillah*, "prayer," which is expressed in *Devekut*, in intimate adherence to God.

In truth, the supreme goal of the Hasid is *Devekut*; he yearns to "cleave" to God, to be *near* to Him; he longs to be *with* Him.

When the Hasid studies Torah, it is not to acquire knowledge, which in the case of every other science, comes to him from without; by the study of the Torah he seeks to "cleave" to Him that gave it, who is Present within it, who is Present to those who study it.

The Hasid observes the mitzvot not to gain advantage from them, but to be *be-zavta*, "together with," to be an associate with Him who has given them.

The Hasid *mitpallel*, "prays," less to obtain the fulfilment of his wishes (although he acknowledges he is addressing the "Master of all," Him upon whom everything depends) than to "cleave" to Him, for prayer is *Devekut*: "*naftulei Elokim niftalti*" (cf. Targum Onkelos to Gen. 30:8: "I struggled in prayer with God").

It is then that "God's Torah" becomes *his* Torah; God's mitzvah *his* mitzvah, and God's prayer *his* prayer. The Hasid himself becomes an embodiment of Prayer and can say in truth, like King David, *va-ani Tefillah*: "as for me, I am prayer" (cf. Ps. 109:4).

Faith and Trust; Faith and Assurance

"Light is sown for the *zaddik*, the 'righteous', and gladness for the upright in heart," declares King David (Ps. 97:11).

The Hasid experiences this *Emunah*, which is "uprightness of heart," in the joy, peace, and *Bitahon* (trust or assurance) that the *Emunah* gives him, for *Emunah* and *Bitahon*, "faith" and "trust," "faith" and "assurance," are kindred spirits. The *ma'amin*, the "believer," trusts in God. "If he is not a *ba'al bitahon*, if he has not implicit and unquestioning assurance and trust, he is not a *ma'amin*, a true believer." Now, joy itself is also a sign of the love of God and men. Thus *Emunah*, at its optimum, is an essential characteristic of the true believer's close relationship with God and with his fellowmen.

> The *zaddik*, the "righteous man," is the heart of the Hasidic community.
> Each individual man is created in order to put at least one thing in this world to rights again.
> So "the world needs every man just as every man needs the world."

"Those who have an upright heart are joyful" (Ps. 97:11). "Light is sown for the *zaddik*" (ibid.), and the *zaddik*, the "righteous" man, "sows" this light for others; he disseminates this light of *zedakah*, of "goodness," to all who come to him, those who surround him, and those whom he encounters.

At the heart of that democratic, popular society, which is

the Hasidic community, the *zaddik*, the spiritual leader, the Rebbe, occupies a central place, which, however, does not distance him from his followers. They in turn, therefore, think of their *zaddik* as the "heart" that gives them life, jointly and severally.

The Hasidim see in their *zaddik* "the foundation of the world" (Prov. 10:25). It is he who by his prayer, his study of the Torah, and his observance of the mitzvot links the lower to the higher world. He causes divine grace, "blessing," to rest upon his people. In addition, he himself "goes down to his people" like Moses (cf. Ex. 19:25); he is "in the midst of his people." Yes, he literally comes down to them, for when he sees Jews fallen into the Gehenna of sin, he forsakes the purity of the heights and, for the "love of Israel," he "humbles himself," not hesitating to "obscure" his holiness temporarily. He comes down into the abyss, where the "wicked" have fallen, to help them rise again (cf. I Sam. 2:6) to the world of Torah and mitzvot. He submits to "making a descent, with an ascent in mind." He agrees to descend into the grave and to "bring up" (ibid.) those who had buried themselves therein. Led by his love for them, he finds them; he stoops over the thick "crust" that covers them and discovers the "holy sparks" hidden in them (every Jew has "holy sparks" hidden in him). He releases the sparks and brings those who held them captive back to the way of *Teshuvah*, of "Return" to God. "No one should be repulsed...." (II Sam. 14:14).

It is thus that Jews coming "from far and near" (cf. Isa. 57:19) again find tranquillity in the ambience of the *zaddik*. They press round him, eager to study the Torah with him, share in his prayers, warm their souls at his inner fire, find comfort in his radiance and draw upon his *Emunah*, his "Faith," for "the *zaddik* shall live by his *Emunah*" (Hab. 2:4).

But even when the Hasidim are reunited around the *zaddik* and are associated with his *avodat ha-Shem*, his fervent "service of God," each Hasid must keep present in his spirit this teaching of the Sages: "Every man must think, 'It is for me, for my sake, that the world was created.' " The teachers of Hasidism have elaborated this teaching by continuing, "Every man has been created to 'repair' one thing in this world. The world, therefore, has need of him, just as he has need of the world."

When each man individually, and all men together, are attentive to this teaching, the world will rediscover its harmony and will be able to ascend again to its Creator.

CHAPTER ONE

In What Sense Is the Kabbalah Knowledge?

The Kabbalah makes man aware of the mystery within him and around him.

Ha-Sod hu ha-yesod: "Mystery is the foundation," says the Zohar. It is the foundation of everything.

The whole of Jewish mystical thought rests on this principle. The whole Kabbalah is called *ḥokhmat ha-nistar*, "wisdom of that which is hidden," *ḥokhmat ha-emet*, "wisdom of the truth." These names do not mean that the Kabbalah has uncovered all that is hidden and possesses the whole of truth. In their works, "the men of the mysteries," *anshei ha-sod*, share with us their unwearying attempts to "look in through the windows and peer through the lattice" — to use the phrase they have taken from the Song of Songs (2:9) — so as to discover a little of the "splendour," the "brightness," and the "truth" hidden in everything that exists. They have an ardent desire to delight their souls in those things and to transmit the little that can be transmitted to those who, living in sanctity, are worthy of it. They realize they are incapable of seeing face to face "the hidden light," of penetrating the unfathomable truth. However, they unremittingly pursue their quest. Light will be revealed in all its brightness, and Truth will appear in its totality, in the days of the Messiah, in the days of the solemn, visible inauguration of the reign of God. Then "all flesh shall see" (Isa. 40:5) the "Light which enfolds His creation" and "will know" that Alone "the Lord God is *Emet* (Truth)" (Jer. 10:10).

To reach the shores of salvation, the quest and the "labour" of the masters of the Kabbalah are not enough. These masters know that every man, each according to his powers (the "higher powers and roots of his soul"), should play a part in bringing nearer the messianic age. Indeed, says Rabbi Naḥman of Bratslav (18th-19th centuries), every man must do his best, according to his capability, to keep watch on that element of the Messiah which is within him and preserve it from every attack, in an attempt to contribute to the service of God and integrate this service into the Kingdom of God.

This is why the masters of the Kabbalah are not content to concern themselves merely with the "roots" of things: they also see to it that the branches of the tree grow and spread....

By drawing man's attention to the mystery that he bears within him and that surrounds him, they enable him to understand the superficial character of his own learning and observations. They then invite him to turn his eyes to the inward nature of things, for what he sees, touches, knows, is only the appearance of the things that truly are, of the things that ought to be known. They try to make him perceive that what he sees is only the "shell" of that which contains the "bright kernel" of the "thing." Their desire is that man will thus become aware that he is living in an unknown world and will be disposed to raise fundamental questions, such as "Where have I come from and where am I going to?" — questions about the *who* and the *what* of existence. He will then begin to understand that everything is a mystery, that the life in him and around him is a mystery, and that this mystery extends to the mystery of God, the Life of Life, from which all life proceeds and to which it returns. Truly, everything is a mystery that surpasses man's understanding.

The thought of the Kabbalah is concerned with the dialectic of "inward nature" versus "outward nature," of the "hidden" versus the "revealed."

In the Zohar, as in all Jewish mystical literature, everything that exists is considered as both "hidden and revealed," "inner nature and outer nature," "light and vessel," "soul and body," "body and clothing...."

This contrast, this correlativity within unity, is written into the heart of reality.

Jewish mystical thought is concerned with the dialectic which this correlativity involves, for that which is hidden is being made manifest.

To surmise how this can be, let us consider the "realities" constantly present in our mind: God, the Torah, the World, Man, Israel.

God is the "Most Hidden among things." Our thoughts cannot grasp what we may be tempted to call His nature, His essence, and our deficient and limited human language allows us to designate Him, with reverence and as from a distance, by none other than the word "He." However, God manifests Himself in His works: "He surrounds them and fills them"; "He is omnipresent." He is very close to us, which is why we can turn our hearts to Him and say to Him, "Thou."

Nevertheless, "the glory of the Lord is that He surrounds himself with mystery," "He keeps things hidden" (cf. Prov. 25:2). He is the *Ne'elam*, the "Hidden One," from whom everything that exists "emanates," though He, in His "essence," remains hidden. His works — the Torah, the World,

Man, Israel — "speak" to us of Him. Within them His Name is hidden, but we are far from being ready to utter or to pronounce It. For the time being, we can only "read" It, "inscribed" in substance, sculpted in stone, or written on parchment. For us humans, for us Israelites, His Name is still *alam*, "Hidden," but "in the time to come," in the messianic age, we shall be able to "utter" It, for then we shall know Him; we shall grasp His "essence" in celebrating His glory. A name, says the *Sefer ha-Bahir*, reveals the essence, the soul, of him who bears it, and the Ramban (12th century) stresses that the Name of God, *Elohim*, specifies and governs the forces in action in the world. Rabbi Joseph Gikatilla (13th century) tells us that the Divine Name is not a simple naming word describing God: it is the very Reality of God.

In the days to come, "the Lord shall be King over all the earth...the Lord shall be one and His Name shall be One" (Zech. 14:9).

In these words, the prophet Zechariah foretells that in the messianic age, when the reign of God will extend over the whole earth, the Essence of God and the Name of God shall appear in their intrinsic Unity, if one may call it so, in their true identity.

The letters of the Torah await our exegesis, which can be endless.

The Torah, which existed prior to the Creation and which is the Charter of the Creation, is full of the Names of God. "There is no word of the Torah that does not contain the Name of God," says the Zohar. God created the world through the *zeruf*, the "combining" of the Torah's letters. These letters are the body, and the "vowels" and "accents" that embellish them are the soul. In the original text of the Torah, as in the *Sefer Torah*, the "Scroll of the Torah" used for the liturgical reading of the Torah, the letters are not "punctuated"; this suggests that their "nature" is not limited but infinite, for it proceeds from the Infinite; this teaches us, too, that the letters await our elucidations, and that these may be endless. Thus, tradition relates that the Torah's letters, revealed on Sinai in the presence of 600,000 adult Israelites, allowed for 600,000 commentators, each of whom was crowned with seventy crowns. In fact, the scholar who enriches one word of the Torah — which has seventy branches, seventy facets — with a new insight receives, in his turn, seventy crowns. The "unpunctuated" letters of the Torah, the *gufei Torah*, the "bodies of the Torah," wait for us to reveal their *neshamah*, their "soul," by the *nekuddot*, the appropriate "vowels" and "accents." These letters say to us, "shed light on us," and our interpretations can be infinitely extended without ceasing to be correct, for when our intelligence is purified and enlightened by observing the Torah's precepts, it is attuned to, and united with, the higher, Infinite Intelligence.

> "God's Torah is perfect."
> No one has yet succeeded in reaching its "innermost" nature, its essence.

"I have seen an end to every purpose, but Thy commandment is exceedingly broad" (Ps. 119:96).

In fact, every word of the Torah and each of the letters composing it have already been scrutinized in their "innermost" nature by the Sages, who have extracted from them invaluable material; yet, each word and each letter still contains uncounted riches waiting to be gathered. For each word of the Torah can be understood at four levels of meaning, beginning with the *peshat*, the "literal" sense, and through to the *sod*, the "secret" meaning.

Having probed these four "degrees," one finds, like the

Gaon of Vilna (18th century), that the *sod* contains the *peshat*, and the *peshat* includes the *sod*. In their "inner nature" they match one another perfectly and are inseparable, validating each other to the degree that they become identical.

Similarly, the *Halakhah*, Jewish religious law, is corroborated and illuminated by the *Kabbalah*, Jewish mystical teaching, and vice versa. This rapport between Halakhah and Kabbalah was suggested and understood by the renowned codifier, Rabbi Joseph Caro (16th century) and his fellow countryman, the Ari ha-Kadosh; many representatives of the different kabbalistic schools have taught this and demonstrated it, down to modern times with Rabbi Naḥman of Bratslav (18th-19th centuries) and Ben Ish Ḥai (19th-20th centuries).

And yet most of the *sitrei Torah*, the *razei Torah*, the "secrets of the Torah," remain hidden in the Torah's "innermost recesses," in its *penimiyyut*. There they continue to exist almost completely in their "pure state," which allowed the Ba'al Shem Tov (18th century) to repeat the words of King David: *Torat ha-Shem temimah*, "The Law of the Lord is perfect" (Ps. 19:8). No one has yet penetrated into its essence, and it will remain inviolate until the days of the Messiah, at which time the Torah will be wholly understood and its precepts perfectly respected.

In those days, the Jew shall see at last the fulfilment of the wish that was on King David's lips: "Open thou mine eyes that I may behold wondrous things out of Thy Law" (Ps. 119:18).

The world itself is also a mystery. The world, which seems to us exposed, is called *olam*, "hidden," because it is thanks to Him who is "Hidden" that the world exists. In its inner nature, the world conceals the presence of the *Ne'elam*, the "Hidden One," who gives it life. The *olam* leads us to the *Ne'elam*, the Divine Spirit, which gives it its *ḥiyyut*, its "vitality."

The Spirit fills the body of the world as the soul fills the body of man, while neither the one nor the other can be seen or located. "It is present everywhere and visible nowhere." Just as man is man through his soul and without it he is a dead man, so the world is world, not by its nature, but by its Spirit, and without it, it is a dead world.

The mystery of the *olam*, the "world," will remain until the days of the Messiah; then, what is hidden and what is unveiled in the world shall merge in a perfect unity; what is unveiled shall be hidden and what is hidden shall be uncovered. This is how the Shelah ha-Kadosh (16th-17th centuries) and Rav Kook (20th century) describe the world in the days of the Messiah.

The World, "Open" and "Closed."
Man, a Microcosm.
His "Conscious" and his Nonconscious State.
Dreams.

The world seems to be "open" but in reality it remains closed to man, who himself is a miniature world. The scientists of our own time are beginning to recognize these truths, these realities.

Man is incapable of penetrating another person's thought entirely or even of knowing himself completely. He cannot grasp his own thought down to its roots, for thought cannot be reduced to its cognitive dimension. "In the height of its depths and in the depth of its heights," his own thought escapes man. Thought, as an object of rational knowledge, is only a part of the whole of thought. A great part of the latter remains buried in man's nonconscious state, in the depths of his being; it cannot be grasped in the waking state and appears only fleetingly in the "subconscious." Man's nonconscious state is sometimes more powerful than his "conscious" thought, and the domain of the former is much more extensive than the cognitive field of the latter. The nonconscious state knows man's whole being, "it sees that which man does not see" — his present, emerging from his past and linking up with his future.

This is why the Sages of the Talmud and the kabbalists so frequently considered the meaning of dreams. They gathered together all that the nonconscious state revealed to them about the human personality when it makes itself present within the subconscious. The dreams retold in the Bible enabled them to understand that a man's dream is an opaque mirror from the depths of his being, and that the content, quality, and range of a dream are dependent upon the moral status of the dreamer. The kabbalists therefore paid great attention to the science of dreams, venturing to decipher them, analyzing their images and words, and thus "interpreting" them. The nature of the truths and teachings they drew from them was certainly psychological, but above all it was religious and moral, for the kabbalists recognized that there is a hierarchy in man's psychic world.

The mystery of man remains. In the days of the Messiah, when man's body and soul will become one, the body "spiritualized" and the soul "materialized," only then will the mystery of man be disclosed.

Israel is called Man for it is the incarnation of the mystery of man.

"Israel is called Man." It is so called because its vocation is to fulfil in itself everything man ought to be, to be fully that which the Creator wished when He created man. This is why in messianic times every man will be able to recognize himself in Man, Israel.

However, if Israel is called Man, this is, above all, because it is the incarnation of man's mystery: a visible body and an invisible soul marvellously, "mysteriously," united by the Creator as the ReMa* points out in his commentary on a daily prayer. As a people and as an individual — the Jew too is called Israel — Israel personifies man's mystery. The people of Israel alone of all peoples personifies this mystery to the highest degree, existentially as well as historically.

The representatives of the different historical schools have tried in vain to find a rational explanation for the singular phenomenon of the perpetuation of the people of Israel. None of their answers is pertinent. The laws of history and sociology cannot account for the "supernatural phenomenon" of the life and survival of the people of Israel. The *sod ha-kiyyum*, the "secret of the existence" of this people in spite of so many vicissitudes, remains intact. The masters of the Kabbalah tell us that only the special relationship existing between Him who is the Mystery of Mysteries and His people — in whose name, IsraEL, His own Name is inscribed — can throw light on the mystery of this people's "going out" — like Abraham — beyond the norms, transcending the "natural order."

The mystery of the people of Israel will be "divulged" only in the days of the Messiah, when the "peoples of the earth" will recognize the perfect union, in Israel, of body and soul in the service of God. Then they shall cry: "Come and let us go up to the mountain of the Lord and to the house of the God of Jacob, so that He may teach us of His ways, and we may walk in His paths: for the Torah shall go forth from Zion and the word of the Lord from Jerusalem" (Mich. 4:2).

---

* Rabbi Moses Isserles (1525-1572).

The "Days of the Messiah": Expectation and Preparation

The masters of the Kabbalah, the *anshei ha-sod*, the "men of the mystery," do not postpone the entire revelation of the Mystery, and the mysteries springing from it, until the days of the Messiah. For were it so, man would have no desire to hasten the time of that revelation by his "labour." He would undertake nothing and would make no plans; the life of the mind and history would be paralysed, as it were. Future revelation would be an event that we passively "waited for," "hoped for," thinking we could have no influence upon it. To the contrary, Jewish mysticism, the Kabbalah, is distinguished by its active, creative character, by its constructive will, in the spiritual and material domains, which are united in the "service of God," and consequently in the service of mankind.

Of course, the days of the Messiah will come "suddenly," *be-hesah ha-da'at*, "unexpectedly," "when no one is thinking about this." However, they will crown a period of "waiting" and "hoping." This waiting and hoping is best expressed in "the study of the Torah," by introducing study periods into the eternal time of the Torah, and by an intensification of mental activity. This activity, this life of the mind, is guided by the Torah and the commandments and must lead to the concrete expression of *Emunah*, "Faith" in God and "confidence" in man. *Hayyei Olam*, the "eternal life" in the Torah, which binds a Jew to God, unites with *hayyei sha'ah*, "temporal life," which binds a Jew to his fellowman; together, they prepare for *Hayyei Olam ha-Ba*, "the life of the world to come."

The Mystery and the branch mysteries will be revealed "soon," when "His kingdom shall be made manifest." The Sages hope this *Gillui Shekhinah*, this "revealing of the Divine Presence," of the *Malkhut*, the "Kingdom," will happen "soon, in our days." But whether this revelation be "delayed"

or "hastened" depends on man's "labour," on his collaboration with God, on the Jew's perseverance in thorough study
of God's Torah and sincere observance of His mitzvot.

The Jew is not only permitted, but is even obligated, to try
to penetrate, or at least to recognize, a great many mysteries
even before the days of the Messiah. The masters of the
Kabbalah urge their followers to enter, as far as they are able,
into the mysteries that are within and around them. They will
be enabled to do so by "hallowing themselves by what is
permitted to them" in daily life. For this work of hallowing,
God has given man the powers of "reason," and man ("the
image of God") must use this gift with reverence.

Pure reason and practical intelligence together lead to
da'at, "knowledge." It is the Messiah himself who personifies
this *da'at* in the highest degree, for it is *Da'at ha-Shem*, the
"knowledge of God," with which "the earth shall be filled"
in his days "as the waters cover the sea" (Isa. 11:9). The
teaching of the masters of the Kabbalah is that "man" — the
man of the "practical ideal," who is called upon to work for
the coming of those days — "is only man through *da'at*,"
through "knowledge."

"Knowledge" is Indefinable.
Intellectual Ability and Ethical Values.

But what is this "knowledge" that is man's glory?

It is indefinable both in relation to the external object that
it scrutinizes and in relation to itself when it "thinks about
itself." Knowledge is an act of thinking whose purpose is to
investigate things. Yet, as Spencer has already stated, "Things
in themselves are unknowable" (and today's representatives
of physical science confirm this observation); and "knowledge" itself, as an instrument of investigation and explanation, remains a mystery.

Da'at, "knowledge," proceeds from yedi'ah, "knowing." And yedi'ah itself, say the masters of the Kabbalah, is never complete, never sure; it is a "knowing" of "probabilities." (This is also the language used in this context by Werner Heisenberg, the celebrated physicist of our own times.*)

The da'at to which yedi'ah leads is an even greater mystery when it seeks to be "pure thought."

"Thought" itself is a mystery which modern science, while making progress in the study of the "miraculous" human brain, has nevertheless not succeeded in isolating.

But there remains "self-knowledge," which Jews are exhorted to explore. The masters of the Kabbalah, the anshei ha-sod, the "men of the mystery," who are also yode'ei hen, "those who know grace," and yode'ei hokhmat ha-nistar, "those who know the hidden wisdom," and following them, the masters of the "moralist" intellectual movement called Musar, which originated in Lithuania in the 19th century, all urgently recommend this self-knowledge, which has profound religious implications and extensive moral applications.

For good reason they are called "those who know grace," because for them, knowledge is far more than an intellectual faculty. It is an ethical value, it "puts wisdom into man's heart." In acknowledging that the Lord is God, that His Torah is the supreme Wisdom, we arrive at this knowledge. It is written (Deut. 4:39-40), "Know this day...that the Lord He is God in heaven above, and upon the earth beneath: there is no other. Thou shalt keep therefore His statutes and His commandments, that it may go well with thee...." In truth, the da'at Torah, the "knowledge of the Torah," is clear and sure. For the masters of the Kabbalah, as for Maimonides, da'at is the link uniting man with his God, for it is a grace which "Thou, the Creator, givest" to the man who is worthy of it.

Furthermore, da'at means union. Ve-ha-Adam yada et

---

* Cf. Alexandre Safran, The Kabbalah, op. cit., Appendix, pp. 277-283.

Havah ishto (Gen. 4:1), "And Adam *was united* with Eve, his wife."

The *da'at* between human beings, between spouses, is a reflection of the *Da'at* which links God to man and to His people. Thus God said of Abraham, *"ki yeda'ativ,"* "for I *know* him" (Gen. 18:19), "I *know* him by My *love."* Similarly, *"va-yeida Elohim,"* (Ex. 2:25), "and God *knew"* the deplorable situation of Israel enslaved in Egypt: He "turned His *heart"* towards them.

Da'at is therefore "knowledge" gained both through the heart and through reason. For Maimonides the rationalist, the man of science, as for the masters of the Kabbalah, *da'at* has an ethical import and aim, and where the moral intention — that is, the intention to use knowledge for the benefit of mankind — is lacking, science is likely to become, in those who possess it, an "intelligence for doing evil."

Da'at, "knowledge," is therefore not a perfect intellectual category, but a perfectible ethical value that the "scholar" must pursue, knowing that his knowledge can never attain perfection. It is a virtue that the "intelligent" man, constantly motivated by the desire to know more, endeavors to exploit through his *Da'at ha-Shem*, his "knowledge of God." In "knowing God" he will know things better as they will become more "transparent" in his eyes, and through improved insight, he will have better knowledge of his fellow-man.

Thanks to the *Da'at ha-Shem,* man will be devoted to the Creator and Possessor of all things and all mankind, he will be devoted to His creation and His creatures. He will "emulate God," and there is only one *Imitatio Dei* that the Sages of Israel know and recommend to man: the emulation of His goodness and mercy.

Nature and Society.
The former is not chaotic matter; the latter is not
a conventional organization.
Man bestows upon others the "goodness" that is
his bounden duty.

The *Da'at ha-Shem*, the "knowledge of God," "links,"
"binds" man to Him who creates everything and from whom
everything is derived, to Him who "in His goodness daily
renews the marvels of His creation" and "in His beneficence
nourishes and sustains all." Thanks to this "bond" with God,
man "relates" with an ennobled love, purified of all egoism and
all *amour propre*, to himself, to his own being, which is rooted in
the Being of his God. He also relates with a more enlightened
and a more penetrating love to everything that exists. For all that
there is, exists both through God, who transcends every creature,
and in God, who is immanent in every creature.

Man should not attempt to dominate, exploit, or possess
nature. His only wish should be to draw near peaceably to that
which God has created, to those things that obey God's will by
following the immutable laws that He has prescribed. In approaching all things, man will remember that in the depths of
all that exists is hidden the Divinity, to which he himself is bound
and by which he knows he is invested. He feels that the Divine
presence, the Shekhinah, desires to dwell in him.

Man should not try to confront society with hostility, but
neither should he blindly submit to it. He should only attach
himself to that which God has formed and associate with those
who voluntarily do His Will, respecting His moral laws of
"justice and goodness" (Mich. 6:8), so that He may live "among
them" (cf. Ex. 25:8).

In the eyes of such a man, nature is therefore not chaotic
matter but an organism given life by Him who has created it. (The
numerical value of His Name, *Elohim*, "God" is the same as that of
the word *ha-teva*, "Nature": 86.) Nature has its own personality, just
like Jerusalem, its focal point, "the Throne of God."

For such a man too society is not a conventional organization formed artificially by men to safeguard their common interests. It is a living, coherent organism ruled by Him who has formed it and given it life. Society — the nation — has its own personality, just like Israel, "the heart of the nations," "the people of God."

Such a man marvels at the diversity of the elements that make up the natural world and harmoniously enhance their disparate qualities. He thanks the Creator for the riches He offers him through nature, and which he must use in moderation and in peace with his fellowmen.

He appreciates the society of his fellowmen and its diversity in unity, into which he willingly integrates himself, for he loves to be of their company. He praises the Creator for having given each man individually his own identity within society, each man being different from his fellowman and yet equal before the Creator and Father of all. He thanks God for putting into each man the "wanting" to bring to his fellowman whatever the other "lacks," for in this way each man can, and must, prove his goodness and justice. God "created a multitude of beings, each lacking in something." Each serves his own needs by his own efforts, yet above all, it is to the honour of man that with mutual trust he also serves his fellowman, a situation practically unknown in the animal world.*

Hence, each man without exception is supposed to *"bestow on others the goodness* — the thanks — *that he owes them"*: he must be a *gomel ḥesed,* one who *pays a debt of charity* to his fellowman.

Abraham the Hebrew, the Father of the people of Israel, "the first believer," who "knew God" and "made Him known

---

* God created this wonderful world and the marvellous higher worlds, but He intentionally left some things "lacking," so that man might have the privilege of providing them, or "restoring" them, of carrying out their *Tikkun.*

to the world," had as his principal characteristic the virtue of *gemilut ḥasadim*, of "rendering favours." It is with an example of *gemilut ḥasadim* that the Torah of Israel "begins and ends."

In society, just as in nature, mutual dependence acts as a constraint, but in a society where *gemilut ḥasadim* is practised, a person is esteemed for his share in this practice. Every man, whoever he may be, should place himself at the disposal of his fellowman. This mutual responsibility was inscribed into the nature of human society by the Creator, who willed man to be both receiver and donor.

In such a society, the individual is neither effaced nor crushed by the masses. Each is able to develop morally and to satisfy his material needs in a moderate way; the material or political interests of a minority will not be served to the detriment of the majority. There is a place for everyone, and none may say of the other that he is dispensable. Each may say to himself, "I am a creature (of God) and so is my neighbour." Both by the nature and by the status that the Creator has given him, each man is at the same time "a stranger and a sojourner" (cf. Gen. 23:4). For "the earth is the Lord's and the fulness thereof" (Ps. 24:1); "Thine O Lord is the greatness, and the power, and the glory...thine is the kingdom.... and Thou reignest over all" (I Chron. 29:11-12). "What is man (then), that Thou art mindful of him?" (Ps. 8:5).

Man and Nature.
Ecological Necessities.

King David was conscious of the precarious nature of human existence, for he asked anxiously, "What is man, that Thou art mindful of him?" (Ps. 8:5). And yet immediately afterwards he marvelled at the signal honour that the Creator paid man in entrusting this world to him. Transported in admiration, King David exclaimed (Ps. 8:6-10): "Nevertheless,

Thou hast crowned him with glory and honour. Thou hast given him dominion over the works of Thy hands; thou hast put all things (in subjection) under his feet: all sheep and oxen, and also the beasts of the field; the birds of the sky and the fishes of the sea; and whatever passes through the paths of the seas; O Lord our Ruler, how majestic is Thy Name in all the earth!"

The power that the Creator gives to man must neither intoxicate him nor make him proud; on the contrary, it urges him to remain humble, the Creator Himself setting the example: "There where His greatness is, there you will find His modesty."

Humble before his Creator, grateful for all His goodness, man regards nature with reverence, approaches it without intent to any injury and contemplates it with admiration as the magnificent handiwork of His Creator: "How great are Thy works, O Lord!" (Ps. 92:6).

The reverence that he feels for nature equally applies to its Creator. In nature he respects everything that moves and lives therein, hence also the very conception of its Author: "the marvellous thoughts" at the origin of His work. He respects the work of the Artist, its order, its content, its variety, "each in its own shape." God "has made them all in wisdom" (cf. Ps. 104:24) and "has created nothing in vain." However, while he contemplates these wonders, man hears his Creator's admonition: "See how good My work is! All that I have created, I have created for you. Take care not to sin — not to destroy My creation — for if you sin, if you do destroy it, no one after you will be able to restore it!"

That is why the masters of the Kabbalah are particularly attentive to the biblical and talmudic injunctions that enjoin upon the Jew reverence for nature in its totality, in its global personality, as much as in the peculiarity of each of its "varieties" and its components.

For this reason, the teachers of Kabbalah are deeply concerned with the Torah's prohibitions regarding the cross-breeding of vegetables and animal species. They see a serious trespass in the mingling of plants and in the hybridization of animals of two different species. For it is the integrity of the "being" of each that is affected (deep within each, as "in all things," lies hidden a spark of the Divine), and above all, it is to their Creator that outrage is done, since He has created them "each according to its kind."

If the masters of Kabbalah judge so severely such unnatural cross-breeding of vegetables and animals, it is because they consider that all the "elements" that make up and populate the natural world are virtually present in man. Man incorporates and represents them; he is responsible for them, for it is he who is summoned to lead them back to their Creator, each in its individual integrity.

When he performs unnatural operations upon plants and animals, he not only harms those he handles as disposable objects. Indirectly, such manipulations affect man, who is their ultimate target, in so far as his dignity is concerned. Furthermore, they may grievously hurt him in the depths of his being, in his heredity, once they result in bewildering genetic experiments, in tests carried out on human beings. These consequences were foreseen and feared by the teachers of the Kabbalah.

The modern biologist, who arrogates to himself the right to try to transform the fundamental structures of the human being, is indulging in genetic manipulations that may result in some advantages of a medical kind, but may also — when they exceed the bounds of "what is permitted" or established by the Creator — do grave damage to the human genetic inheritance. By disturbing the latter, by mutilating it, these manipulations put at risk man's delicate psychosomatic equilibrium and may even destroy his freedom of judgment, thus eventually depriving him of his freedom of movement.

The wrong inflicted on a person is akin to the damage done to any article.

The principle of "damage," its basis and applications, play an important role both in halakhic and in mystical literature. An inner link unites the halakhic commandments and their juridical motivation with the mystical reflections and their ethical and philosophical justification. In the writings of both groups, the wrong inflicted on a person is akin to the damage caused to an object. According to the teachers of Kabbalah, man does wrong to his fellowman when in his mind he "slights or despises" him, by treating him as an insensitive "thing"; when he relates to the *davar* — the "word" spoken to him by his fellowman, the "word" that expresses the other's spirituality and uniqueness, his soul and his intelligence, which are all worthy of respect — as a *davar*, as an inert, confused "thing," as something to be scorned. When a man in his own mind treats any object as if it were a dead thing, he damages that object. In fact, the things we wrongly call "animate beings" and "inanimate things" are part of the same cosmic reality, the whole of which is "animated" by the divine breath that flows through it. True, this breath is manifest more clearly in man than in animals, more in the animal than in the vegetable kingdom, and more in the vegetable than in the realm of minerals, but all these realms constitute a coherent unity, where the various elements are closely linked.

Today's scientific philosophy has been liberated from classical, dogmatic determinism. It gives due regard to the role of energy from the infinitely small to the infinitely large, without which "matter," so-called, does not really exist. It thus recognizes a progressive freedom at every level of physical reality, bringing it closer to the scientific philosophy of the Kabbalah.

Taking their stand on the legal prescripts contained in the

Torah and the Talmud, the masters of the Kabbalah liken the damage caused to nature in terms of its "person" and its "property" to the wrong done to man, to himself and his property. The way man behaves toward nature is judged with the same severity as his behaviour towards his fellowman.

> In polluting the natural world, man defaces the "work of God"; in striking a neighbour, he "disparages" the image of God.

In a word, it is another aspect of his behaviour in relation to God, "Creator of the world" and "Master of all things."

In polluting nature, man defaces "the work of God"; in striking his fellowman, he "disparages" the image of God. When he displays the anger he feels against his fellowman by "smashing something," man infringes the commandment "not to destroy," *bal tashhit,* and becomes "guilty of waste"; he is like an idolator who only yesterday venerated certain objects and carefully preserved them, while today he is destroying them.... When he throws food away, when he neglects to gather up "crumbs of bread" and keep them for those who may need them, man becomes guilty of waste and of a "trespass in regard to foodstuffs," *bizzui okhel (bizzayon be-okhalin),* thus committing an outrage towards "Him who feeds and cares for all, who provides sustenance for all the beings He has created."

The Importance of Trees in Kabbalistic Thought

Both Jewish religious law and Jewish mystical thought base the prohibition against harming anyone, including oneself, and against vandalism, on Deuteronomy (20:19-20), which says: "When thou shalt besiege a city...thou shalt not destroy its trees...."

Indeed, the tree, friend of man, is the symbol of life; it is "the tree of life." It is the incarnation of life in the broadest sense, embracing animate beings and inanimate objects. Reverence for all life and all things is modelled upon the reverence we owe to the tree, which in the Kabbalah is a symbol of the Creator and His creative powers, the Tree of the *Sefirot*.

Consequently, from among all the parts of the natural world that are unjustly called "inanimate," the tree is the one selected by the Torah, the Sages, and the kabbalists. They are truly concerned with the protection of all of nature, and resolutely oppose its misuse, its senseless exploitation, but it is the tree they seek to protect with special insistence, not only in times of peace, but particularly in exceptional circumstances such as those created by war. The Torah itself clearly says, "When thou shalt besiege a city for a long time...thou shalt not destroy — *lo tashḥit* — its trees by forcing an axe against them : for thou mayst eat of them and thou shalt not cut them down; for the tree of the field is man himself" (Deut. 20:19-20).

The kabbalists are insistent upon the care we should give to trees, upon the responsibility incumbent upon us for their well-being. Rabbi Judah he-Ḥasid, "the Pious" (12th-13th centuries), strictly forbids the cutting down of fruit trees and even strongly advises against felling sterile trees — *ilanei serak* — except in case of man's great need; for man's life is bound up with that of the tree.

Man lives with the tree. The man of the Kabbalah talks to the tree; with his lips he speaks to it, with his ears he hears the rustling of its foliage, and with his eyes he follows the flexible lines of its body. He "blesses" it and he includes it in his prayers, he rejoices with it when it grows, and he suffers with it when it dies. Therefore the man of the Kabbalah is as emotionally upset at the violent death of a tree as he would be at the death of a fellowman. He discovers that "there are times when cries traverse unheeded from one end of the world to the other, namely when a fruit tree is felled and when the soul quits the body."

Trees and Man: Their Common Destiny

As we have noted, the Kabbalah pays special attention to trees because of the similarity it sees between trees and men. This is more than a mere resemblance, for there is an actual affinity between the crown of the vegetable world, the tree, and the crown of the animal world, man. This affinity between the friendly representatives of these two worlds is expressed in their appearance and their vocation. Both are "upright," both are "bearers of fruit," and both offer protection to those who need it.

Standing vertically, the tree looks to heaven; man, "standing up before God" (cf. Lev. 9:5) "lifts up his eyes to the heights" (cf. Isa. 40:26). The tree nourishes and comforts man with its fruits; man, and especially the righteous man, the *zaddik*, helps and strengthens his fellowmen by his fruits, namely his "good works." As the Bible says, "There is fruit (reward) for the righteous" (Ps. 58:12), and "the fruit of the righteous is a tree of life" (Prov. 11:30). With its shade, the tree protects man from the heat of the sun; man, and specially the *zaddik*, who "flourishes like the palm tree" (Ps. 92:13), "protects" his followers, his contemporaries, his "generation," from the "fire of passion"; he purifies and cools the "breath of their life."

Yes, the Torah affirms that "the tree of the field is man himself" (Deut. 20:19). With one difference, the Maharal (16th century) points out: the tree has its roots buried in the earth and raises its branches towards the heights, whereas man has his roots in heaven and directs his branches downwards....

However, a certain common destiny is established between the tree and man, of which the latter is conscious and accordingly he expresses his affection for the tree. In addition to celebrating man's New Year, *Rosh ha-Shanah la-Shanim,* "Head-of-the-Year for the Years," the Jew confirms his bond with the tree by celebrating the New Year of the trees, *Rosh ha-Shanah la-Ilan* (or *la-Ilanot*), "Head-of-the-Year for the Tree" (or "for the Trees").

Rosh ha-Shanah la-Ilanot is a great favourite among the men of the Kabbalah. They have created a *tikkun* for this "feast," a special ritual of prayers, and have decreed that on this joyful day one should enjoy fruit, especially the produce in which *Erez Yisrael,* the Land of Israel, takes pride.

The New Year of Years and the New Year of Trees are distinguished from each other by the season in which they are celebrated, the former being celebrated in the autumn and the latter in the spring. Autumn reminds man of his mortality and his limited life span; spring offers him the "rebirth" of the tree, the renewal of life. So on the one hand, man is reminded that he is mortal and on the other, the tree — in its return to life — is a sign for man that his death may not be final.

After each of its repeated "deaths" (like every phenomenon in the history of the natural world), the tree gives evidence of its "resurrection," which takes place before our eyes. It proclaims it in its coming back to life, albeit unchanged; yet "in the days to come, in *Erez Yisrael,* it shall produce fruit every day...."

As for man, he must wait till the "time to come" to "be resurrected" as he was on earth. Indeed, after one single death, his body must first be almost completely destroyed, "purified" in the earth, becoming one "with the dust out of which he was taken" (Gen. 3:19). Only after the "sowing" of the "little bone" that remains, will man "be born again," "be raised to life," and will appear on earth the same as he was during his "lifetime." It is from almost nothing that he will be reborn.

Thus the present life of the tree on the physical plane is a guarantee of man's future both on the physical and on the metaphysical planes.

A Jew walking in a field, who "*sees*" — with his bodily eyes — the rustling of foliage, the trees in blossom, or luxuriant fruit trees, "blesses" God, thanking Him for His goodness in "having created good fruit-bearing trees for man to enjoy," praising Him because "thus it *is* in His world."

On the other hand, when the Jew enters a "field of the dead," a cemetery, he "blesses" God for "having created men and taken them from among the living, so as to call them later back to life" and praises God who "*is (now) bringing* the dead to life again."

In his faith, in his certainty, a Jew sees now, in the present — with his spiritual eyes — the future resurrection of the dead, of which the rebirth of the tree — that symbolic element of nature — is an augury. He experiences "the daily renewal, by His goodness, of the Primal Works," of the "works of Creation." Today's present miracle, the daily re-creation of the whole of nature, which only yesterday seemed "dead," is a promise of the *future* miracle of tomorrow, of the "rebirth of the dead," who have departed this world in the course of innumerable "yesterdays."

Thus the life of the tree and its resurrection are symbolic of man's life and his resurrection.

God himself is the foundation and the guarantee of the kinship between man and tree and their common destiny. This is seen in His Names, which describe Him as the Creator of the World and the Lord of History. The disciples of the Ari ha-Kadosh have shown that the numerical value (91) of the Hebrew word *ilan*, "tree," is the same as that of the combined names *HaVaYaH*, the essential Name of God, which means God as Creator, and *Adonai*, "my Lord," the personal Name of God. Now, the numerical value (45) of the Hebrew word

Adam, "Man," is connected with that of the combined names *EHYeH* and *HaVaYaH. EHYeH,* "I shall be," is the Name that designates God at the origin of the *thought* of the creation of the world and man in his *future* "return to God," his *teshuvah* to the non-time preceding the time of the world's creation ("when" the Teshuvah was conceived). *HaVaYaH,* the Tetragram, is the Name which denotes God at the origin of the actual creation of the natural world and His entry into man's history. However, the numerical value (47) of *EHYeH* and *HaVaYaH* exceeds by two (represented by the letter *Bet,* or the preposition *ba-*) the number 45, which is the numerical value of the word *Adam,* "Man." This is because these divine Names live within the man who is worthy of them; they are *in* man, *ba-Adam* (2 + 45), thanks to the divine image in which the Creator has made him and which he must reveal through his conduct.

Adam, the name of this "Man," prefigures *IsraEL,* into which God has inscribed, has "singled out," His own Name: *El,* "God."

God, the Torah, and Israel are all designated "Tree."

God, who has inserted His Name into that of the people of Israel, declares, "As the days of the tree are the days of My people" (Isa. 65:22). Indeed, like the tree, which having survived the winter, comes to life again, the people of Israel too "comes to life," blossoms, after living through rough, dark, wintry periods; it "changes" while remaining constant.

This people, which resembles the tree on the plane of its "natural" *existence,* is connected, on the plane of its spiritual, historical *life,* with the Torah, which is also "likened to a tree," for it is "a tree of life to those who lay hold upon" it (Prov. 3:18).

In fact, the "Torah of *Life*" "was given to Israel" to ensure its life and its perpetuation, for it is the Work of the Lord, the Expression of His Will. Thus Israel *lives* within the "shade of the Faith" in Him who is the "Source of Life," "the Great Tree": God.

This is why the *Zohar Ḥadash* is able to affirm (on the basis of indications supplied in the Torah): "Three stages (of reality) are linked with one another: The Holy One, blessed be He, the Torah, and Israel, and all three are called Eẓ (tree)."

The Tree of Israel must be planted in the Land of Israel.

In their turn, these three stages — God, the Torah, and Israel — are linked, each separately and all three together, to the "Land of Holiness," to the "Royal Residence."

Indeed, this Land is the land where "God is King," the land which He has "chosen" in order to "promise" it to Israel, His "chosen people," so that they may fulfil the Torah there. It is the land where the Torah is studied and observed and thus the very land of the "*Knowledge* of God," the *Da'at ha-Shem.* For God is "King in Zion"; His people Israel is the "People in Zion"; His Torah is the "Torah in Zion."

This Land was prefigured and created in the garden which "the Lord God planted...in Eden," where He placed Man, and where He "caused to grow every *tree* that is pleasant to the sight and good for food; the tree of *life* also in the midst of the garden, and the tree of the *knowledge* of good and evil" (Gen. 2:8-9).

God planted.... Therefore Israel, the Man called to "cleave to" God by emulating Him, is told: "Just as God, at the creation of the world, first planted, as it is written, 'And the Lord God planted a garden in Eden,' so you, Israel, when you enter into the Land, your first concern must be to plant, as it is written (Lev. 19:23), 'And when ye shall come into the Land

and shall have planted all manner of trees for food....' " (What the "fathers" did in the past, the "sons" have done in our own times; the *ḥalutzim*, the "pioneers," have undertaken the restoration of the Land of Israel by the reforestation of the desert land.)

The Tree of Israel must be planted in the Land of Israel. Indeed, Moses pleaded with God to "lead" the people He had freed from slavery in Egypt "and *plant* them in the mountain of Thy inheritance" (Ex. 15:17); and he ordered the men whom he had sent ahead to explore the Promised Land, to see "whether there are *trees* in it, or not" (Num. 13:20) ("trees," say the Sages, in the double sense of plants and *zaddikim*, "righteous men").

The Tree of the Knowledge of Good and Evil and the Tree of Life

In the perspective of the Kabbalah, the symbol of the Tree, beginning with the Tree of the *Sefirot*, plays a particularly important role in the development of the destiny of Man, of Israel, and of Humanity.

The attitude of Adam, the First Man, to the "tree of the knowledge of good and evil" is initially an expression of his will to be disobedient to God. God had forbidden him to eat (the fruit) of that tree and bade him to be content with the food He gave him in abundance, permitting, even begging, him to eat the fruit "of every tree in the garden," with the sole exception of the "tree of the knowledge of good and evil" (Gen. 2:16-17; 3:3,6). But the attitude of Adam was also an insult to the "peculiar character" of that tree, which the Creator had entrusted to Man's personal protection.

This outrage inflicted by Man on the tree of the knowledge of good and evil led to the fall of Adam. This in turn brought down the "curse" upon the earth, which should have satisfied man with the abundance of its fruits. Adam's fall was likewise the cause of man's being condemned to "death"; indeed, not to that death which had been foreseen for him, and which he might have regarded and even accepted as a "godsend" (just as the *tanna* Rabbi Meir (2nd century) regarded it), but to the pangs of death.

The thirst for pleasure, the wish for power, the ambitious desire for the "knowledge," both intellectual and sensual, of good and evil, did not bring to the First Man (nor to the "presumptuous overweaning generation" of the "Tower of Babel") the much sought-after physical, material, or intellectual satisfaction. On the contrary, his immoderate desire to possess and to consume, and his insatiable drive for limitless growth have produced in man only sorrows, torment, and anguish. In fact, his temptations and his excessive claims make him even less inclined to accept "the day of death," the arrival of which will compel him to put an end to his greed, to abandon his gains, his possessions, to quit his physical life, in short, to die. Now, "man dies without even the half of his desires being satisfied." ·

Nevertheless, at the very hour of his "sin", Adam, Man, did not have to bow to the weight of an irrevocable curse, a final condemnation. God's reproof, the consequence of human sin, already contains the seed of His grace; it opens up the road that can lead man to regeneration and even to his elevation. Though he may have committed no grave sin, truly every man is called to go through a process of *berur*, "clarification," which continues and deepens throughout his life. This means that if he is rational enough to wish it, he can always "clarify" even further "the mixture of good and evil" that is in him and around him. If he is sufficiently "intelligent," he is able to "distinguish" good from evil, separate the one from the other, perceive the good that lies "inside" the evil, extract it and transform it into something good that constantly gains in strength. Thus man is able freely and lucidly to choose "good," to choose "life," as he did before he allowed himself to be led into error, into the confusion that the "mixture of good and evil" provokes in him. For "evil" does not exist in a "pure state"; even from an ontological point of view, there is no absolute, definitive, independent evil. Evil is potentially found in a state of "mixture" with good. In man, who is called to detect it, evil is nonexistent at his birth, for, says the Maharal, if it so existed, it would act from the moment of birth, which is not the case. Evil becomes manifest "in the dawn of man's youth" (cf. Gen. 8:21), when his desires, his passions, drive him in the direction of that which is potentially evil. Yet even here, the roots are pure and holy. Initially it is "good" that feeds a man's desires and passions, which may lead him to further good and holiness if he uses them well. Furthermore, say the Sages, "if it were not for the so-called evil instinct, man would build no houses, never marry, produce no children, undertake no trade...."

Thus, according to the teaching of the masters of Hasidism, evil *does not exist* in man, but there are in him "degrees of goodness." When man acts well, potential evil becomes good; his ardour and enthusiasm are necessary for him to do good truly and fully. When man does wrong, the potential evil becomes evil in fact; indeed, his ardour and enthusiasm make the evil thus accomplished gravely injurious.

Sin and Death

The story of the Tree is the story of Man, his fall and regeneration; it is the history of Israel, its *Galut* and its *Ge'ullah*, its Exile and its Redemption.

Adam's sin, allied to his disregard of the nature of "the tree of the knowledge of good and evil," led to his eviction from the "garden of Eden." Having transgressed the commandment not to eat the fruit of the tree that contained the *sam mavet*, the "poison of death," "the admixing of good and evil," Adam was sentenced to exile.

Similarly, sin allied to the disregard of the nature of the tree of the Torah, the "tree of life," led to the eviction of Israel from "the garden of Eden," the Land of Israel. Having transgressed the commandments of the Torah, of that tree which contains the *sam ḥayyim*, the "elixir of life," Israel was sentenced to exile.

These exiles, however, are not permanent, for "Behold, the *days* are coming" when man will be able to "distinguish" good from evil "intellectually," to "clarify" the mixture, to separate the one from the other "in practice," as stated above. Man will succeed in transforming evil into good (darkness into *light*, night into *day*), and he will crown this work of transfiguration by converting the "tree of the knowledge of good and evil," the "tree of death," into the "tree of life" (Gen. 2:9), of whose fruit he shall eat, as Rabbi Moses Cordovero (16th century) taught. In the future, in the "garden of Eden," these two trees will become "one tree," *ez eḥad* (an image to be found in Ezekiel's vision, Chap. 37), and this will be the "tree of life," the "tree of the Torah." The world, which consists of a mixture of good and evil, will undergo a metamorphosis and become Torah. Matter will be spiritualized; it will be clear and simple. It will become alive.

The victory of man over sin will be a victory over death (for "without sin there is no death"). God "will destroy death forever," and "the Lord God will wipe away tears from off all faces," as foretold by the prophet Isaiah (25:8). Man will reappear in all his beauty, in all his dignity. The outrage of death will be abolished; the rebellion that death caused in man will end; "and the insult of His people" — brought on them by death — "shall He take away from off all the earth, for the Lord hath spoken it" (ibid.).

That tree which was present at man's fall, Israel's fall, will be present at the time of man's, Israel's, regeneration.

The prophets of Israel bear witness to this, and the Kabbalah plays a large part in this witness.

"Behold, the days are coming, says the Lord, when.... I will return the captivity of My people of Israel.... And I will *replant* them upon their land, and they shall no more be plucked up out of their land which I have given them" (Amos 9:13-15). "And thou, son of man — *ben Adam* — take one *tree* (stick) and write upon it.... Thus says the Lord God: Behold, I will take the children of Israel from among the nations, into which they are gone, and will gather them from every side, and bring them back into their own land.... And they shall observe...My statutes, and do them.... And My servant David shall be their prince forever" (Ezek. 37:16-26). And David is the Messiah!

The Days of the Messiah

The days when the "tree" shall be "replanted" foretell the days of the Messiah; they precede them, prepare the way for them, make the conditions fit for them. The Sages remind us of this when they write, "If you are planting a tree and somebody comes to tell you, 'The Messiah is here,' do not break off. You shall go to greet him when you have finished planting your tree." Indeed, the planted tree is the personification of the Messiah, of whom Isaiah said (11:1), "And there shall come forth a shoot from the stock of Jesse, and a branch shall grow out of his roots."

The Messiah is this shoot.... The tree from which this shoot emerges will be cherished, not so much for its external "beauty" as for the "nourishment" it will give to men (see Gen. 3:6), for the "fruits" which it will offer them. For the "fruits of the *zaddik*, the 'righteous' man, are his good deeds."

The Light of the Messiah.
God's Revelation of "Power."
God's Revelation of the "Word."

The *days* of the Messiah will be accompanied by the *light* of the Messiah. This will materialize from the place where God "concealed" it on the very first day of Creation "for the sake of those who devote their energies to the Torah" (by studying it deeply and observing its mitzvot, in the fear and love of God who ordained them), for the sake of the *zaddikim*, the "righteous."

The light of the First Day was intended to unite with the light of That Day, of the End of Days.

It is this light of the first day of creation, the "light of the Torah," which reveals the Creator's "intention" in creating the world, and the objective to which He is directing His creation. This intention, this objective, He expressed thus (Isa. 43:7): "I have created (all) for My glory — *li-khvodi!*" The supreme purpose of creation is the revelation of God's "glory." Now, the Kabbalah teaches us that the *Kavod*, the "glory" of God, expresses the *Malkhut*, the "kingship" of God. His "glory" will be finally established, His "kingship" permanently founded, when the "light of the Torah" (of the united Torah: heavenly and earthly), the light that was "hidden," has reached its culmination and has become wholly visible and accessible. The Torah, Charter of the world's creation, will preside over the founding of the Kingdom of God throughout the world in the union of the world below and the world on high.

God's first revelation by the light of the "First Day" was also the revelation of His "Power": it was expressed in the analogous divine Name: *Elohim*. Now, in this world, God's spokesman is man; it is to him that God *speaks* so that in turn man shall make known what has been revealed to him. But man was not yet present at this first revelation; therefore, when God made the world and said, "Let there be light," in that light He marked out Abraham, the "great man," who would make Him known to the world. Thus God's revelation became the "Word," revealing to man by the Name *Elohim* and by the *Shem HaVaYaH*, the Tetragram Name, that He has created and is creating all things, and by the Name *Adonai*, that He is his "Lord."

With the name *Adonai*, observes Rabbi Eliyahu, the Gaon of Vilna (18th century), God makes known to man the "goal" of the revelation, namely, that man shall accept His Sovereignty, that with man's aid, His Kingdom shall be established. For in order to reign, the King needs a people; "there is no King without a people."

To exercise His Sovereignty, God chooses Israel and makes them a people; he proclaims them God's people at the foot of Mount Sinai. There He reveals Himself to them through His Word. This Word is the moral Law He inscribes into the hearts of His people, thus completing and making meaningful the Law He has inscribed in Nature. The revelation of the divine Word confirms and justifies the revelation of divine Power. The revelation of the Word is directed to man. It is he who must live it. It is Israel, Man, who receives it; it is he who is called to reveal God's revelation to the world. The Kabbalah truly calls man the "foundation of revelation within the universe."

Withal, enjoying the degree of freedom the Creator has given him, man does not loyally fulfil his vocation to spread the divine revelation of the Word. On the other hand, the natural world does faithfully and unfailingly witness to the divine revelation of Power. The glory and reign of God are "waiting" only to be "fulfilled," but this "waiting" must be activated by diligent preparations for the arrival of the days of the Messiah, when the glory of God will be made manifest and His reign established.

In this world, called the "world of action," it is Man, Israel, who acts, co-operating with God, to hasten the coming of the days of the Messiah. Their coming will mark the advent of the Last Days, which will be the First Days of a new era, that of God's glory and God's reign.

The Messiah personifies the "Mystery of Knowledge."
Seeing and Hearing.

These will be the days of the Messiah, of Man, in whom the human race will have attained maturity by giving its wholehearted reverence to the revelations of the Power and Word of God. The proof of this maturity will be the ability to see God's glory and to live under His royal power.

These will be the days of the Messiah. Now, in kabbalistic teaching, the Messiah personifies the *sod ha-da'at*, the "mystery of knowledge." And it is precisely through *da'at*, through "knowledge," that the Messiah will accomplish the *gillui*, the "revelation" of this mystery. At the revelation on Mount Sinai, it was Moses who received the *Mattan Torah*, the "gift of the Torah." He, the precursor of the Messiah, was an *ish ha-da'at*, a "man of knowledge." This revelation prefigures the "time of the Messiah." And the characteristic of the Sinaitic revelation was the synthesis of sight and sound. During this event, says the Torah, "all the people saw the sounds," whereupon the masters of the Kabbalah pronounced that "the *gillui ha-da'at*, the 'revelation of knowledge,' enabled the people to see what they heard."

The *gillui sod ha-da'at*, the "revelation of the mystery of knowledge" by the Messiah, heralds the *Gillui Shekhinah*, the "revelation of the Presence of God."

Then the "Mystery of Mysteries," God Himself, will be seen and heard through His Torah, with which He is One. On

"That Day," as on the day when He revealed Himself through the Torah on Sinai, "they shall see what they hear"; the visual faculty — of the body and senses — shall be one with the aural faculty — of the spirit and intellect.

Then we shall see the "Words" of God illuminated in all their depths; then we shall understand His "command-ments" with all they contain, in all their clarity. Not only shall we "hear" them, not only shall we "listen" to them as they come to us from without, but we shall also confirm them by our *da'at,* our "knowledge." We shall experience this knowledge as much in our mind as in our heart, for it will imbue the innermost parts of our whole being.

In addition, *da'at* will reveal to our spiritual eyes the reasons for all God's actions regarding ourselves; those we have accepted, judging them to be good, and those we have submitted to, judging them to be bad. For *all* His actions regarding ourselves, we shall thank God, who "is Good and does Good."

In fact, when one is in a position to "look" at the different parts of a *whole,* discovering them and "knowing" them and their inner structure, this *whole* seems good to us. Man, "living with God," can then grasp the sense of those words that crown the biblical account of Creation, "And God *saw every-thing* that He had made, and, behold, it was *very good*" (Gen. 1:31). God gave us to understand that the *whole is good,* moreover, "it is *very good....*" As Adam did before the Fall, so, in the days of the Messiah, a man will be able to "see the world from one end to the other," to embrace time in a single glance, unifying in his spirit the different parts of which it is com-posed. For the sight of a man who "lives with God," the Almighty, is clear and is "illumined by His light" (cf. Ps. 36:10). This light makes the *unified whole* visible so that appar-ent antinomies are removed and unity appears in all its simplicity. This ultimate light is above the light that is the opposite of shadow, above the light regarded in relation to the dark; it appears here in its pristine purity, without reference to anything but itself. For "here all light is one," "here (in Him, in the Source of the Godhead) all is in unity. One sees neither mercy nor severity (the Manifestations of the Godhead); one does not see light as if it were emerging from the dark, for here there is no darkness, there is no severity." Thus, the *tanna* Rabbi Simeon bar Yoḥai (2nd century) describes for us that supreme, ultimate state where pure light reigns.

"In the future,..." in the days of the Messiah, when the revelation of the Word of God shall be wholly fulfilled, this light will be the quintessence of Light, the radiance of God Himself. It will excel the light that God created on the First Day, the light "with which He enwrapped Himself" and from which He withdrew as His power became manifest. In fact, the light of the "Work of Creation" had replaced the darkness, the void, as it is written at the beginning of the Book of Genesis (1:2-3): "...and *darkness* was upon the face of the *deep*.... And God said, 'Let there be *light*,' and there was light."

Few people attain this high level of perception of the super-light. The great mystic Rabbi Simeon bar Yoḥai was one of those few, and he himself stated, "I have seen some Men of Grandeur (men able to raise themselves spiritually very high), but they (those who are worthy to welcome the face of the Shekhinah) are few in number."

Nevertheless, in the messianic times, when, according to the prophet of Israel (Isa. 60:21; 40:5), "Thy people shall be all righteous," for "the glory of the Lord shall be revealed, and all *flesh* shall see it together, for the mouth of the Lord has *spoken* it"; when, according to the vision of Rabbi Moses Hayyim Luzzatto (18th century), "the heightened power of the soul will have weakened the dark forces of matter and the human body will have become transparent" — then "man, radiant with brightness, shall be able to raise himself to this quintessential light." He will return to the garden of Eden, from which he was evicted, to himself, to his roots from which he had severed himself, to God from whom he had removed himself following his sin — his repudiation of the Word of God — and he will "lay hold on the tree of life" (Prov. 3:18), on the Torah. Then he will begin to live his real life, for hereafter he will live "with the fountain of life"; "in Thy light shall we *see* light" (Ps. 36:10). This man will experience "knowing God," who is the "Life of Life." In truth, "knowledge is life," *ha-da'at hi ha-ḥayyim*, thus teach the masters of the Kabbalah. It is the *ḥiyyut*, the "vitality," the very essence of life, states the Gaon of Vilna. And life is the unity which results from the harmonizing of the different and opposing forces that animate it. As the Maharal observes, the Hebrew word *ḥayyim*, "life," is in the plural, meaning one life in its unity.

The Principle of Contradiction and the Ideal of Unity

Man achieves this harmonization of the forces which animate his life by applying the precepts of the Torah. The Torah is a "Torah of Life." Its precepts bring to those who observe them the serenity celebrated by King David in his Psalms (19:9): "The statutes of the Lord are right, rejoicing the heart: the commandment of the Lord is pure, enlightening the eyes." In observing the mitzvot of the Torah, the Jew succeeds in mastering the antagonistic materialistic forces by reducing, simplifying, and finally eliminating them. Left unchecked, these forces are evil; they must be controlled and dominated by man.

Thus, the principle of contradiction, which the Creator inscribed in human beings so as to impel them "to choose," to exercise their free will — that principle, when it is properly understood by man, contributes to his development.

The messianic era, which man will have prepared for by study of the Torah and observance of the mitzvot, will be the era of perfect, and yet dynamic, unity in man; that unity is animated by the beneficent forces that flow through the Torah-observant being.

Having conquered within himself, and so around himself, those evil antagonistic forces that bring death in their train, man will be re-established in the garden of Eden, where the "tree of the knowledge of good and evil" becomes one with the "tree of life," thus affirms Rabbi Nahman of Bratslav (18th-19th centuries). For evil is a contradiction of good; death is the contradiction of life. Both evil and death, adds Rabbi Nahman, are a "contradiction" of the will of man, of his will to be in the pure, unified state inscribed by the Creator at the very root of the opposing forces that should test him. It is that will which man is called upon to project, to emphasize, freely.

That evil is the contradiction of good, and death is the contradiction of life, the Book of Deuteronomy (30:15,19) states clearly for us: "See, I have put before you life and good, and death and evil.... therefore, *choose* life, so that thou mayst live." So it is up to man to surmount this contradiction, which the Creator has inscribed into the heart of the human condition; nevertheless, he will not be able to do so without God's help.

When the contradiction shall have thus been overcome, God will suppress "evil," violence; "He will swallow up death for ever, and the Lord God will wipe away tears from off all faces" (Isa. 25:8). The salt of their tears, adds Rabbi Nahman, will be transformed into the "sweet water of the knowledge of God"; "The earth shall be filled with the *knowledge* of the Lord, as the waters cover the sea" (Isa. 11:9).

Evil will have rediscovered Good, its root; death will have rediscovered its own root, which is life.

All this will come about thanks to the "knowledge of God," who is one, the perfect One, in whom there is no contradiction, states Rabbi Naḥman, and adds that all evil arises in man from his separation from the One. He goes on to recall the thought of our Sages, may their memory be blessed: " 'On that day the Lord shall be one and His Name (shall be) One' (Zech. 14:9), that is to say, He shall appear to us as He is, 'entirely Good, He who does good,' for in the One there is no evil. Wherefore 'in the imminent future,' evil shall be destroyed, contradiction suppressed, and that which is written shall be fulfilled: 'Truth stands firm for ever, but lies live only for a moment' (Prov. 12:19); for truth is *one*, it is forever, but a lie is motley and is gone in the twinkling of an eye."

Deterioration and Restoration of God's Creation by Man

In that marvellous description of "That Day," which the brilliant master of Hasidism, Rabbi Naḥman of Bratslav, has bequeathed us, it is striking that in the days of the Messiah, thanks to the "knowledge of God," each thing will appear to us good in its essence, while evil, naturally supposed to be the opposite of good, will cease to exist. Each thing in its manifestation will seem to us to be pure, while impurity, the natural opposite of purity, will not endure. Everything will appear to us transparently clear.

The unified creation will be led back to its original Source, there where it existed before becoming "separated," "liberated," "distanced" from its Creator, before "going off" into "division," "scission," "rupture"; before being "divided" by the ontological "breach" in the cosmos brought about by the "breaking of the vessels," and by the moral "rupture" brought about in man by his "sin." Then, only the good will exist in the worlds that have been pacified: in the external world outside man as in man's interior world. The spirit of truth alone will endure, that truth which is at the root of all phenomenon, both visible and invisible.

The "deterioration," the "breaking down" of the Creation, has been caused by man, but its "restoration" and "repair" is led by the work of Man, Israel. For the process of the world's "restoration" and "repair," according to the Kabbalah, is a process of *berur*, "clarification," performed by man. This "clarification" having been achieved, "the glory of the Lord will be revealed," and "His reign shall begin." A perfect unity will become manifest: between soul and body; between the *orot*, the "lights", and the *kelim*, the "vessels"; between the "closed" and the "open"; between the "inward" and the "external," the illusory and the rational, the poetic and the scientific, the imaginary and the real. (In fact, man can only imagine what is possible, what is virtually real, observed Maimonides the rationalist (12th century) and Rav Kook the mystic (19th-20th centuries).)

Man, whom God "has made to be straightforward," will no longer "seek out endless artifices," a procedure condemned by King Solomon (cf. Eccles. 7:29). For the upright man, everything is upright.

The Jew who is searching the Scripture and probing its biblical depths to reach the *sod*, its "secret" sense, will understand the Gaon of Vilna's warning: it will not be possible for him to penetrate the Scriptures, even to scratch the surface on the level of *peshat*, the "plain" sense, unless he has looked for and found the intrinsic agreement of the *sod* and the *peshat*, for each completes and qualifies the other. Similarly, the scientist who is investigating nature at the surface level in an attempt to fathom its secrets, the scientist who is exploring immediate reality, trying to discover there the properties and laws given by the Creator and to understand their interrelations

— the scientist of our own time — would be willing to adopt (as his predecessors of less than a century ago would not have dared to do) this statement, made by the Gaon of Vilna (who excelled both in the domain of the Kabbalah and that of pure and natural sciences): "He who does not believe in the things that are 'hidden' does not believe in what is 'revealed.' " For the "hidden" and the "revealed" are linked together; they constitute a unity.

In fact, everything is joined together in unity. The Torah, which was made for the world, constitutes a unity in itself; the world, governed by the Torah, constitutes a unity in itself; the Torah and the world together form a unity in which each supports the other. They are brought together by Man, Israel, who constitutes a unity and who was created to live simultaneously within the union of Torah and world. Hence the unity of each and all things, of all existence, derives from the Unity of the one God and aspires to return to the one God and find itself again in His Unity.

The Meeting of Kabbalah and Science

Into its doctrine of unity, the Kabbalah has inserted its teaching concerning the unity of the Kabbalah and science. Indeed, the latter occupies a central place in the doctrine, for the Kabbalah aims to discover the *razei Torah*, the "mysteries of the Torah," in the Torah, which it is carefully examining, and, hidden in the depths of the Torah, the *razei olam*, the "mysteries of the world." For between the Torah and the world there exists a close relationship, an inward bond. The Torah was the Charter for the creation of the world, and as long as the world exists, the Torah must be — for all its inhabitants and, in particular, for Israel, its guardian spirit — the basic constitution that guides their behavior. The Kabbalah, being the supreme expression of the Torah, scrutinizes the "inwardness," the essence of Reality; it penetrates its invisible "kernel." Science studies the "external evidence" of the real world, examines its visible "shell." Now, the "internal" and the "external," the kernel and the shell of all that exists, form a unity.

The complementarity of the Kabbalah and science is particularly evident when the Torah, the object of kabbalistic research, unveils its inner secrets, while science, penetrating the surface of the material world, the immediate object of its study, tries to get down into its invisible, immaterial reality. Today, Kabbalah and science meet and merge, displaying their harmony to those who are worthy of it and privy to its knowledge; they thus confirm their unity, for both of them share in the same reality that the Creator offers as an object for study to man's intelligence and intuition.

This coming together has its origin in the acceptance of the Kabbalah by science, which concedes that in principle it is not opposed to the Kabbalah. Quite the contrary, when science has made progress in its *fundamental* research into reality, it will recognize that the Kabbalah and itself both draw from the same divine Source and are travelling towards the same ethical goal appointed by the Creator while taking parallel roads of research and using parallel methods of investigation.

Such meetings between the Kabbalah and science have occurred throughout their long history. But there never was a real convergence of ideas, for the vision of the world held by the Kabbalah and that held by science were fundamentally different.

According to the Kabbalah, the Creator has established in the world that He freely created a determinist system which, by means of the laws He has ordained, makes certain that the world will proceed in a "regular," "normal," "natural," course. But within this determinist system, the Creator has placed a "psychic force" that gives a certain special self-determination to everything that exists, from a grain of sand to a distant planet, from the smallest insect to man. This latitude is evident in every rank of existence, from inert matter to human beings.

According to natural, physical science, from its Greek origins to the beginning of this century, an absolute, all-powerful determinism, with neither beginning nor end, rules the entire world. This latter governs *itself* according to a system of immutable laws that it has given itself and that strictly regulate everything that exists. Man is not exempt from these laws, for he is no more than a "physical fact"; his "freedom" is only one link in the chain of general determinism. Thus man is only an insignificant particle of matter (or again, an anonymous part of the social machinery).

Not until modern times has there been the beginning of an agreement between the Kabbalah and science, especially physical science. Such an agreement could eventually lead to a harmonious accord on the essence of scientific thought.

The Kabbalah teaches that there are moments "selected" by Divine Providence for the revelation of certain truths contained in its teaching. Such "moments" betoken a deeper examination of the "mysteries of the Torah," a greater penetration of the Torah's "inner wisdom" by those who devote themselves to this in holy living: the *anavim*, the "humble," the *aniyyim*, the "poor" (these two Hebrew words reflect two virtues that are combined in the *zenu'im*, the "pure," who thus "respond" to God's call). By their assiduous study of the Torah and their scrupulous observance of the mitzvot, these *zenu'im*, these "pure" men, succeed in penetrating the "mysteries of the Torah." As these secrets rise to the surface, though without being "revealed to others," they awaken in "the others," in the non-initiated, a growing interest in the Kabbalah's values, as much among Jews as among non-Jews.

This could result in a rapport between the scientific conception of the Kabbalah and that of science, especially in the realm of cosmology, out of which — once the idea of the *creation* of the world has been accepted (a free, *ex nihilo* creation) — there might evolve a philosophy of science and ethics reuniting the two conceptions.

"Exceptional Moments" in the History of the Kabbalah.
Their Eschatological Significance.

Some of these "exceptional moments" in the history of the Kabbalah have been pointed out by the kabbalists themselves and they invite us to deduce the lessons they contain.

The first great moment was that of the "revelation," the appearance of the *Sefer ha-Zohar*, the "Book of Splendour," crowned with the halo of Rabbi Simeon bar Yohai, the *tanna*, the great Sage and leader, who lived in Galilee in the 2nd century. The "revelation," that is, the dissemination of this basic book of the Kabbalah, took place in Spain in the 13th century.

The second great moment was that of the "revelation," the appearance of Rabbi Isaac Luria, the *Ari ha-Kadosh*, the "Sacred Lion," the father of Jewish mysticism, in Galilee in the 16th century.

The third great moment was that of the "revelation," the appearance of Rabbi Israel Ba'al Shem Tov, the "Master of the Good Name," the father of Hasidism, in the Ukraine in the 18th century.

The Zohar itself is evidence of the importance of the first great moment and its eschatological significance. It asserts that "in the future," "in the time of the King Messiah," Israel shall taste of the tree of life, which is the Zohar, within which the Holy One, blessed be He, has hidden the deep mysteries of the Torah. These, Israel will discover and, accompanied by divine grace, it will finally emerge from its *Galut*, "exile." In fact, "it is the thorough study of the Zohar that will make possible the final deliverance."

Witness to the messianic relevance of the second great moment is the disciple of the Ari ha-Kadosh, Rabbi Hayyim Vital. He states that thanks to Rabbi Isaac Luria's commentaries on the Zohar, this holy book has become accessible to those who are worthy of it due to their holy way of life, namely to those who work for the glory of God and the redemption of Israel and the world.

The messianic relevance of the third great moment is evidenced by Rabbi Moses Hayyim Ephraim of Sudylkov, grandson of Rabbi Israel Ba'al Shem Tov and commentator on his teaching. He writes in his *Degel Mahaneh Efrayyim* that the messianic era will begin when the "sources" of the Ba'al Shem Tov's teaching "shall spread outwards" into the world. (The Hasidism of the Ba'al Shem Tov emphasizes and popularizes the ethical and practical aspect of the abstract doctrine of Rabbi Isaac Luria.)

These three great moments were accompanied by a deeper examination and an "uncovering" of the mysteries of the Torah; thus they contributed to the outpouring of the *da'at ha-Shem*, the "knowledge of God." They paved the way for the coming of messianic times, they hastened the time of redemption. Some famous masters of kabbalistic thought, in particular Rabbi Isaiah Horowitz, the Shelah ha-Kadosh (16th-17th centuries), and Rabbi Shneur Zalman of Lyady (18th-19th centuries), delight in dwelling upon the historical significance of these great moments.

The "Mysteries of the Torah" and the "Mysteries of the World"

Da'at ha-Shem, knowledge of God as the Creator of the world and Giver of the Torah, is the ultimate expression of all knowledge. In order to attain this, it is necessary to acquire *da'at*, "knowledge" of the divine Torah, clarifying the scientific knowledge of the divine Creation of the world. In the Bible, God is called *El De'ot ha-Shem*, "the Lord is a God of knowledge" (I Sam. 2:3). And the Sages add, "Science is great when it is placed between the two Names of God: *"El... ha-Shem"* (thus showing, says the Zohar, that "the two Names form a Unity: there is no separation between them").

From Daniel to Maimonides, from Maimonides to Rav Kook, encompassing all the Jewish mystics and rationalists, the "increase" of *da'at*, of "knowledge" — especially knowledge of the sciences — occurs under the aegis of the *hokhmot*, the "wisdoms" of the Torah, which the Kabbalah has closely studied. These *hokhmot* reflect the *Torah Ila'ah*, the "higher Torah," the "Torah above," and the *Torah ze'ira*, the *Torah tata'ah*, the "lower Torah," the "Torah here below." The *Torah Ila'ah* contains the *razei Torah*, the "mysteries of the Torah"; the *Torah ze'ira* contains the *razei olam*, the "mysteries of the world." The former includes the latter, which is linked with science. The totality of these mysteries finds its place in the ethical, practical ideals proclaimed by the Torah.

On the abstract, "sefirotic" plane, *da'at* unites *hokhmah* and *binah*: the first may be likened to inductive reasoning, a process of mental synthesis; the second, to deductive reasoning, an analytical mental process; *da'at* unites them, reveals them and also represents their crowning goal. This must be a religious and moral goal, which means *da'at* as understood by the prophets of Israel, in particular Isaiah and Jeremiah: a *da'at* leading to *da'at ha-Shem*, as clarified by the Zohar and Maimonides. This *da'at ha-Shem* will eventually lead Israel (and all humanity with it) to ultimate deliverance from the Galut, from both a material and spiritual exile, as in the times past it led Israel to its first deliverance from slavery in Egypt. A verse of the Book of Exodus (6:7) is evidence of this, says Rabbi Naḥman of Bratslav. It reads: "...and I will take you to be my people and I will be your God, and you shall know that I am the Lord your God who brings you out from under the burdens of the Egyptians...."

"Physical Reality" interconnects with Metaphysical Reality.

The accord between Kabbalah and science is happening at the "given moment" when the latter — the science of life, physical science, experimental science — is converging in its basic conceptions with the Kabbalah's scientific conceptions; when science even seems disposed to assimilate such conceptions into its own vision of the *created* world, its specific mode of apprehending reality.

Today's scientist is spellbound when he is confronted by the *sod ha-Ḥayyim*, the *"mystery* of life," its beginning and its end, and especially so with the *sod ha-maḥashavah*, the *"mystery* of thought," in other words, with the *"mystery* of man." According to the masters of the Kabbalah, the essence of man is *yedi'ah*, "knowledge"; now, this is *not knowable*—man cannot grasp it, just as he "cannot grasp the essence of his own soul." The modern scientist recognizes that what is known is infinitely small beside the immensity of the unknown. He admits that that which is known, visible, tangible, encompasses immeasurable areas that are invisible and inaccessible to our perceptions. He conjectures and even assumes that beyond the phenomenal reality are hidden invisible realities. His research leads him to adopt a point of view that is basic to the Kabbalah and makes distinctions between several levels of reality, namely that the "*physical reality*" in the classic sense of the term extends into *metaphysical reality*.

Today's man of science already recognizes absolutely that the physical, material world would not be what it is without the immaterial force of energy which permeates it. He is thus not far from being able to adopt the Kabbalah's basic thesis, which states that "in each thing there is an internal point, a 'spark', which animates it and represents the life force with which the Creator has endowed it," and which He maintains and "vitalizes." This "spark" embodies the power of God acting within that which suffers His action. These *orot*, these "inner lights," are concealed behind the *'orot*, the "outer shells." (The Hebrew word *orot*, meaning "lights," begins with the letter *Alef*, representing *Alufo shel olam*, the "Master of the world"; and the Hebrew word *'orot*, meaning "outer shells," begins with the letter *'Ayin*, representing *olam*, the "world"!) According to the teachers of the Kabbalah, "nature" does not really exist; what really exists is the *ḥiyyut*, the "life-force" that animates nature from within; without this *ḥiyyut*, what we see from the outside would not exist. In fact, the *ḥiyyut* reflects, as it were, the Life of Him who is *Ḥayyei ha-Ḥayyim*, the "Life of Life"; it resides, hidden, within what exists, waiting until man, in particular the Jew, brings it to light by fulfilling the mitzvot.

The living, personal God, is therefore revealed as Hidden Life, which nourishes the life of all that exists. In every thing there is a kind of soul, of spiritual *ḥiyyut*; each thing incorporates a specific characteristic showing, in increasing order of intensity, some degree of freedom. The *ḥiyyut*, says the Ba'al Shem Tov, recalls the "letters" of the Word of God, for the world "was made by the word of God" (Ps. 33:6) and it continues to evolve by the Word of God. The *ḥiyyut* actualizes the "Ten Utterances by which the world was made," whereby lives everything that exists, everything we see, whether animate or inanimate. God, transcendent, invisible, incorporeal, "encompassing the world," manifests Himself in this way by His life-giving, immanent reflection in the "world that He fills," investing it with its content and its life.

Through Kabbalah in particular, Judaism aspires to discover the *penimiyyut*, the "inner nature" of things and their essential meaning. Hellenism, whose spirit shaped men of science down the centuries, confined itself to displaying visible things, ranging them in order of "beauty." But nowadays scientists no longer have a Hellenic, mechanistic vision of the world, of a world formerly regarded as immobile and static. Following the masters of the Kabbalah, today's scientist recognizes the dynamic and evolutionary character of the world. Einstein's Theory of Relativity and Heisenberg's Principle of Uncertainty put the contemporary scientist in an "uncertain reality." He is aware, therefore, that his mental processes, and the actions that flow from them, take place in an "uncertain reality."

The "certainty" that for centuries scientists proudly paraded when they were examining the world with the help of their reason is now giving way to a modest estimate of "probability." This is the only judgment they put forward, having examined the world and explored what they call "reality." In fact, reality can no longer be precisely circumscribed as it was previously. The real world is transcending the "unreal" world, which the scientists are not able to describe. Man can only analyse what he is able to discover with his reason. He is not able to define what cannot be grasped. Reason, therefore, is not the only road that leads to the knowledge of reality.

In Contemporary Science, absolute Determinism
is in doubt.
Now the New Physics is catching up with the
Kabbalah.

Finding himself in an "uncertain reality," which is that of
"probabilities," the scientist today no longer dares show the
same pride as his predecessors did, nor disdainfully state that
in the natural world, within which he lives and which he can
easily investigate, everything is foreseeable and therefore
knowable. *In fact*, his predecessors saw in the origin of everything a fixed, immutable *cause*, inflexibly governing the *evolution* of all things. Nowadays, absolute causality and
absolute determinism are in serious doubt. In modern physics indeterminism prevails over determinism, but without
parting from it; therefore, it is converging *grosso modo* with
the Kabbalah, which recognizes no impersonal *causality* —
either fixed, or constraining, or perpetual — impassively
governing the world.

As for the Kabbalah, it highlights the *Creation* — the
world's creation which He, the Creator, freely and voluntarily undertook, to which He gave a "beginning" and placed
within "Time." The Creator, "Cause of Causes," "Root of
Roots," is the Being above all beings, who Himself is watch-
ing over His "Primal Work," whose beginning, hidden from
men, cannot be fathomed; yet, in His goodness, He renews it
every day so that in the course of time, man may come to
visualize and understand it.

The Kabbalah does not disregard the precise laws of
determinism, which the Creator himself has established and
continues to maintain in the visible world. Nevertheless, in
this same visible world, and above all in the invisible world,
He leaves plenty of room for indeterminism.

The Kabbalah also recognizes an "evolution" in the world,
but not that evolution presented by the classic scientific image,

unidirectional and leading automatically from "cause" to "effect." The evolution recognized by the Kabbalah is a *hishtalshelut*, a "series," like a voluntary "descent" followed by a voluntary "ascent," a "moving away" from the "Root" and a "return," a *teshuvah*, coming back to the "Root." The *Sefirot*, representing Man, are evidence of this evolution. This twofold "movement" of His creation, of His creatures, willed by the Creator, has been discovered by man through his learning and determination, for this movement must lead him to his ultimate destiny.

Science, being infinite, is unattainable in Infinity.

Scientists today, thanks to their growing humility, are coming closer to the masters of the Kabbalah, who, when their spirit reaches a high degree of clarity, cry out, "But where shall wisdom be found? — *Ve-ha-hokhmah me-ayin timmaze?*" (Job 28:12). Kabbalistic thinkers take this verse out of its narrow, literal context and give it a much wider interpretation, having found in it a meaning of great philosophic import. They have interpreted it as follows: wisdom — science — which comes from the *Ayin*, "Nothingness" (the equivalent of *Ein-Sof*, "Infinity"), should be greeted with great humility by the Sage as by the scientist. Wisdom — science — can be "found" wherever the searcher recognizes it as being submerged in "nothingness." Hence, he must look upon himself, too, as an *ayin*, a "no-thing," and regard his wisdom as "nothing" in relation to total and all-embracing Wisdom. For God and Wisdom are One, whereas human wisdom cannot become one with its subject, however great its bearer. God, who is Knowledge, knows Himself and knows everything that exists, for everything that exists, "exists through Him," says Maimonides, "and in Him," add the kabbalists. He, the

Ein-Sof, the "Infinite," is above all the divine Names by which He communicates with men. He has no Name, wrote Joseph Gikatilla (13th-14th centuries). Science, which comes from the Infinite and extends to infinity, will have no name either, says the Gaon of Vilna, for the more a thing is elevated, the less can it bear a name. Today scientists recognize that science, being infinite, is unattainable even in infinity. Reaching out into regions that are more and more inaccessible to human perception, science escapes man. Today they acknowledge that they have no intelligible way of capturing the infinite, no adequate semantic means, not even a mathematical language to express the science of the infinite; thus, they can give it no name. They attest to this fact even when they are on the way to attaining heights of knowledge and technical achievement of which their predecessors never dreamed.

"Reason itself enables us to perceive its limits."

As stated, the most eminent scientists today admit that they are incapable of meeting the requirements of true science, that is, of touching the essence of reality, of grasping it in its entirety, of expressing it in an adequate language and so, of precisely formulating its unity, this of course being the ultimate goal of science.

In every age, reason has been regarded in the scientific world as the sole route to attain this goal, which researchers thought was within their grasp. Consequently, they used to celebrate the absolute, exclusive, intellectual omnipotence of reason. They proclaimed its pure, "impartial" objectivity, free of all personal or contextual influence. Now, for some time past, the "impersonal" objectivity of reason has been in doubt; man's character, his inclinations, and his prejudices do not allow the completely free exercise of reason. It is admitted that a certain subjectivity intervenes in the exercise of reason, in its approach to reality, in its apprehension of living beings; a certain scission separates the subject from the object: the object is what the subject would like it to be... Man understands that his reason will not help him satisfy his justifiable wish to gain a global, clear view of reality. In the critique of systems aiming to explain reality, the value of reason no longer appears incontestable, compelling, or primordial; reason no longer enjoys the infallibility attributed to it in the past; in the future, its universality will be disputed.

For scientists up to the last century, as for the Greeks long ago, there was no criterion of truth without rational demonstration and experimental proof, but today there is ceaseless and many-faceted questioning of the ideas of reason and truth, of experiment and proof. There are no definite answers to the philosophical-scientific problems that confront researchers. They are compelled to doubt the value traditionally ascribed to reason, to which their predecessors attributed the power of explaining everything, of sustaining great material and technical undertakings, and of leading to truth. Reason can no longer guide researchers to the goal of their quest. Some eminent scientific philosophers, doubting the efficacy of reason and the validity of its results, even speak of a "crisis of rationality"; others do not hesitate to speak of its "bankruptcy." One renowned thinker and scientist is happy just to put forward a "revision of rationality" in recommending a new approach.

And so, today's men of science are discovering the sense of mystery!

As for the Kabbalah, it underestimates neither the value nor the function of reason. It recognizes that reason has an important role, both in intellectual scientific research and in man's religious and moral conduct. However, the Kabbalah never gave it primacy in the realm of science as did the Greeks.

The Kabbalah appreciates reason as a "gift of God to man" to help him to understand His creation and to take care of His universe, in the midst of which God has placed him and given him responsibility. The kabbalist does not forget that reason clarifies man's service both to God and to his fellowman. When man neglects reason, he is more exposed to "sin," and, in fact, he "does not sin" against God, nor does he commit any fault against his fellow creatures, "except when a breath of foolishness enters into him."

On the other hand, man should not trust exclusively to reason, either in his intellectual, scientific researches or in his religious and moral conduct; for reason alone might lead him into error.

A century before the criticism of reason began to be heard in philosophic and scientific circles, one of the masters of Hasidism, Rabbi Zevi Elimelech of Dynow (19th century), stated that "reason itself shows us its limits"; it shows us the way that can lead us beyond itself, that can raise us "above reason," but it also tells us that this "supra reason" completes rather than contradicts reason.

As much on the intellectual, scientific plane as on the religious, moral plane, the mission of *sekhel*, "reason," is to lead us to *da'at*, to intellectual-ethical knowledge. In its turn, the mission of this knowledge is to bring us to the *da'at ha-Shem*, the "knowledge of God," the source of the "science of brain and heart."

Today's man of science is discovering the sense of mystery. But he cannot yet show us where the mystery must lead us. Rav Kook, who lived through the beginning of the "scientific revolution" of our time and saw its material, moral, and social consequences, has defined the meaning of this mystery. He writes, "As science progresses and grows stronger in its evolution, so man grows nearer to the divine light."

The Bond Uniting Science and Ethics

Today's scientist, therefore, is receptive to the transcendent. But the transcendent is inseparable from ethics.

The Kabbalah requires man to consider the "hidden things" from a religious, ethical point of view, for the "hidden things" are bound up with "those things that have been revealed." The latter must be seen by man in the perspective of the Torah and its commandments. The Kabbalah bases this doctrine on the verse in the Book of Deuteronomy (29:28), which says: "The *secret* things — *ha-nistarot* — belong unto the Lord our God, but those things which are *revealed* — *ha-niglot* — belong to us and to our children forever, that we may do — *la-asot* — all the *words* of this Law."

A bond thus exists between the "hidden things," *ha-nistarot*, and the "things that are revealed," *ha-niglot*. Man is called to demonstrate this bond to the world through religious, ethical *action*, *la-asot*. By this *la-asot*, a Jew discloses to the world that the "hidden things" and the "things that are revealed" do not belong to two different orders of things, to two separate worlds, but to one and the same world, which is waiting for its unity to be revealed. Both the individual Jew, by study of the Torah and observance of its mitzvot, and the Jewish people, must labour to bring to light the *Yiḥud*, the "unification" of this apparently divided world.

When the Torah recommends the Jew to "do," to "act," *la-asot* in accordance with the mitzvot, it consoles him for his "ignorance," his inability to pierce the mysteries of the *nistarot*; it encourages him in his "knowing," in his ability to develop his knowledge of the *niglot*. In truth, the *olam ha-maḥashavah*, the "world of thought," of pure spirituality, is there, completely impenetrable, but man receives "sparks from the Torah" that help him to implement the *olam ha-asiyyah*, "the world of action" — action that is thoughtful and sustained — which is his world, reserved entirely for him.

The more man acts in the *olam ha-asiyyah* in accordance with the Torah's mitzvot, the more he develops his spirituality. The purification of his body and the refining of his mind increase his intellectual perspicacity, strengthen his cognitive power and enable him to "look at" those things which ordinarily "the eye cannot see."

When God gave the Torah to His people on Sinai, Israel proclaimed, "All that the Lord has said *na'aseh* (will we do) *ve-nishma* (and we shall hear and obey)." And the Sages comment on this verse of Exodus (24:7), saying, "At the hour when Israel put the *na'aseh* before the *nishma* [when they said first *na'aseh*, 'we shall do,' and then *nishma*, 'we shall hear and obey'], a divine echo was heard which asked, 'But who *revealed* to My children this *raz*, this 'mystery', which is shared by the angels, as it is written (Ps. 103:20), 'Bless the Lord, you, His angels, you mighty ones, *osei* (that do) His biddings, *li-shmo'a* (to hearken) to the voice of His word?'" First *osei* (those who "do"), then *li-shmo'a* ("to hear").

First "do," then "understand." With what result, what reward? When the *asiyyah*, the "doing," the action, precedes the *shemi'ah*, the "hearing," the understanding, only then, according to the Zohar, can man exercise his intuitive faculty, which permits him to penetrate the world of pure, "angelic" spirituality, there to discover the "mysteries." Among the kabbalists, those that have attained the status of "true humility" have sometimes had this experience to which the Zohar refers.

Today's man of science can no longer fail to recognize the influence of the transcendent upon him and his conscience, especially in regard to his extraordinary responsibilities in a world where science and technology offer humanity so many promises of fruitful development and so many threats of extermination.

It is not so long since scientists refused to acknowledge

any connection, any link between science and ethics. They believed that what they termed *pure science* could not be linked with ethics without the former losing its sovereignty. According to them, pure science, being sufficient unto itself, was not only able but had the right to respond to the moral demands resulting from its objectivity. But science being exact and autonomous, it can in no way of itself engender moral values. The proof is the state of the contemporary world, where science is pre-eminent and where prodigious scientific progress not only brings with it no spiritual, moral progress but, on the contrary, is linked with a baleful regression on the spiritual and moral plane, with disastrous consequences.

Today, when scientific objectivity is in question and the scientist's subjectivity is no longer denied, it seems that, little by little, it is being admitted that there is an intrinsic bond uniting science and ethics (an inner, rather than disciplinary, link between the so-called exact sciences and human sciences). Both are a part of the *mystery* of the infinite.

In contrast to the contemporary scientist, who is becoming progressively more open to the *mystery* of the infinite, the layman in general still seems to be indifferent, if not hostile, to the world of *mystery*. Yet there are indications that, disillusioned by materialist rationalism and a stifling technology, the layman is trying to throw off these constraints. Among young people in particular, an earnest quest for spirituality is beginning to take shape. This search being still unclear, unfortunately, some of the young people are sinking into a morbid obscurantism, but others are discovering the gardens of a real spirituality and tasting its perfume.

The scientist who is ready to live in the unified world of science and ethics would be able to help such young people (many of whom have a thirst for both science and faith) to break out of their confusion; he would be able to "enlighten" them, that is, to arouse in them what the Kabbalah calls *berur*, "clarification." Moreover, this clarification is necessary and even beneficial in order to overcome the "separation" between man and God, between man and himself, and between man and his fellowman, and as a result, to discover the "roots" of true life.

The Reconciliation of the Two Scientific Concepts: that of the Kabbalah and that of Contemporary Science. The Kabbalah's "Modernity."

The contemporary scientific world, and consequently the entire world, is at a critical turning point: its concept of science is moving towards that of the Kabbalah. Now, the Kabbalah's concept of science is inseparable, on the plane of religion and philosophy, from its concept of ethics; they interpenetrate one another to form one single concept.

Nowadays, at the end of the 20th century, the scientific conceptions of our age are converging with those of the Kabbalah of every age, now that the deep affinity of their cardinal features is being revealed.

Is this a chance event? Decidedly not. Why should this meeting be taking place just in the very days when science, having quickened its advance more than ever in the past, is reaching impressive heights with an astonishing speed? In a very short span of time relative to its long history, it has enriched itself in an astounding manner, almost in one step, in ideas, inventions, discoveries, and technical achievements. Why has this fertility of imagination, this explosion of ideas, this revolution in techniques occurred only now?

From the point of view of the Kabbalah, this accord between its own scientific concept and the ever-changing one of contemporary researchers does not seem to be fortuitous

—quite the contrary. It compels our consideration and demands to be explained.

Again, from the viewpoint of the Kabbalah, this meeting between the closer study and dissemination of its teachings and that of scientific enlightenment — both unique in their kind — is the Will of the *Hashgahah*, "Providence." It provides the justification of what can be called the "modernity" of the Kabbalah. In the past, this term could not have been applied, either from a scientific or a philosophical point of view, to any "contemporaneity" between the Kabbalah's conception of science and that of the scientists.

The accord between these two concepts comes at a moment of which the Zohar says that it would bring about a deeper awareness, an "unveiling" of the *razei Torah*, the "mysteries of the Torah," by "humble" kabbalists, and a growing interest in the Kabbalah, especially in the Zohar, among a great many intellectual circles.

This "moment" of meeting, which, according to the Zohar, is charged with eschatological meaning, will take place, it says, at the end of the sixth millenium (to the creation of the world), which corresponds to the present time by the Jewish calendar! Then, continues the Zohar, "there shall be opened the gates of *Hokhmah* (Wisdom) on high and the springs of *hokhmah* here below [this term suggests the idea of investigative reasoning, leading to religious, moral values]. It is thus that the world will prepare to enter the seventh [sabbatical, messianic] millenium." However, "it is the Will of the Holy One, blessed be He, not to reveal to the sons of Adam [to men] [the time of] the advent of the Messiah." "But when the days of the Messiah are near, even children will be able to calculate the end."

We do not wish to transgress the interdict, many times expressed by our Sages, forbidding us to "calculate the end" or to claim to be able to find the numbers and numerical combinations in the sacred texts that would permit us to "calculate the end," the moment when the messianic age will begin. Far be it from us to be so presumptuous! Those who believed they were able to "calculate" and succeed in such a delicate arithmetical computation "fell into error." (Although it is true that the "upheavals" of the present day could be likened to the pre-messianic "upheavals" predicted by our Sages!)

As we have said, the fact remains that this turning point in the history of science which we are experiencing corresponds to an undeniable reconciliation of two scientific trends of thought, that of the Kabbalah and that of contemporary science.

This reconciliation is occurring both on the plane of scientific theory and thought and on the plane of the ethical, historical, and religious corollaries which necessarily arise from them, as people are beginning to recognize. In fact, science today has the power to be either a *sam ḥayyim*, an "elixir of life," or a *sam mavet*, an "elixir of death," for man as an individual, for humanity as a whole, and for the ecological and physical life of the world.

The Kabbalah repeatedly emphasizes this corollary; it shows the connection between Israel's coming out of *Galut*, "exile," and the (messianic, eschatological) victory of "knowledge," of *da'at* (a word encompassing the notions of science and ethics). Now, the Galut of Israel, of Man, symbolizes both the inner galut of every man and the spiritual exile of all humanity. "The whole world is in exile," proclaims Rabbi Moses Cordovero, and with him so many other masters of the Kabbalah down to our own times. Israel's deliverance from Galut will mark the deliverance of mankind from its Galut and the beginning of the messianic age.

"Messianism," writes Rav Kook, "is, in essence, a value originating in Israel [a value which was revealed to the people of Israel and which they have presented to the world]. Among this people, in fact, the heavenly kingdom and the earthly kingdom are one whole." Consequently, the people of Israel, guardian of the Torah, bears a great, indeed an extraordinary responsibility in the world, because the *Tikkkun,* the moral and religious "restoration" of the world, is dependent upon the moral and religious "restoration" of the people of Israel, declares Rav Ashlag (20th century), following the teaching of Rabbi Hayyim ben Attar (18th century).

Israel will be qualified to secure this "restoration" when it has achieved the highest degree of *da'at,* "knowledge," and *da'at* is perfect when, above its attainment on the human level, it reaches out to the *da'at ha-Shem,* the "knowledge of God."

The *da'at ha-Shem* is defined by Maimonides as *hokhmah amitit,* "true wisdom." (In this, the famous philosopher and rationalist is in harmony with the great thinkers of the Kabbalah.) From the religious point of view, this supreme wisdom clearly has an ethical, human compass. Maimonides confirms this by referring to the words of the prophet Jeremiah (9:22-23): "Thus says the Lord, Let not the wise man glory in his wisdom.... but let him that glories glory in this — that in acting wisely, he *knows* Me, that I am the Lord who exercises loving-kindness, justice, and righteousness, in the *earth*: for in these things I delight, says the Lord."

How can one glory in wisdom, in the *hokhmat ha-emet,* the "wisdom of truth"? ask the masters of the Kabbalah. We know that the *truths* we affirm are far from *The Truth,* and that our "scientific truths" often contradict each other. The history of science is full of examples of theories put forward as being *the truth,* the one and only truth, followed by other truths, totally different, which replace and cancel the former. Nevertheless, the ambition of the respective branches of science, from the Greeks down to our own times, has been to recognize *the* truth, the sole truth, for there can only be one Truth.

This *ultimate* goal of science will never be within man's grasp; it is always "hidden" from him. However, man must search for it constantly; this is his mission.

Consequently, the Kabbalah concludes that *Truth* is unknowable, unattainable. Nevertheless, man must always be searching for it, reaching out towards it, even though he knows that its essence will remain inaccessible to him.

Then where is *The Truth*? It is in Him and in Him alone. As the prophet Jeremiah (10:10) proclaimed, "The Lord God is *Emet* (Truth)." These words of the prophet of Israel are repeated with humility and certainty by the masters of the Kabbalah and all true believers. For them, *Emet* and *Emunah*, "Truth" and "Faith" (which have the same root) together lead man to the *Da'at ha-Shem*, the "knowledge of God." Yet King Solomon the Wise reminds us that "the glory of God is to *hide* things..." (Prov. 25:2).

The Zohar bids us to end this chapter with the words with which it allowed us to begin: *Ha-Sod hu ha-yesod*: "Mystery is the foundation." It is the foundation of all things and everything is a mystery.

CHAPTER TWO

In What Sense Is
the Kabbalah Wisdom?

**Wisdom is the essence of the Kabbalah's teaching
and its goal.**
**Wisdom has its roots in the divine Will and
Thought, which are "concentrated" in the Torah.**

Wisdom is not simply one of the Kabbalah's values; it is
not just one aspect of the Kabbalah's doctrine, but forms the
very essence of its teaching and its goal, for Wisdom is at its
beginning.

Wisdom is the Kabbalah.

So what sort of wisdom are we concerned with?

The stream of Jewish mystical, meditative, contemplative,
and even speculative thought spreads like a river of life. In
action, this thought offers us a particular model of wisdom,
that is, carefully considered moral conduct for both individuals and society. Eastern, Christian, and Muslim mysticism
also lay down principles of wisdom and construct ethical
systems claiming their origin in a higher moral will and
favouring an ascetic life style. But Jewish mysticism is unique
both in its form and its basis. Even the Hebrew term that
defines it, *Kabbalah*, is unique. This word, which means

"reception," teaches us that the theory of the Kabbalah is based on the Hebrew Torah revealed on Sinai and "transmitted" "by word of mouth," so that by interpreting it, one may penetrate its "mysteries." It is unique, again, on account of its practical applications, also founded upon the Torah.

The theory and practice of the Torah are united in _Hokhmah_, from which they derive and in which they meet in perfection.

In Hebrew, _Hokhmah_ means "Wisdom."

In its origin, _Hokhmah_, "Wisdom," is _ila'ah_, "supreme," for its "roots" lie in the divine "Will" and "Thought," even before they have been revealed; since their revelation, the position of _Hokhmah_ is very close to the summit, to the "Crown" of the primal, "sefirotic" order of divine manifestations.

> The Creator has put man at the centre of the universe.
> He makes him responsible for the world's destiny.

These primal manifestations of the Creator led to the creation of the world, which was crowned by the creation of man. The Creator put this creature, this extraordinary being, at the centre of the universe. He made him responsible for the whole world and everything that is in it. He purposely made man from all the spiritual and material elements that make up this world, and from all the elements making up the other worlds and corresponding to our world (the world of spiritual "emanation," the world of "creation," and the world of "formation"). Those worlds are reflected in this world, and this world in them. Indeed, this world is the material outcome of the higher worlds, with which it must combine. Man, whom the Creator sent down here below, and in whom He has gathered together the elements of all the worlds, is responsible for their cohesion. He is not only the guarantor of their order and responsible for their disorder; he has, in addition, been given the task of leading the world within which he lives, which is the world of "action," through the higher worlds and back to the very source of the worlds in <u>H</u>ai Olamin, in Him who "lives forever," in Him who "gives life to the worlds." Man's task consists of "putting right" the "maladjustments" that may have resulted from the original world's differentiation and diversification into several worlds, by "restoring" them to the unitary fullness of their life in Him who is the <u>H</u>ayyei ha-<u>H</u>ayyim, the "Life of Life," the unique One (before the numerical one could have been conceived).

"What is man that Thou art mindful of him?" (Ps. 8:5). How can such an enormous task have been entrusted to this frail being? How can such a prodigious mission have been given him, to the point of saying of him, "yet thou hast made him a little lower than God" (Ps. 8:6)?

God does not ask of man anything that would be beyond his strength. He asks him to "act in accordance with the strength" that He has infused into him. Though at times man may be tempted to shirk this task, judging himself incapable of bearing so heavy a burden — a cosmic burden — or of attempting the "impossible," the inconceivable from a human point of view, God has given him sufficient strength to carry through such a task.

> The Creator has put at man's disposal the Torah, the divine Teaching, and the Mitzvot, the divine Commandments, so that he can accomplish his calling in the universe.
> Israel is the repository, guardian, and fulfiller of the Torah and the mitzvot.

In reality, man is qualified to respond to the calling that God has given him. It was with a view to the fulfilment of such a calling that God created the Torah, the Charter of the world. This preceded the Creation, and, as it were, "looking into the Torah" and guiding Himself thereby, God proceeded to build the universe. This Charter of the world is also a "teaching," a Torah, for man's use, for through it he, in turn, will be guided to ensure the existence of the world by revering, and making others in the world revere, the "Will" and "Thought" of his Creator.

Consequently, the Author of the Torah has endowed it with *mitzvot*, "commandments," that is, duties that man must perform to preserve order in the world, and prohibitions that he must observe to remove disorder from the world; it is due to these mitzvot that man is able to cause harmony to reign between the worlds.

Moreover, "from the beginning," when God was looking into the Torah, the expression of His Will and Thought, in order to create the world, He provided a partner for it, a trustee, a guardian, one who would fulfil it: Israel. So in the "beginning" of the world's creation, the Torah, called "beginning," and Israel, called "beginning," collaborated in the hands of the Creator. In these two, Torah and Israel, the Creator envisaged the development of the world from the outset. He also inscribed in them the end of the world, tracing the eschatological coming together of the "beginning" and the "end." Therefore, the history of the world is a process that develops between two poles, the "primordial state" and the "messianic state," enjoined to coalesce "on that day," "at the end of days." It is a continuous and difficult process of messianic inspiration and messianic order. The primordial ADaM returns in the final ADaM. At the threshold of history, Adam recognizes himself in David, who is at the centre of history, and who is perfected in the Messiah, the end of history (see footnote, p. 215).

According to the plan of His Providence, God permits the world, "the work of His hands," to "descend" from its original, spiritual height. When He gives it life, He fills it with the "desire" to return to Him, the Creator, the Lawgiver, the Redeemer. Man "will return" to Him enriched, thanks to the free and just use that he will make of this world, and thanks to his beneficence in this world of "action" — which will be reflected in the other worlds. Thus man acts, remaking the worlds, restoring them to their initial state of "perfection," enriched by their historical, human experience. (The human soul, rooted in the spiritual world, sent into a human body and so destined to "descend" into the material world, "will return" to its source doubly enriched, but only if it deserves to do so, after fulfilling its earthly calling, that is, after "mastering" and spiritualizing the body in which it has been dwelling.)

> The Jew is called upon to live within the Torah, to live by the mitzvot.
> In this way, he will contribute to the consolidation of the worlds.

Man, every man, is called upon to see that the worlds do not "become separated" or corrupt one another in the course of their History; man must work towards their consolidation, so that they become indissolubly "linked" together.

However, Man-Israel — the individual and the community — is held responsible in particular for carrying out this universal, cosmic plan, which "though last in execution, was first in God's design"; he is destined to be "associated with the Holy One, blessed be He, in the work of the Creation."

Is this impossible? No. For God has given Israel the Torah, the *Hokhmah ila'ah*, the supreme Wisdom, wherein are inscribed the supreme "Will" and "Thought" so as to be within man's comprehension in this world of "action." (Each world has its Torah, similar to the Torah revealed in this world, but their letters are differently arranged, "combined" according to the nature and needs of each of the worlds.)

The Jew (individual and people reflecting each other) is called upon to study the Torah "for its own sake," with impartiality and holiness, to study the Torah, which is full of the Names of God; to try to penetrate its "innermost mystery" and reveal its "hidden truth." He must clothe himself with its divine "garments," the mitzvot, so as to reach their "roots" in the higher worlds, to adhere to those roots and introduce their "vitality" into the material aspects of the mitzvot, to live by them, to live within the Torah. Such a Jew will become aware that by each of his thoughts, words, and deeds, conceived and carried out within the *hokhmah*, "wisdom" of the Torah and the mitzvot, he is able to co-operate in the consolidation of the worlds, commencing with this world, the "earth which God founded in wisdom" (cf. Prov. 3:19). Conversely, by each of his attitudes or movements that might upset the harmony of this world, he can endanger the harmony of the other worlds. By each *het*, "sin," that is, by each misdirected thought, word, or deed that could destroy the order of this world, he brings confusion into the order of all the worlds through the mixing of "good and evil," as did the First Man with his first sin. And, "if the shadows are already there, he is called to transform them into light."

> **Torah and mitzvot require the Jew to unite his will and thought with those of God.**
> **Free Will.**
> **Ethics and Holiness.**

Through study of the Torah in depth, and application of the mitzvot in detail, the Kabbalah penetrates Wisdom so that finally it is identified with Wisdom.

The Torah and the mitzvot require men, the Jews, to unite their will and thought with those of God, to harmonize them with those of the Creator so that they become identified even to the point of total effacement, thus entering into the luminous space of absolute, divine Liberty.

To penetrate into the space of this pure, simple liberty, man uses one of the prerogatives granted him by the Creator: that of free will, that is, the power to choose from among the different — and generally contradictory — possibilities that are offered to him for action, the one that seems to be right and pleasing to himself and most in accordance with the divine Will.

Most certainly, the liberty given to man by the Creator is relative, limited by his physical state, by the material conditions in which he lives, and by his natural and social environment.

Nevertheless, one cannot evaluate man's activity in thought and will in terms of plain "ethics." For, having made proper use of his liberty, the Man of the Kabbalah is forever drawing closer to the spiritual, metaphysical "area of holiness," whose boundaries lie within the absolute Holiness of God, who alone is called "the Holy One, blessed be He."

In fact, if one were to judge in terms of ordinary ethics the actions of such a Jew, who is ready to yield up his own liberty to the divine Liberty, to "offer his soul," that is, his "will," to God in an act of *mesirut nefesh,* one would be ignoring the autonomous nature of this action and be tempted to regard it as being influenced, or even governed, by heteronomous — howbeit religious — demands, overruling his will.

Yet the act of *mesirut nefesh* does override the usual distinction between autonomy and heteronomy.

Through the Torah and the mitzvot, a Jew can establish a personal relationship with God, whose beneficent action he tries to imitate.

Thus, man frees himself from the status of creature, "receiver," and rises to the rank of creator, "giver."

We are in the presence of a human being, submissive to God, who Himself is One with the Torah and whose mitzvot are, so to speak, His "garments," which are likewise destined to be the "clothing" of the soul of the man who performs them. It is with this God that man is able to establish an "enlightened" and "loving" personal relationship.

Consequently, when the Creator greets His favoured creature, he who studies the Torah and observes the mitzvot for His Name's sake, He takes into consideration the fervour of his wanting — coming from this world "here below" — to come to Him, the strenuous efforts he has made, and the "trials" he has undergone to reach Him. God judges them independently of the fulfilment of man's wishes which, in the case of the man who is searching for Him, cannot be, nor should ever be, complete. Man was purposefully so created that by progress in the knowledge of Torah and observance of the mitzvot he could aspire to come close to God.

However, God the Creator, the Giver of the Torah, responds to man's "wanting" from below with His own will from on high. He liberates man from his status as creature and raises him to the rank of creator, like Himself. He raises him that high, because man's wanting God is pure — devoid of all desire for physical or material well-being, or even for spiritual happiness. Indeed, man aspires to come close to God, not for the sake of the joy he might feel in his closeness to God, but to imitate Him in ways that He may be imitated: for the Creator Himself offers as model His most perceptible activity, that of spreading good. He who has created the world in order to communicate good to His creatures is the example man must follow. What raises man from the rank of creature to that of creator are his acts of benevolence. In ceasing to be purely a "receiver" like all the creatures that benefit from the good showered on them by their Creator, he too, by emulating the example of His Creator, becomes a "giver," as far as possible impartial like Him — not expecting reward, with only the impulse to do good. The *nahat ru'ah*, the "satisfaction" that he automatically derives from his deeds is not an indispensable condition; for likewise, the Creator gives man everything needed for doing good, independently of the *nahat ru'ah* He derives from the deeds of His creature, man. The *nahat ru'ah* is a gratuitous "satisfaction." "If you are upright — if you do good — what do you give Him?" (Job 35:7).

Such a man, who emulates God in the good he does, is a *zaddik*, an "upright" man, capable of "founding" a world and renewing it by his goodness, as the Creator of the world "by His goodness, daily renews the primal deeds" of creation.

> God exists outside what we call existence in space and time.
> Man can conceive of Him and His numerous "outward" manifestations by an unbounded "inner" knowledge.

The man of the Kabbalah, the man of Wisdom, is one who "recognizes" his Creator; in knowing Him, he loves Him and, by extension, he loves his fellowman, created in God's image.

His love of God is nourished by cogent reasoning, the fullness of his senses, and the richness of his imagination. Accordingly, he "sees" — with the spiritual intuitive vision of the eyes of the spirit, of "knowing" — Him who "cannot be seen" by living man; he "touches" — with supersensitive "feeling" — Him who cannot be touched, for He is not perceptible to our senses either here below or in the other world. Ordinary man cannot "see" God, "touch" "His

garments," "embrace Him"; he has only a very vague perception of Him. For man cannot know God with the outward,
precise knowledge proportionate to an object, because in this
case, the object of his "knowing" — God Himself — is infinitely greater than he is. He can only perceive God with an
"inner," "intuitive," unbounded knowledge, which itself can
hardly be formally realized, for its object is the *Ein-Sof*, the
Infinite, which "exists" beyond our existence in space and
time, totally beyond any human comprehension. " 'To whom
then will you liken Me, that I should be his equal?' says the
Holy One" (Isa. 40:25).

Of course we wish to attain *the Truth*, the Truth of the only
existence that is true, that is, "the Lord [who] is the true God,
Elohim Emet" (Jer. 10:10). But who can lay claim to have
grasped Truth as it is? Who can apprehend by power of
reason that which alone is true, when reason, being itself a
gift of God, recognizes — precisely out of "rational consider-
ations" — its inability to do so?

Who can attain the Truth? Not even the "humble" men
who, nevertheless, devote their lives in secret to the Hokhmat
ha-Emet, the "wisdom of the Truth," namely, to the Kabbalah.
However, they have great merit, for they never abandon their
assiduous and fervent search for Truth and steadfastly advance along the road that leads to Truth and brings them,
little by little, nearer to "the true God." Being unable to attain
sublime Truth, they are content to grasp those immediate and
infallible truths that emanate from the "God of truth." Thus
they "grasp" God — awed at being able to "capture" His
"light"; delighted to "touch" His "garments"; full of wonder
at discovering His life-giving Presence everywhere and in
everything; happy to feel His close proximity. Most certainly,
they grasp Him in His many and varied manifestations, but
they make no pretensions to grasp Him in what we call, in
our imperfect terminology, His "essence." For no thought is

capable of grasping what is beyond our thought, beyond even our ability to express our own thought. "No thought can grasp Him," "can take hold of Him," for "My thoughts are not your thoughts, neither are your ways My ways, says the Lord" (Isa. 55:8).

> **To "know-and-feel" God, "to know-and-love" God, leads to the "service" of God.**
> **Man then recognizes and feels his constricting "liberty" to be a liberating "constraint."**

The Torah and its rabbinical, mystical, and philosophical commentators invite us all to "know God"; they exhort us to acquire a *Da'at ha-Shem*, a special "Knowledge of God." In the language of the Torah, the verb *yado'a*, "to know," means "to know" as well as "to feel." This "knowing-and-feeling," this "knowing-and-loving," this "intellectual love," has as its corollary a readiness to "serve" and to devote ourselves to Him completely, with all our intellectual faculties. "Know thou the God of your father and serve Him" (I Chron. 28:9). This readiness to serve leads to the "Covenant," the "choice," the personal "bond" freely entered into, between the Father and His son, between the Master and His servant.

At the moment when man senses within himself this "knowing-and-feeling," this "knowing-and-loving," his intelligence, sensibility, and imagination merge to form an actual living unity. Understanding, perception, and vision become a concrete entity. Reality and the imaginary complement each other; reality is clarified by the imaginary, and the imaginary becomes realized in actuality.

At the very moment when man senses this "knowing-and-feeling," he feels his freedom to be a "constraint," though one which frees him from the anxiety provoked by his uncertainty and the fact of his mortality. He knows and "feels" himself to be free. Henceforth, he will perforce have to establish and maintain an equilibrium between these two apparently contradictory realities: liberty and constraint. Whereupon, everything within and around him will seem so clear, so luminous, that he can cry out, "Within my flesh shall I see God!" (Job 19:26). From out of his now transfigured and transparent physical being, he perceives the Divine Presence. He lives "in the light of the King's countenance" (cf. Prov. 16:15). He directs his clear-sighted and loving gaze towards the King, who has been King forever, but whom he now enthrones as God and King over himself, joining "the multitudes who confer His majesty upon Him" (cf. Prov. 14:28) in resolving to belong to His people, Israel.

> **A Jew knows that the mitzvot of the Torah, coming from the Infinite, themselves have "reasons" that derive from the Infinite.**

The King in turn, by virtue of His royal power having been accepted by man, makes known His decrees to His subjects, to Israel.

Man — both son and servant — asks no questions about the "reasons" for these decrees, nor about their "usefulness." He is content to know and to feel that they come from Him who is "knowing-loving," who created the world in order to do good to His creatures, who created the "Torah and the mitzvot to bestow them upon Israel." Man knows that the mitzvot coming from the *Ein-Sof*, the Infinite, themselves have "reasons" that derive from the Infinite. It is not these "profound" reasons — which the Kabbalah in particular tries to penetrate — that convince the man of the Kabbalah to respect and fulfil the mitzvot. To him, everything seems so clear and totally good that he feels voluntarily constrained to accept His precepts and respect them (knowing himself "constrained" by Him who loves him the most and knows him the best, and who only desires his true good). This man, who has accepted first the "yoke of the Kingdom of Heaven" and then the "yoke of the mitzvot," freely gives his consent, while knowing himself bound to accept the mitzvot of his Creator, as in the past did Man-Adam and Man-Israel. Before Adam's outlook and judgment were obscured by his allowing evil — which hitherto had been external to him — to enter into himself, and before he exposed himself to the struggle which those two "foes," good and evil, would wage within him, he had accepted, both voluntarily and under duress, the single mitzvah, the only "command" that God his Creator had given him. Before Israel "corporealized" its concept of God and obstructed its communication with Him by making the "golden calf," they had accepted at the foot of Mount Sinai — both voluntarily and under duress — the Torah and its numerous mitzvot. God, who delivered them from slavery in Egypt, revealed to them the mitzvot by concentrating them in the letters of the Ten Commandments, which He, the Lawgiver, had engraved on the Tablets of the Law.

> Though their source is in the Infinite, the Mitzvot are accessible to Man, Israel, in this finite world, and he can fulfil them using the material means provided by the Creator.

God has "concentrated" His Will and His Thought in a significant but limited number of letters in the Torah and the mitzvot. Thus, although the source of the mitzvot is in the Infinite, they are accessible to Man, to Israel, in this finite world. By the *Zimzum*, the "concentration," the "contraction," which God, the Author of the mitzvot, effects upon Himself — if one dare say so — Man, Israel, can perform them in this material world with which they come into contact. For it is here that man finds the material means provided for him by the Creator, those which he needs in order to realize the Torah and its mitzvot. In fact, most of the mitzvot are of a practical nature; they involve both the physical body — by "hallowing" and "spiritualizing" it — and the human soul — by "substantifying" it; they involve man's whole being, that is, his unity. That is why Man, Israel, is called upon to identify himself with the letters of the Torah and "inscribe" the mitzvot "upon the table of his heart" (cf. Prov. 3:3). He is directed to identify the number of mitzvot with the number of organs in his body and with the number of days in the year.

God "concentrated" Himself in the Torah and the mitzvot, a finite work limited by shape and form, but one into which He breathed His infinite power. This "concentration" is analogous to the concentration that He effected when He created the world. For to create the universe, He "concentrated" Himself, as it were, so that the world about to be created would be able to withstand the powerful radiance of His light without disintegrating. He "compacted" the world and "halted" its tendency to extend into the Infinite, from which it originated. God said to it, "Enough!" He gave the world a "shape" so that it could exist within its boundaries.

Time, Created by God.
Time and Man, before and after His Sin.
"Cyclical" and "Differentiated" Time: *Shanah*
and *Shinnui.*

In creating the universe, God created the "beginning"; He created time: "In the beginning God created..." — God created the "in the beginning"; He thus created the beginning.

Before Adam sinned, he lived hours of true "knowledge," true "good" and true "life"; he lived them in the "present," his "time" reflecting the time of the higher worlds, where "present" is eternal, for it exists in the light of the Eternal God, who is above time. Similarly, before the sin of the "golden calf," during the revelation of the Torah on Sinai — a revelation which "completed" the act of the creation of the world in its spiritual finality (and in the course of which "reparation" was made for Adam's sin) — Israel lived hours like those that Adam lived before his fall. The substance of "good" was then still pure, and no evil opposed it; the light of "knowledge" was then resplendent, and no shadow obscured it. Those were hours of liberty and constraint.

Following the sin of Adam and the sin of the "golden calf," man must study the Torah and fulfil the mitzvot in precarious conditions, torn between the contradictory tendencies that confront one another within him. He has received from his Creator free will, the "power to choose" between good and evil; he has to remember that it is a gift of God. Through free will, God offers him the possibility and the merit of putting an end to the struggle waged within him between good and evil, between (true) life and death, and of emerging victorious. At the same time, he will have the merit — with God's help — of having listened to His recommendation to choose the good, to choose life. Now, every choice between good and evil leads man to recollect the past, to clash with the present, and to turn towards the future. For man, time is henceforward divided into three periods, which, while they follow one another, should not however replicate one another. The Hebrew term *shanah*, "year," signifying a unit of time, recalls both the cyclical, successive "repetition" of time and the *shinnui*, its "differentiation," its changing character in its particular epochs.

Man is the only being to have an idea of time, to be conscious of passing time. Nevertheless, he is apparently unable to stop time. Man lives time in his mind, but he also lives within time and, above all, with time, his travelling companion in this world. Time forms the framework within which the events of his life take place, within which he undertakes his activities. All the same, though living within time, man ought not to submit to it; on the contrary, he should dominate it, shape it, give it a lasting content. He should not allow time to escape, but hold it securely in place within the province of eternity. This he is able to do thanks to the Torah and the mitzvot, which come from eternity. In fact, the *zaddik*, the "righteous" man, embraces each "day" by filling it with Torah and mitzvot; he retains each "hour," for it offers him the chance to "gain a world" — his "world to come" — "in a single hour." He transmutes the present, the immediate moment, into a "blessed" and fruitful finale of the past and a wellspring for future "blessing" (otherwise the present would lack consistence, being placed on the periphery where a past is coming to an end and a future is being roughed out). For the *zaddik*, therefore, the monotony of successive and repetitive time does not exist; he is constantly ready to renew time.

Israel is directed by a religious command to "renew" time, by "hallowing" it through the Torah and the mitzvot.

The first mitzvah laid upon the whole people of Israel is that of renewal, analogous to the reappearance of the moon. Now, renewal implies "hallowing." That is why Israel is called upon to "hallow the times," the *zemannim*, in particular the special, meaningful *zemannim*. Thus, Israel makes itself master of time. Israel's vocation is to give time its whole value through the Torah and the mitzvot. As these originate in eternity, a Jew can introduce them into time, particularly during the "times" of Sabbath and Festivals, which are reflections of eternity and offer us a foretaste of the "world to come" even during our lives here on earth. They constitute an *'Et*

Razon, a "time of (good) will" and grace, the time when God's benevolent love for man, for Israel, and the welcoming love of Man, Israel, for God meet and unite. The *'et* may also include all the *zemannim*, each of those times when man "here below" manifests his sincere and pure "desire" to meet the "desire above," and when the "(divine) desire above" responds.

> The time wasted in the pursuit of vanities is not irretrievably lost.
> Man can replenish the emptiness of that time by *Teshuvah*, his "Return" to God, the source of time.

Having been created by God, time has its "source" in the higher world of the Infinite. By giving to time all of its value, through the Torah and the mitzvot, a Jew leads time back to its source; he reintroduces it into eternity, enriched by the good use he has made of it. In "hallowing time," Israel links it to its source and to its end, to its origin and to the ultimate purpose of holiness, which likewise dwell in the higher worlds.

In those worlds, time witnesses the successes and failures of man. Says the Zohar, "Observe the days of man! If he has merits, if his works in this world are good, his days rejoice in them on high, there where the source and number of his days are to be found." But they also testify to man's failures. His failures are heavy with all the regrets, disappointments, and anxieties resulting from "time" wasted in vanities. Yet this time is not irretrievably lost or spoiled, for man can obtain the *Tikkun*, the "restoration" for it, by his *Teshuvah*. In fact, *Teshuvah*, the "power of Return," which was created even before the world's creation in order to offset man's predisposition to sin, can, if he consents, "return" him to the roots of his soul, to the source of time, to God Himself. But first, man must prove his unshakeable will to perfect his *Teshuvah*, his "Return," by the "purity" of his thoughts, words, and deeds.

Then he will be freed from the sorrow caused by his remorse and will joyfully recover the time lost in the pursuit of vanities. *Teshuvah*, created before the "beginning" of time, permits the *ba'al teshuvah*, the "returnee," thanks to the Creator's grace that he has evoked, to redeem his time. The profound meaning of *Teshuvah* is expressed in the words "And now" (cf. Deut. 10.12), which encapsulate the "present." That is why he who does *Teshuvah*, henceforward attains eternity in the "present"; even here below, he gets the foretaste of the "world to come."

When he attaches himself to the root of *Teshuvah*, acting out his remorse with true humility, man erases the evil of his deeds in this world, which were recorded in time. By the intensity of his thought and the strength of his will in fulfilling this important mitzvah, by this very mitzvah itself, man is able to redeem the time wasted. While man, by his sin, introduced a void into the time that was allotted him and that accompanies him, he can fill that void with good deeds. God promises him, "The number of thy days I will fill up" (Ex. 23:26). The man of *Teshuvah* is thus able to act retroactively, in a positive way, in regard to time past. He revives it, gives it a new content, brings it back into the present and, above all, transforms it into a "becoming", thus unfolding it to the future.

"To Be" and "to Become."
Man lives in a continual "beginning."

The Torah teaches us that if one "adds" a letter to the Hebrew verb "to be" in the past tense, this tense is transformed into the future.

The verb *hayoh*, "to be," really means much more than "to be," "to exist," in the passive sense of the word; it means above all "to become," that is, "to live" in a highly active way. This verb *hayoh* is not conjugated in the present tense, for in reality the present has no time for being: it has hardly left the past when it at once meets up with the future. "Even a single instant does not constitute the present!" And yet, it is that instant which is the "here and now," the starting point of future action: "if not now, when then!" (Avot 1:14). For it is in this moment of the present that issues from the past, it is in this "today" that man acts, "does," directing his efforts towards the future. "There is a tomorrow which is the present."

So man lives in a continual state of "beginning." "God created the beginning." He bids man always to remember that he is only "in the beginning"; his "work" is never "finished." At every moment, he must take into account the coming time that awaits him. It is certainly a moral becoming — in the Bergsonian sense of the word — but even more, it is an eschatological one. The "eschatological becoming" leads to the "days of the Messiah," to the "day which is entirely Sabbath." Messianic time is made up of the sum of the "becomings" that end in it and depart "afresh" from it.

> **The man of the Kabbalah devotes himself unceasingly to *Avodat ha-Shem*, the service of God with fear and love.**

The effort that the man of the Kabbalah, the man of Wisdom, constantly puts forth is directed to the future and is called *avodah*. This effort is made in depth: it reaches "the depth of what is on high and the depth of what is below."

The *avodah* is, therefore, an *avodat ha-kodesh*, a "labour of holiness," which strives towards becoming a true *Avodat ha-Shem*, a "service for the Name," a constant "service of God." The more we enter into the mystery of God, the more we wish to serve Him, and the more we serve Him, the deeper will be our understanding of Him, until we enter into "intimacy" with Him, into His Palaces, the Palaces of the King, when our understanding of the Torah will be clearer, and our fulfilment of the mitzvot improved.

This *avodah*, this "labour," is done in "fear and love," in sorrow and joy, dutifully and willingly. It is accomplished with the left hand and with the right hand and is expressed both through the feminine and the masculine principle. This labour is undertaken by one whom "the yoke of the Torah and the mitzvot" compels to look earthwards, for the Earth offers him all that is necessary to fulfil the mitzvot. He is the same one who — as he conscientiously performs his service — stands and raises his head heavenwards, "lifts up his eyes to the hills" (cf. Ps. 121:1), from whence he hopes to receive inspiration and "help."

> Through *avodah*, the man of the Kabbalah contributes to the realization of the *Yihud*, the material and spiritual unification of the worlds, the "unification of the Names of God," which give life to these worlds.

All of these spiritual states, inner attitudes, and gestures, which are characteristic of *avodah*, contribute to the realization of the *Yihud*, the spiritual and material "unification of the worlds," the "unification of the Names of God," which give life to these worlds. These "Names of God" designate the only God, transcendent, distant Creator, of the furthest imaginable distance, yet at the same time the living, life-giving God, immanent, near, closer than anything that is near, God who "encompasses all worlds" and at the same time "fills all worlds" and gives them life; God who "from afar appears" (Jer. 31:2) to man and is very close to him, closer to man than man himself. By His *Hashgahah*, by His "Providence," by His "Vigilance," God follows man like his shadow; as long as man follows his God, he is told, "The Lord is thy shadow" (Ps. 121:5). By virtue of the Torah and the mitzvot that man fulfils,

God is with him and within him; but when man separates himself from the Torah and the mitzvot, God separates Himself from him.

Avodah, "holy service," "work consecrated to God," "service of God," is not the privilege of the kabbalists alone, of the *yode'ei ḥen*, those who have penetrated the mystery of grace, those versed in the *ḥokhmah nistarah*, the "hidden wisdom."

It is true that these "men of great worth," these "spiritually exalted men," the men who ceaselessly strive upwards, will do "all their deeds for the sake of the Name of Heaven," because they live "in holiness and purity" (in an ascetic state, in the sense of extreme moderation in enjoying the material things of this world, so as to raise themselves upwards towards their roots in the worlds above). Their only wish is to contribute to the *Yiḥud*, the "unification of the worlds," the "unification of the Names of God."

**Avodah is demanded of every Jew.
There are several degrees of Avodah.**

No Jew, however, must shirk his duty to practise the *avodah*, because each Jew is born to be an *oved ha-Shem*, a "servant of the Name." For this, it is sufficient to have a pure heart, acting with sincerity, to guide it heavenwards; and in order that his heart may be truly pure, each Jew must pray, "Create in me a clean heart" (Ps. 51:12).

Numerous and precise *kavvanot*, "intentions," fill the heart of the *yode'ei ḥen* during their *avodah*, accompanying their prayers and directing their actions heavenwards. The *yiḥudim*, the acts of "unification" they perform during their prayers and actions, are themselves also numerous and precise. But these are compensated for by the spontaneity of heart of the Jew during his prayers, the Jew who offers his heart to his Creator, for "God desires the heart."

Because of the simplicity and integrity of his conduct, such a Jew is considered worthy of the "company" of the *yode'ei ḥen*, the *ba'alei avodah*, the "masters of *avodah*." In fact, the latter give him the benefit of their own *kavvanot* and *yiḥudim*. The *zaddik*, the "righteous man," makes them spiritual partners in his own *avodah*, allowing them to share the fruits of his deeds; he is the "channel" whereby the abundance of "blessing" flows for them from on high, and they themselves become *anshei ma'aseh*, "men of deeds," good deeds.

Thus, the *avodah* is required of every Jew: "Know thou the God of thy father and serve Him with a perfect heart..." (I Chron. 28:9).

Most certainly, there are several degrees of *avodah*, according to the intensity with which a Jew serves God. *Avodah* may also assume a variety of faces: one person may give it a more intellectual face, by studying the Torah; another — a more meditative one, by prayer; yet another — a more charitable face, by loving his fellowman. However, while each may favour one aspect of *avodah* in particular, no one will thereby neglect the other aspects. The Jew follows the example of Abraham, Isaac, and Jacob. All three served the same God and served Him in the same way; nevertheless, each of them gave his service a special character, relevant to his unique relationship with God and conforming to his personal conception of the only God. That is why during our *avodah*, in our prayers, we, their descendants, "the offspring of the Fathers," invoke "the God of Abraham, the God of Isaac, and the God of Jacob." When we invoke His Name, we do not say, "O God of Abraham, Isaac, and Jacob," but, instead, we put the accent on the unique relationship, the special bond that each of them had, and on the personal testimony that each of them gave of the one God. Abraham, the first of the patriarchs, served God above all through the "tenderness" of love, through his love of God and of his fellowman; the second —

Isaac — through the "strength" of worship, even to the extent of sacrificing himself; the third — Jacob — through the "beauty" of the study of the Torah, though this had not yet been revealed. Each of the patriarchs, while personifying a particular aspect of *avodah*, also observed all the mitzvot, even before they had been laid down; they perceived them all, thanks to their intuitive understanding of their importance and necessity. The Torah and the mitzvot form one whole; they are not just linked together — they are interdependent. Moreover, each mitzvah contains the germ of all the others.

Each of the Hebrew patriarchs had his own way of approaching God, of looking for and finding his way to God and of serving Him. Similarly, each Jew, servant of God, can realize his *avodah* in a way that is his own, that suits his personality, his psychological make-up, his spiritual aspirations, his moral affinities, the "root" of his soul.

It is as a function of his own particular relationship with God that a Jew "knows and serves God." He serves Him in the light of the Name, the cognomens of the "attribute" that reveals that manifestation, that Face of the Godhead which particularly attracts him. "The righteous man lives by *his* faith" (Hab. 2:4), the faith that is distinctive of him.

> During the *avodah*, a Jew is "alone" with his God, but also "in the midst" of His people.

The *avodah* of each Israelite is, therefore, a service to a personal God, but, also, it is necessarily included in the service that *kelal Yisrael*, "the whole of Israel," renders to God. This is the condition which gives value to individual service, for no one is capable of responding on his own to all the requirements of the *avodah*. So a Jew finds himself *yaḥid*, "alone" with God, but *yaḥad*, "together with," and "in the midst of," His people. Linking himself to Israel, he binds himself more firmly to God. For by its very nature, Israel is linked to the Torah, and the Torah, by its very essence, is linked to God, who "dwells" within the Congregation of Israel. The *oved ha-Shem* is thus doubly and wholly linked to his God.

The *avodah* accomplished by a Jew has a personal value in that it responds to the needs that the "root" of his soul in the higher world stimulates in his soul here on earth. By his service, a Jew ascends to the sources of his being, renews his bond with the "root" of the soul. The latter responds to this ascent by transmitting light to "illumine," to spiritualize the body that here below shelters its extension, the human soul.

The body has great need of the soul. Being the physical, material instrument of the "bodily" realization of the mitzvah, it must be made worthy and capable of collaboration with the soul. From the soul comes the necessary "spiritual" *kavvanah*, so that he who fulfils the mitzvah, though it be in the physical sense, may be able to direct his "inspiration" toward the heights where the mitzvah has its "root." Actually, nothing exists "here below" that does not have its spiritual likeness on high.

Through his *avodah*, a Jew becomes more deeply aware of his God, and God regenerates the revelation of the Torah and the mitzvot in him, personally. In truth, man would not even be aware of his "self" if he did not know his origin and his end in the "I am" of his God, if he did not draw his strength, his "vitality" from the "I am" of Him who, when giving the Torah on Sinai, revealed himself as "I am." The human "self" draws all its value from the divine "I am." Without Him, he would not be.

All that concerns man finds a place in the *avodah.*
"In everything in this world God has hidden a
mitzvah for Israel."

However, the *avodah*, the service of God, is not limited to
the three great ideals that the three Hebrew patriarchs per-
sonified, as well as inscribed into the hearts of their children
and descendants for ever, namely: "love," through the gen-
erous practice of good deeds; "strength," through the fervour
of prayer; and "splendour," through the assiduous study of
the Torah. It is true, "they established the world on these three
pillars." However, the man of the Kabbalah knows, as did the
patriarchs, that in this world, where they lived and where we
live now, the Torah and the mitzvot involve the whole of his
being and demand all of his time. Everything that concerns
man has its place in the *avodah*; everything that touches his
life, in the integral sense of the word, exists in it. His very
existence must be a continual *avodah*. Certainly, the *avodah*
comprises several ascending stages, according to its purity,
its complete devotion, and its quality, but considered quan-
titatively, the *avodah* concerns every Jew. These exhortations
are directed to each of them: "In all thy ways, know Him"
(Prov. 3:6); "Know thou the God of thy father and serve Him
with a perfect heart..." (I Chron. 28:9).

In the man of the Kabbalah, the desire for knowledge and
the willingness to serve are directed towards God alone. The
wise man must "have God always before his eyes" (cf. Ps.
16:8) and must always remember that "His eyes are on him"
(cf. Ps. 34:16). He does not forget for an instant that he is
before God. Every breath that passes his lips, every heartbeat,
declares God's praise; every word he utters extolls God's
marvellous works; each gesture recalls that God accompanies
him. When he falls asleep, he knows that his soul "ascends to
give an account on high of his behaviour during each day."
He consoles himself for having to break off his "conscious"

avodah by remembering that sleep will enable him to serve God the next day with renewed strength. The wise man of the Kabbalah, the man of Wisdom, knows that every thought, every word, every single action "is recorded on high in a book" and has repercussions throughout all the worlds, even as it reaches God himself. "In everything in this world, God has concealed a mitzvah for Israel."

Thus, every person, every thing a Jew meets, may be the object of a mitzvah, potentially capable of being integrated into the *avodah*. Should he thirst to fulfil even more mitzvot, God will give him the opportunity to do so. He will provide him with new ones and He will "enlighten" him so that he may pronounce "one hundred blessings" every day. If he proves worthy, God will lead him to discover places and persons that "hold the sacred sparks captive." These he will help to do *Teshuvah*, to find their way back to their own origin, to their proper being, which they have abused, to God whom they have offended; thereby he will liberate those "sacred sparks." Thus, every action may constitute a mitzvah which will enrich his *avodah*. Making a thorough study of the Torah to discover its mysteries and so to be raised on its wings in heavenly bliss to the higher worlds; or descending to the material, physical world intentionally, to spiritualize it and raise it to the higher worlds — both are part of one's *avodah* and lead to holiness. For *avodah* includes both "small" things that may seem unimportant to us and "great" things that may seem to us very important; all without exception wait for us to "hallow" them. By this "thoughtfulness" that we give to both "great" and "small" things, a human being will be emulating his Creator, who "in His greatness and His modesty" pays equal attention to all things through His *Hashgahah*, His "Providence" and His "Vigilance." Moreover, our care for both the "small" things and the "great" ones calls for and elicits God's providential intervention.

Even the act of eating, when carried out in holiness, is highly spiritualized.

"One whose *kavvanah*, whose "intention," or thought, remains bound up with His Name, may It be blessed, during his material occupations, achieves a perfect *avodah*, a perfect service of God. On the other hand, he who does not keep his thoughts and intentions thus bound up while devoting himself to the study of the Torah and prayer, does not respect the Name, may It be blessed." This teaching concerning spiritual *avodah*, which was handed down to his followers by a holy disciple of Rabbi Israel Ba'al Shem Tov (18th century), is connected with and completes the teaching that his master, the father of Hasidism, had entrusted to him concerning down-to-earth, material *avodah*. He stated in particular, "By the manner in which you eat, you serve God." With these words he wished to say that insofar as you understand how to eat (in holiness), "you serve God" in holiness. If not performed in holiness, the act of eating is simply an instinctive act necessary to preserve life in our bodies, or solely a means of satisfying our greed. The First Man committed his first fault through the act of eating; the Israelites, coming out of Egypt, "did reparation for his fault" by eating unleavened bread, the "bread of faith," the "bread of healing"; in messianic times, too, salvation will be celebrated by feasting.

When it is performed in holiness, the act of eating is highly spiritualized (the word *ma'akhal*, "food," is composed of the same letters, differently arranged, as the word *mal'akh*, "angel"). This act must be performed according to the rites laid down by the relevant mitzvot. It must be spiritualized by the *Divrei Torah*, the "Words of Torah" that we speak at the table, and by prayers that remind us that it is God who "brings forth bread — specifically human nourishment — from the earth" and who "nourishes the whole world with His goodness." (By these *berakhot*, these "blessings," we acknowledge that everything comes from Him and belongs to Him.) Thus, our souls will be nourished by prayers and *Divrei Torah*, and our bodies will be sustained by the nourishment they need to serve God. Now, the soul and the body constitute a single entity. Should the body not receive its material nourishment (which conceals within itself a spiritual element, which we evoke with the *berakhot*), it would no longer be able to shelter the soul and thus jointly perform the *avodah*. Man, as a being conscious of his vocation to serve God, is called *nefesh*, "soul," "vital spirit," and he must subordinate his body to his soul in order to approach holiness. This does not mean depriving the body of its moral dignity, or of its natural rights; the body must be respected, for as the "little world," it symbolizes in its marvelous construction and form the "greater universe." The two constitute the magnificent world of the Creator. Nourishing the body, caring for it, keeping it "clean," making it worthy of the "purity" of the soul and capable of participating in its "holiness," all of this constitutes a mitzvah. To watch over the well-being of the *nefashot*, the body and the soul, and that of the "animal" and the "divine" spirits, which together reside within man, constitutes a mitzvah. This body, "hallowed" by practice of the Torah and the mitzvot, has become spirit itself.

The man who fulfils his *avodah* must, therefore, be considered as a whole being, in his physical and psychic totality. First within himself, then through himself, within the greater world, that which is physical, material, visible, and external becomes spiritual and inward, and the spiritual, inner element becomes visible. The supreme (messianic) goal of *avodah* is to disclose the perfect, intrinsic harmony between the outer, "carnal" element, which is material and visible, and the invisible, inner, spiritual element. The visible "enters into" the invisible and the invisible is made manifest. This state of holiness is the paramount goal of *avodah*.

Praying and Eating.
Man is judged in his spiritual and physical totality.
The Unity of His Activities.

How can such a high goal be attained? Only by taking seriously the exhortation, "Hallow yourself by what is permitted to you!" Hallow yourself by what you are, by what your Creator offers you!

Here is an example of sanctification. To eat, man uses his mouth. To study the Torah and recite prayers he also uses his mouth. The mouth serves to fulfil two acts of different values. Now, a Jew prays standing "before God"; he lays his table and eats "before God." Praying and eating are ritual acts. Both the "prayer" and the "table" recall and replace the sacrificial ritual of the Temple of Jerusalem. When he prays, the Jew prays "for the sake of the Name of God"; he eats "for the sake of the Name of God." It is not only in studying the Torah and reciting prayers that he invokes the Names of God; when he carries the *ma'akhal*, the "food," towards his mouth, he also invokes the Names of God. In fact, the numerical value of the word *ma'akhal* (91) is the same as that of the divine Names *HaVaYaH* and *Adonai* put together (the one denoting God as Creator of the world and the other, God as Master of the universe). The same human mouth has to perform acts that seem to be different in nature and import and that nevertheless are complementary and demonstrate the unity of man, the intrinsic unity of his activities and his calling.

Rabbi Simeon bar Yoẖai, the great Jewish mystic of the talmudic era (in the 2nd century), shared with God his regret that He had not given two mouths to him whom his Creator calls "son" and "servant," namely, one for studying the Torah and reciting the prayers and another for eating. Now God, in His desire that man be one and serve Him in his totality, has given him a single mouth for a variety of activities, which are to be fulfilled according to the Torah's precepts. "His mouth will become a Torah." God requires of man that by this very organ he shall sanctify both that which is material and that which is spiritual in nature, so as to form one whole. Thus will be achieved the very high goal of *avodah*: to unite its material and its spiritual functions in a single act of sanctification, performed by the "total" man.

Correlation between Brain and Heart, Two Essential Factors in a Human Being's Spiritual Life

The unity of the one who is an *oved ha-Shem*, a "servant of God," is realized by means of the living relationship that links the different organs of the human body, all working together for a perfect *avodah*. Thus there is a correspondence, a correlation, between the "cold," glacial, "thinking" brain, which commands man to execute a mitzvah with "meticulous precision" in the "fear" of God, and the "warm," glowing, "feeling" heart, which incites man to fulfil the same mitzvah with "goodness" and "enthusiasm" in the "love" of God. The "cold water" that comes from the brain is directed towards the "burning fire" in the heart, though without extinguishing it. Both water, which cools, and fire, which warms, are integrated into the very tissue of the mitzvah and reinforce it.

This correspondence, this correlation, between the brain and the heart, two factors essential in the spiritual and psychosomatic life of a human being, entails the exchange of their properties and a permanent complementarity of their faculties. Thanks to this correlation, a man devoted to God, a man who is spiritually whole and well-balanced, is able to offer His Creator an *avodah*, a total service. When the "brain," the "seat of the Divine Spirit," receives the influence of the "heart," it is "warmed," it shares its tenderness and it begins to "feel." The "glowing heart," in turn, influenced by the "brain," "cools," reflects, begins to "reason." It becomes the "heart of a wise man," a heart that "thinks," "understands," "knows," "speaks," "sees," and "hears." These virtues appear in its "right-hand chamber," the "seat of the spirit"; the latter faces the blood-filled left-hand chamber, which is the "seat of the animal spirit," the "evil inclination." These two chambers in the heart are linked, and yet they are opposed to each other by all their dispositions.

The opposition between these two sides of the heart was foreseen and desired by the Creator. If He has formed man in this way, it is so that within him, within his heart, there may lodge two "creatures," termed the good and the bad inclinations. In truth, in the Book of Genesis, the Hebrew word that indicates the creation of man, and, more precisely, his "formation," is provided with a doubling of the *Yod*, the first letter of its root. This letter is the smallest and the most concentrated of all the letters of the Hebrew alphabet, which served to write the Torah and create the world. The Yod is one single point that emerges from nothingness and is condensed; it reveals the first thought, the original intention of the Creator, who presided over the creation of the "highest worlds" and of the "world to come," which is the goal of "this (human) world." The letter *Yod* is "the principle and the foundation of the world." That is why this letter *Yod*, the first of the "Four Letters" composing the Name of God, is also the first of the five letters composing the name *Yehudah*, which contains the "Four Letters" that form the divine Name. *Yehudah* is he who "gives thanks to the Lord." He is a symbol and a description of the Jew, the *Yod*, the *Yud*, called to "celebrate God" in this world. The *Yod* also personifies Man, who is summoned to recognize God and to serve Him. "The letter *Yod* is also the sign of the Covenant" between the God of Israel and the people of Israel.

Two "creatures" coexist in man's heart: the "creature that is good" and the "creature with evil potential."

The two *yezarim*, the two "creatures" symbolized by the double *Yod*, coexist in man's heart. On the "right" side of the heart dwells the *yezer tov*, the "creature that is good," and on the left, the *yezer ha-ra*, the "creature" with the potential of becoming "evil." The latter is not "wicked" in origin, but is capable of becoming so, of "tending" towards evil, of changing sides and eventually turning to the other, evil side. Through the harmful influence he is able to exert upon this creature, man can corrupt it and debase its original good nature ("everything God made was very good!") (Gen. 1:31). Fascinated by the images that come to him from without and excited by the ensuing exaltations, man is led to make of this second *yezer* an actively wicked "creature" to the extent that it will be nicknamed "the wicked creature," *yezer ha-ra* (whereas the "creature that is good" remains what it is intrinsically, in its immutable essence, *tov* and not *ha-tov*: "good" without being "*the* good").

Thus, though both are works of God, "Creator of All," because of man's thoughtlessness and fickleness, they do not live in harmony. They agitate, each in its own "house"; they riot and quarrel over the ascendancy each would like to have over man.

In the conflict that takes place between these two adversaries, the *yezer tov* and the *yezer ha-ra*, on the battlefield of man's heart, it is the latter which holds the initiative. The *yezer ha-ra* hits out in its fight against the *yezer tov*, to reduce it to silence and thus to gain complete control over man and do with him as it wishes. From being the *yezer ha-ra*, it changes to being simply a *yezer*, which "takes possession of man" — *yizro shel adam*. Indeed, man often succumbs to the passions which the *yezer ha-ra*, "the evil tendency," unleashes in him, inflaming his instincts, promising him all kinds of delights and pleasures. The *yezer ha-ra* often succeeds in its endeavour, for it is "older" and more experienced than the *ye̱zer tov.* The *ye̱zer ha-ra* is at work "from the moment man enters this world," at which time it identifies with his instincts alone, and it continues to exert pressure throughout the adolescent years. The *ye̱zer tov* is younger and does not appear effectively until the boy is thirteen and the girl is twelve years old, when they receive help from above. It is generally less vociferous, less hasty, less passionate, calmer, more moderate, and more "thoughtful" than its "elder" enemy. The latter, though it is "an old and foolish king," has recourse to various means of "seduction," various "wiles," the more firmly to dominate man.

Thus, to deceive man regarding its intentions, the *ye̱zer ha-ra* suggests that he obey some mitzvot, some precepts of the Torah, and do "good deeds," but in reality those "good deeds" proposed by the *ye̱zer ha-ra* conceal just as many incitements to commit *averot,* to transgress the commandments of the Torah, as would a multitude of "bad deeds." A pious, honest man, trusting in his *ye̱zer tov* with little knowledge of the "tricks" of his *ye̱zer ha-ra,* frequently falls into the traps set for him by the latter and cannot free himself except, in his turn, by having recourse to "wiles."

Divine "Knowledge" and Human "Choice"

At the cost of numerous efforts, man can succeed in "holding his *Ye̱zer* in his hands," in becoming its master. The question is, how is he to emerge "victorious" from this seductive and seditious, covert and overt "battle," which his "enemy" the *ye̱zer ha-ra* is waging on the uneven terrain of his heart?

In consultation with his reasoning powers and his *neshamah,* his "spiritual soul," man calls upon his "ability to choose," that faculty which the Creator has bestowed upon him. This divine gift enables man, alone among all the other creatures, to choose between "the blessing and the curse," between "life and death" ("death is the *yezer ha-ra*"), between good and evil, knowing that God recommends him to "choose life" (cf. Deut. 30:19) ("life is the road which the Torah shows him"), to "choose good," to choose that which is truly good for man, whom his Creator, who made him, knows better than he himself.

Acting on the advice of his intelligence, man is ready to use the free will which the Creator has, as an exceptional measure, given him. In making him this precious gift, the Creator wishes to enlighten man as to what he is, to "let him know" that he is "created in His image, after His likeness" (Gen. 1:26), that he has received immense power. Although this is only a feeble "reflection" of His absolute Intelligence and Will, man is summoned to emulate them within his potential. God wished to show His "love" for man by thus selecting him, not only above all the other creatures of this world, but even from among those of other worlds who, like the angels, do not have the "power to choose." As He did at the creation of the world, the Creator put into effect, as it were, a *zimzum*, a "contraction" of His own powers, so as to augment those of man. One could say that He renounced part of His prerogatives as the All-Powerful Master of the universe and transferred them to man. By this very fact, man has received the right and the duty freely to determine his own moral conduct. God has chosen to limit His incommensurable Authority in favour of man, knowing at the same time that man will be tempted to rebel against Him.

However, one may assume that this basically relative "freedom of choice," fraught with numerous good and bad consequences for man, is not as determinative as one might hope or fear. Nevertheless, the Torah makes it the incentive for observing the mitzvot; the Talmud and Zohar also regard it as the incentive for applying the divine precepts, and

Maimonides, doctor and psychologist, praises its power and above all its vital importance in man's religious life. But it must be acknowledged that this much-celebrated "power to choose," the *ko'ah ha-behirah*, is largely conditioned by man's apparently unchangeable innate disposition and it is obstructed by apparently impassible physical frontiers and, very often, by social and political obstacles.

Truth to tell, faced with *Yedi'ah*, divine "Knowledge," the *Behirah*, the human "power to choose," which man exercises when he acts, is almost lost in the immense expanse of space and time governed by the divine Intelligence and Will. Nevertheless, it remains true that by his deeds, and even by his thoughts and words, man can exert a good or bad influence upon both the lower and the higher worlds.

This ability that man has, namely, to choose how to act, may seem insignificant in the face of God's foreknowledge and omniscience, which in every way surpass the space reserved for human life and the time divided for man's sake into past, present and future. (A division which in relation to man is even inscribed in the Name of God, the Tetragrammaton.) Divine Knowledge looks out upon infinite space and embraces infinite time. In His eyes, the imagined boundaries within space and time disappear; everything is present. But man's field of vision is limited. He is unable to link organically "the three durations of time — the beginning, the end, and the present." The Gaon of Vilna, Rabbi Eliyahu, remarks what a paradox it is that the present, the meeting point of the two streams of past and future, is for man "precisely the present moment, when he must distinguish between good and evil and choose between them." Whereas for God the present is omnipresence and eternity, for man it is the instant, the "today"; yet how decisive it is for what he must "do"!

The antinomy between divine omniscience and
human choice is a mystery that human reason
cannot penetrate.

How can one explain the contradiction that our reason
observes between the *Yedi'ah* and the *Behirah*, the "Knowledge" of God, and the "Free Choice" of man; between God's
foreknowledge and omniscience and man's "power to choose";
between what is called Divine Providence, and human freedom?

This apparent contradiction has been presented succintly
by the Sages of Israel, who state, in the same phrases, that "all
is foreseen" by God and yet "permission is granted" to man
to act freely; that "all is open" before God and yet "what man
does, he does according to his own intelligence"; that "all is
in the hands of God, except for the fear of Heaven."

Furthermore, it is this contradiction which is regarded by
the Sages as an axiom of their faith in God, yet this antinomy
between *Yedi'ah* and *Behirah* remains inexplicable, a mystery
that human reason cannot penetrate, a fact upon which Jewish philosophers and mystics are fully in accord. This apparently insoluble contradiction is one of those things that, in the
words of Maimonides, "set human reason before sealed doors."
Maimonides the rationalist, like the mystics, convinces us that
man is not able to comprehend, or to grasp, the Knowledge of
God. His Knowledge is unlike our knowledge. His Knowledge is one with Him; ours must relate to something found
outside of itself. The Intelligence and Will of God are One
with Him; our intelligence and will (the one conditioned by
our ability to apply it and the other by our ability to fulfil it)
have as their object something that is outside ourselves, upon
which they are generally dependent. Howbeit, our intelligence and our will must be anchored to, and fulfilled within,
the Intelligence and Will of God.

Yedi'ah and *Behirah*, both severally and in their mutual

relationship, must therefore be viewed as a mystery. "They are part of the foundations of the Torah," wrote Rabbi Zvi Elimelech of Dynow, "although they are in apparent opposition. Our faith should enable us to know the truth of these two contradictory notions, for human reason cannot grasp them. They are unified in the power of His Holy Name, blessed be He. He alone, their Originator, is able to vindicate them, and He alone knows how these two realities coexist, for He alone knows how all things subsist." Ours are deficient, "unlike His Thoughts," which are perfect (cf. Isa. 55:8).

In tackling this difficult question, the Zohar draws support from a verse of Ecclesiastes (3:11), which in its view summarizes the ideas put forward on this subject: "He has made every thing good in its time; He has also set the world (put the idea of eternity) into man's heart, even so, man cannot grasp the work that God has made from beginning to end." Yet there were those that God in His goodness did deem worthy to "grasp His work from beginning to end." The Sages of Israel declare that the "Holy One, blessed be He, showed Adam and Moses all the following generations and those that would lead them"; moreover, He showed Moses "everything that has been and that will be."

Ordinary human reason is incapable of understanding how *Yedi'ah* and *Behirah* can be reconciled. The two ideas cannot even be compared. In essence, *Yedi'ah* is absolutely inaccessible to human reason; in depth, *Behirah* is only partially accessible to human reason. Rabbi Isaac Luria, the Ari ha-Kadosh, states that human reason is totally powerless to perceive *Yedi'ah*, which preceded even the creation of this world. Our reason itself is merely another creation of God set into this world and so is unable to know "what is above and below this world, what was before its creation and what will be after it has ceased to exist." Our reason was created, as were space and time, within which reason acts. Like them, it is limited, and it can only act within them. As for the relationship uniting the *Yedi'ah*, which existed prior to the Creation, and the *Behirah*, which is of this world — how can our reason grasp this relationship, when it cannot fathom even its own dimension or its own manifestation, which we call "free will"? Apart from its status as a creation, reason is bound to, and, moreover, dependant upon, the matter that constitutes our bodies. It cannot disengage itself in order to operate with total freedom; it cannot unburden itself from the opaque matter of our bodies, which obscures its vision and falsifies its judgment.

Divine creation continues in human procreation. "Circumcision of the Flesh" and "Circumcision of the Heart."

According to the *Sefer Yezirah*, there is an affinity, which at first sight seems astonishing, between "two covenants" that God has concluded with the Jews: the *Berit ha-Ma'or*, the "Covenant of the Flesh," and the *Berit ha-Lashon*, the "Covenant of the Tongue."

The Covenant of the Flesh is inscribed into the body of a Jew by the *milah*, "circumcision"; it is inscribed into that part of the body where man transmits life. That is why this *berit* is called *yesod*, "foundation."

As a "symbol of the Covenant" between God and the people of Israel, circumcision requires of a Jew that he "keep the Covenant," that he "watch over the sacred covenant" — *shemirat ha-berit* — especially when in the very act of procreation. The transmission of life has as its paramount objective the *avodah*, the "service" of God, and in fact, in order that God may be served on earth forever, the earth must be peopled by human beings who will proclaim the Creator's Sovereignty. If man "betrays" or "denies" this "Sacred Covenant," his procreation is regarded as "barren," like the earth where, if

God is not worshipped, it is cultivated in vain.

Divine creation continues in human procreation, always with the same goal, to make the Creator and His Will acknowledged, as it is expressed in the Torah and the mitzvot. This is why the Talmud and the Zohar both declare that "if the mitzvah of the *milah* — circumcision — had not been foreseen since before the world's creation, the heavens and the earth could not have continued to exist."

Abraham, who was the first to make sense of the world's creation by inaugurating the process for its completion, was also the first to receive the divine ordinance of circumcision. This command that he received was preceded by God's invitation to him to "walk before Him" (Gen. 17:1). Abraham was thus the first to "proclaim" God in the world. His descendants, the children of Israel, who joyfully fulfil the sacrificial mitzvah of circumcision, are likewise invited to "sanctify the Name" of God in the world, to make Him beloved by their own love for God, which must be proven by their conduct here below. Their life in this world will be an example for others inasmuch as they joyfully fulfil all the mitzvot of the Torah, as well as the fundamental mitzvah of the *milah*. In fact, the Talmud and the Zohar proclaim that the mitzvah of the *milah* is so important that it is equal to all the Torah's mitzvot. "The *berit milah* is itself called, concisely, 'Torah.' "

The world that God created, He "created it for His Glory" (cf. Isa. 43:7), so that His "Glory might fill the earth" (cf. Isa. 6:3); so that men may sing His praises here; so that "Isra-el may sing to the Glory of God here" (cf. Ps. 66:2). It is with this end in view that the children of Israel are born, and it is in order to glorify God that human procreation flows from divine creation and should not be dissociated from it. This is why "the Holy One, blessed be He" declares that He is "a partner with the father and the mother" who beget the child. The child is destined to "honour God, his father, and his mother"; at the same time, father, mother, and child are all "bound to collaborate in glorifying their Creator." In addition, the child is destined to continue with, and to expand the *avodah*, the "service" of God.

Now, a Jew must serve God with all his being, in his psychosomatic unity, which means with a "holy body," in its wholeness, and an upright soul, a "holy spirit."

To fulfil the *avodah*, certain virtues are necessary, and the *milah* is the indispensable condition for acquiring these virtues. The *milah* is an act contributing to bodily hygiene; the goal of the "circumcision of the flesh" is to protect health and at the same time to "weaken man's passion"; but the *milah* is also an act leading to spiritual hygiene. The "circumcision of the heart" (cf. Deut. 10:16) will deepen man's devotion to God.

By the *milah*, a father has the superfluous outgrowth of flesh "excised" from his child. At the same time, it is a kind of a moral operation, for he has broken the "husk" that might bar access to the future spiritual inwardness of his son, who is destined to carry out the "circumcision of his own heart," the "purification of his own heart," thus "opening his heart" to God, to his fellowmen, and to the world at large.

By the *milah*, a "surplus" part of the human body is removed, which in reality constitutes "a lack." This "surplus" was willed by the Creator so that in removing it, man could have the merit of "making himself," of "repairing," or completing, himself thus becoming what God requested of Abraham before commanding him to circumcise, namely, *tamim*, "perfect," whole. The word *tamim* is in the plural, for the "wholeness" that the *milah* brings to a Jew is both physical and spiritual.

> **The married couple celebrate on an equal footing within their sanctuary, within their family home.**

A Jew is commanded to be pure when he "hallows himself during his conjugal service" by intimately uniting himself with his wife with "affection" and "respect." If they are truly aware of the responsibility incumbent upon them in their marital life, both spouses deserve the title that the Zohar confers on them when it calls them *Kohanim*, "priests," who officiate on an equal footing in their sanctuary, in their family home.

Such a "priesthood" was envisaged by the Ramban, who, like other kabbalists, composed a prayer for the married couple to recite before coming together in purity of intention and thought. The latter will have a beneficent influence on the children they beget; they will be fit to become true *ovdei ha-Shem*, faithful "servants of the Name," perhaps even *talmidei ḥakhamim*, "disciples of the sages," who consecrate their lives to study of the Torah; and possibly even more, to becoming true *zaddikim*, "upright" persons, who, by their rectitude, "ensure the existence of the world." The Ramban's prayer, like others of the same type, contains some moving hymns to the glory of God the Creator, the Life of Life, the King of Peace; but it also contains sublime poems dedicated to the beauty of conjugal life, to the love and peace between man and wife. It is a true celebration of human love, proceeding from, and returning to, divine love, a celebration suffused with a breath from the Song of Songs.

Thus prepared by a common wish for "sanctification," their union has the value of an act of holiness.

> A woman "hallows" herself by immersion in the
> water of the *mikveh.*
> Water is a symbol of life, of renewal.

The *milah,* a ritual act with a double connotation for a Jewish man — material in the "circumcision of the flesh," and spiritual in the "circumcision of the heart" — has its corresponding ritual act for Jewish women in the immersion in the *mikveh,* the ritual bath, which is doubly significant in that it is an act of both physical and spiritual "purification."

A woman "hallows" herself by the "purifying" immersion in the water of the *mikveh,* the ritual basin. She generally does so after her menstrual period and after childbirth.

Thus, she "purifies" and "hallows" herself in the water, which is the primordial element in God's creation: "In the beginning" the world was only "water in water," "and the breath of God moved on the surface of the waters" (Gen. 1:2).

Water is a symbol of life; it is a prerequisite for life.

The *mikveh* represents the original waters. That is why some spring water is let into the bottom of the *mikveh* basin. For the water in the *mikveh* must not be only water "drawn from a well" by man, that is, artificial water. The spring water keeps its original property of purity and transmits it to the main *mikveh* water.

Thus, a woman who immerses "her entire body once" in the *mikveh* water is submersed in the original "living water" of creation* "as if she were living through the beginning of Creation," when it was "water in water"; "as if she had gone back to her origin"; "as if she has been born at that very instant"; "as if she bound herself at that instant to the Source of Life, to the Creator Himself."

---

* The numerical value of the Hebrew Word *mikveh* is 151, and if one adds to it 7, representing the seven days of Creation, the result is 158, the numerical value of the Hebrew words *Mayim Hayyim,* "living waters."

The states of "purity" and "impurity" belong to the moral universe of human beings.

Water is symbolical of the "benevolence" and "love" of the Creator, who "founded the world on loving-kindness" (Ps. 89:3). It is a sign of divine grace, which — even as the Torah — "descends here below" and "purifies," as does pure water.

A Jewish woman receives from the purifying waters a token of "joy," of "salvation," "the promise of monthly renewal." This sign, "a source of new life," she brings to her husband, "as a young bride does to her spouse."*

The immersion in the *mikveh* water should not be regarded as a kind of magical practice by which one can free oneself from a state of "impurity." Impurity does not arise from a supernatural world. The states of "purity" and "impurity" belong to the moral universe of human beings. A woman's temporary physiological state of "impurity" is the result of a natural organic function. However, this periodic state, by its very nature, exerts a disturbing influence on a woman's psychosomatic being. The end of this state, therefore, is marked by an act both material and spiritual, which she performs on herself and within herself, namely immersion in the *mikveh* bath. The *mikveh* water exerts a vivifying, renewing influence on her, but only if she immerses herself to demonstrate and fulfil the purification both of her body and her soul. By this immersion, she emerges physically and spiritually purified.

Maimonides called attention to this double function of the *mikveh* in a meditation he included in his Codex, the *Mishneh Torah*. He wrote, "Although nothing is changed in her body,

---

* As the feminine calendar is linked to the monthly cycle, to "lunar time" — the moon being, similarly, the symbol of the renewal of the people of Israel — tradition says that a Jewish woman should observe the first day of the new month, *Rosh Hodesh*, in a quasi-festive manner.

she is pure, she who wishes to purify her soul of its psychic, spiritual impurities, such as evil thoughts, by deciding in her heart to turn from them in immersing her soul in the waters of knowledge, *mei ha-da'at*. About her, God said by the mouth of the prophet Ezekiel (36:25), 'I will sprinkle clean water upon you, and you shall be cleansed from all that defiles you; and from the taint of all your idols will I cleanse you.'"

Original Waters and Messianic Waters

The masters of the Kabbalah took up and enlarged this meditation with which the illustrious codifier and philosopher ended his *Hilkhot Mikva'ot*, his "Laws of the *Mikva'ot*." They saw clearly expressed in it the Torah conception of the laws on "immersion."* The Sages of Israel state that the Torah is a "Torah of Life"; it shows man (considered in his psychosomatic unity) the way he should follow during his life: "The Torah is compared to water." Man should immerse himself into the study of the Torah as he would into the life-giving waters of the *mikveh*. By means of the mitzvot, the Torah illustrates the work of the Creator. He created man, the supreme miracle, and, as observed by the ReMa, He was *mafli la-asot*, "did wonders," in uniting the body and the soul into a mysterious unity that we call life, which we are bade to preserve and transmit in its purity. Man is called upon to link this life with the "beginning of Time," of the Creation, when "the world was water in water" and "the spirit of the Messiah moved on the waters," and to lead it to the "end of time," the messianic days, when "the earth shall be filled with the

---

* The quantity of spring water needed for a *mikveh* is 40 *se'ah* (one *se'ah* is 7.3 litres). The number 40 is a reminder of, among other things, the 40 days and nights that Moses spent on Mount Sinai to receive the second Tablets of the Law, containing the Decalogue, and by the number of its letters, the Decalogue symbolizes the whole of the mitzvot of the Torah.

the knowledge of God as the waters cover the sea" (Isa. 11:9). It is in fulfilling the mitzvot with a pure intent that Man, Israel, will also be found worthy of re-uniting original time with the messianic age, an age of "restoration" and "perfection." This unification of the ages is the destined goal of the world's Creation and of the history of Mankind. Hence it was the Creator's wish at the dawn of Creation that man should work towards, and eventually succeed in, his task of unification.

On the road that leads to those times when life will be lived in "water-like" purity, the transmission of life should continue through the *toharat ha-mishpahah*, the "purity of the family." Each partner in marriage should bear his or her own responsibility and share it with that of the other partner.

So we should not be astonished that the *mikveh* holds such an important place in the life of constant "purification" and "sanctification" of the *zaddik*, the "upright man," who is *yesod olam* (Prov. 10:25), "the foundation upon which the world is based," as well as of the *hasid*, the "pious man," he who is constantly giving proof of his "love," his *hesed*, towards "God and men." For the *zaddik* and the *hasid*, the waters of the *mikveh* form a natural milieu, appropriate to *Devekut*, devotion to the Creator.

The "Covenant of the Flesh" and the "Covenant of the Tongue": Sanctity of the Body and Sanctity of the Spirit

According to the *Sefer Yezirah*, as we have said (see above p. 152), God made two covenants with the Jews, the *Berit ha-Ma'or*, the "Covenant of the Flesh," and the *Berit ha-Lashon*, the "Covenant of the Tongue." These two are closely connected and reveal God's creation, which is at the same time dual and unique: a merger of nature and spirit. These covenants are reflected in the dual and unique structure of man

— a single being, made of a body and a soul permeating each other.

In varying degrees, the spirit resides in every thing, and all matter supports the spirit in varying degrees. It is the "word" that links the material world and the spiritual world. In God, the word is already, in itself, a concrete act. "By the Word of the Lord were the heavens made..." (Ps. 33:6), "for He commanded and they were created..." (Ps. 148:5). Among men, too, the word has both a spiritual and concrete connotation. The "word" seeks to be fulfilled in a physical act: "That which comes out of thy lips thou shalt observe and do..." (Deut. 23:24). The *davar*, the abstract "word," must be transformed into a *davar*, a "physical act."

The inner link between the divine Word that created the material world and the divine Word that created the spiritual world, which are but one and the same Word, is illuminated by Tradition, which says, "The world was created by Ten Utterances" of God, and "the Torah was revealed on Sinai by Ten Utterances" of God. These two divine revelations complement and incorporate each other; they influence and are identified with each other in their common Author. The number *ten* being a symbol of holiness, these Ten Utterances, the former and the latter, unite in a single holy Utterance. They manifest themselves in nature and they can be heard in the Torah calling upon man to strive to emulate God, who alone is holy: "You shall be holy, for I am holy, I the Lord your God" (Lev. 19:2). His absolute holiness, far above us, inspires and sustains the holiness within us.

In man, this holiness involves both the spiritual enlightenment of the body and the physical consummation of the spirit. Hence, the holiness of the body is upheld by that of the spirit, and the holiness of the spirit is heightened and strengthened by that of the body.

This is the basis for the close link binding the two covenants that God has made with the Jew: the "Covenant of the Flesh" and the "Covenant of the Tongue." The first is written into that part of the human body from which physical life is transmitted; the second relates to that part of the body by which spiritual life is communicated. The common aim of the two covenants is to bring human beings together. This coming together must take place in the presence of God the Lord, who is "near to all who call upon Him in truth" (Ps. 145:18), with sincerity, within an aura of holiness that is desired by the Holy One who makes man a participant in His holiness when the former earnestly seeks it and receives it in its purity.

When man neglects his search for this "holiness," this state of "purity," keeping himself apart from it, or even totally rejecting it, then "impurity" invades him.

The Jew, God's partner in this dual covenant, is called upon to answer a dual demand, trenchantly expressed in the word *shemirah*, "vigilance." He must "keep the covenant" — the first demand, expressed in the words *shemirat ha-berit* — by penetrating into the deepest meaning of circumcision; and he must "watch his tongue" — the second demand, referred to as *shemirat ha-lashon* — by delving into the essential spirit of this expression. The Jew must be aware of the serious consequence of rejecting either one of these covenants. To reject the "Covenant of the Flesh" may have "irreparable" consequences for the Jew's descendants; to reject the "Covenant of the Tongue" may have "deadly" consequences for relations between human beings.

Mitzvah and *Averah*.
All depends on the "direction" man imprints on his deeds and words.

Through a "considered" and prudent use of his tongue and his body, a man can be led to great heights of virtue. On the other hand, their irresponsible, thoughtless, or immoderate use can drag him into wretchedness and vice. Everything depends on the "direction" that he imposes on his deeds and words; if he checks and controls them and "orientates" them towards the good that is revealed in the Torah, he is fulfilling the Will of God, thereby fulfilling a mitzvah, which "finds grace...in the eyes of God and men" (Prov. 3:4). But if, dragged down by his deeds and words, having lost all control over them, he causes them to "miss the goal" indicated in the Torah, he "transgresses" the Will of God, thereby committing an *averah*. Having failed to give his words and deeds their true import, their profound meaning, he has become "disoriented," he has failed in his task as a "servant of God," he has committed a *het*, a "sin," towards God and a "fault" towards man in that he has failed to reach the true goal.

Confidence in Man and Man's Doubts

It is true that in the realm of thought, in which man uses his intelligence, as well as in the realm of action, where he uses his will, he is not truly "free" in the exercise of his free will. At all times, he is strictly conditioned, above all by biological factors; neither his thoughts nor his deeds will ever be completely pure or perfect.

Nonetheless, the Sages of Israel have always placed their confidence in man, while at the same time recommending him "not to trust in himself until the day of his death." They have faith in man's ability to keep his intelligence honest and his will unshakeable, although the "upright men" doubt this ability within themselves and even fear it, because, they say to themselves, "perhaps" they may not prove themselves worthy of it; "perhaps" they will not use it effectively. Yet the Kabbalah deems man capable of raising himself to the level of wisdom: he can always consider and choose, that is, he can compare the known facts, evaluate the situations before him, and, finally, overcoming his indecision, he can opt for, and act, in accordance with this choice. For the man of the Kabbalah, the man of Wisdom, this means that he will act in conformity with the demands of the Torah and with the guidance given by the mitzvot. But of course man does not choose once and for all, being beset by contradictions that ceaselesly draw him in all "directions." This is one of the characteristics, indeed one of the conditions of his life, of life itself.

Man, being unified in structure, must reconcile the contradictions that animate him.

Man incarnates to the highest degree, visibly, and on the level of consciousness, the principle written by the Creator into the heart of His Creation, namely, the principle of the contradiction between the fundamental elements upon which nature rests. This principle is a sign of the complementarity of the elements of Creation, which results from their original oneness and leads to their living unity. Thus, fire and water, *esh* and *mayim*, combine to form *shamayim*, the "heavens," and similarly, day and night make time, and heaven and earth form our world. They are all apparently opposing elements and manifestations, but, in reality, they combine to make their original unity and their final unity more perceptible.

The contradictions that animate man are more clearly apparent in him than in all other living creatures, for he alone is confronted by morality problems, and he alone is the superior being that presents deeds of a moral order. These confrontations oblige him to favour one of the these various opposing elements within him. Those that inspire man show their intrinsic unity. According to God's design, they are destined above all to develop in man the exercise of his free will and to throw light on their original and final unity — by virtue of man's intelligence and willingness, and thanks to the awareness of his calling in the universe. This unity, inscribed into Creation from the beginning, must be revealed when Creation is complete. The unity was apparently and temporarily breached so that man can re-establish it in all its brightness. It is with this goal in view that man, in his integral structure, has to reconcile the two opposing elements within him, which are commonly called "body" and "soul" (and, in his psychosomatic life, the two mutually hostile components of the soul itself: the "vegetative soul" and the "spiritual soul"). Man must assist these two elements to interpenetrate and mutually serve each other, thus revealing their active, creative unity. He is called upon to communicate to the body the spiritual sensitivity of the soul and to the soul, the physical strength of the body. (Likewise, he has to communicate to the spiritual soul the feverish zeal of the vegetative soul and to the latter, the serenity of the spiritual soul.) This state of harmony will not be fully attained until the messianic times.

Nevertheless, man must work to establish this harmony as if it could be attained during his lifetime. So day after day he will struggle, first to reconcile the "enemies" face to face within him, and then to lead them to see their respective strengths, closely binding the spiritual and the material factors that they embody. From then on, these two entities will no longer be separated from each other by their differences, but will work together. They will be striving towards unity, as He willed it in His design for them: to serve Him together in peace and in harmony, to serve Him, their Creator, "whose Name is Peace."

Thus, from the beginning, the Creator placed man in a state of tension and dilemma. He intentionally thrust him into a changing, uncertain situation so as to offer him the chance, nay, the privilege, of introducing into it a living stability. So, man will have the joy and the honour of overcoming this state of instability, but without eliminating it. His success will derive from the unremitting exercise of his free will, aided by his intelligence and his energy, and supported by the Creator, to whom man prays to extend to him the help he needs to progress along this difficult road. In fact, "Sin — the evil impulse that leads to sin — is lying in wait at man's door, trying to possess him, but man must succeed in dominating it..." (cf. Gen. 4:7).

Man's Life is a Trial.

The Creator strengthens the power of the *yezer ha-ra*, that spiritual "creature" in man that is capable of awakening and aggravating his inclinations towards evil, towards the shadows, implied in "all that is contrary to that which God Himself has created." It is the Creator who has given the *Yezer* the necessary skill to attack man anew "every day," to "visit" him (a visit which the *Yezer*, as a guest, may prolong until it "becomes a member of the household," if it is well received and welcomed). Through His "envoy," this provocative, irritating *Yezer*, the Creator puts man, His privileged creature, to the test, time and again, making his life a "trial." This is the destiny reserved for His chosen people, in whom He takes pride. He constantly tests them, so that their whole life becomes a "trial," a *nissayon* (like that of Abraham, as an individual, and like that of Israel, collectively). In the trial, His elect grow stronger, distinguishing themselves by their strength of character, so that God presents them to men and to nations as an example of tenacity, endurance, and faithfulness to His Law. So the *Yezer* attacks "great" men by preference. It "grows" in proportion to their "greatness"; it provokes them with particular insistence. It lays siege to their "citadel" with added violence, since this offers greater resistance than the "houses" of other men, which are quickly shattered under its assaults.

The *Yezer* is "sent" by the Creator to rouse man as much when he is plunged into voluptuous rapture as when he buries himself in sleepy indolence.

In fact, God loves those who, like Isra-el, "contend and prevail" (Gen. 32:29). He would prefer not to see the "wicked" submit without a struggle to the *yezer ha-ra*. Nor does He like to see those who, wearied from struggling against the *Yezer*, shut themselves up completely against it by locking up the left side of their hearts to prevent it from entering, thus repelling its assault. Worn out, they sink into apathy and become indifferent to the "lawful" demands of their instincts. They abandon themselves to the boredom of repetitive, colourless "habits" and put up with an unrelievedly monotonous existence. Rabbi Menahem Mendel of Kotsk (19th century), interpreting a verse from the Book of Judges, states that God loves "those upright" men who hold themselves ready at any moment, standing "at their gates" to do battle again with the *Yezer*, and, rather than giving way to an inactive, sterile "process of growing old," keep their "youthful" "freshness." In truth, "the upright have no rest in this world, not yet in the world to come; they go from success to success," for success is never complete, ultimate, and definitive even when, "in the world to come, the upright are seated and savour the splendour of the Shekhinah," of the Divine Presence.

However, the stern Rabbi of Kotsk, like other *zaddikim*, "upright men," did not disregard the benefits of a retreat. On the contrary, during a certain period of their lives, they especially appreciated *hitbodedut*, an absolute "solitude" with God. They kept themselves shut away, safe from all temptation, lowering their eyes, seeking to protect "their hearts and their eyes" (cf. Num. 15:39) from the "many eyes" of the *yezer ha-ra*, which follow man in every slightest move. Nevertheless, they recognized and admired the boldness of those *zaddikim* who, voluntarily and openly, fearlessly face up to the "test" and dare to "provoke the *yezer ha-ra* in its abode," to confront it and overcome it.

> Asceticism is regarded as a temperate manner of life.
> Man transforms what is physical and material — the work of God — into what becomes spiritual — the reflection of God.

The Rabbi of Kotsk and, shortly before him, the Gaon of Vilna (18th century) chose not to confront the *yezer ha-ra*, but rather to keep themselves away from the "vanities of this world," from insatiable appetites ("man leaves this world without having satisfied one half of his passions!"), and from the torments that they bring with them ("man is born to trouble") (Job 5:7). Nevertheless, in observing such extreme watchfulness, they were not trying to secure a peaceful life for themselves. On the contrary, their years of contemplation and meditation, and, above all, of profound study of the Torah — study which helped them to penetrate its mysteries, to scrupulously observe the mitzvot and to fathom their inner meaning — these years passed in an outward calm, which was accompanied by great inner tension and marked by ardent spiritual intensity. The Kabbalah constantly recommends that God be served "with fear and with love" (cf. Deut. 10:12); this requires a concentration of all the forces of the spirit, which permits no rest. Jewish history provides innumerable examples of such "holy men" as Rabbi Judah ha-Nasi ("our holy master") (2nd century), Rabbi Simeon bar Yohai (2nd century), Rabbi Judah he-Hasid ("the pious") (13th century), Rabbi Isaac Luria ("the holy Ari") (16th century), Rabbi Isaiah Horowitz ("the holy Shelah") (17th century), Rabbi Hayyim ben Attar ("the holy Or ha-Hayyim") (18th century), and many other *zaddikim*, "upright men," belonging to the

Hasidic school of Rabbi Israel Ba'al Shem Tov (18th century), who himself was inflexibly against an excessive, total asceticism, which moreover is not approved by the Torah.

In fact, from the perspective of both the written and oral Torah, asceticism is conceived as a temperate and moderate way of life that transforms physical and material pleasures into a means of "sanctification." Thus, that which is physical and material — the work of God — is metamorphosed by man into that which is spiritual — the reflection of God.

"Nothing that God has created is in vain or useless." Each of His visible creations, each of their manifestations, inherently contains the spirituality which gives it life and reflects its "roots" above, in the higher worlds. A "speck," a kernel, is hidden in the depths of God's creation, and man is directed to discover and reveal it, and then to develop it and lead it to its goal, which is to participate in a total material and spiritual "service of God."

For human love to survive, it must lead to the love of God.

Thus the passions animating man contain within their core a spirituality that awaits discovery by man. It is that spirituality, helped by the physical and material "vessel" that "encloses" and expresses it, which man must guide towards the love of God, their Author. In other words, human passions, which are being momentarily realized in human love, must be led towards their source in God, who is Love, and whose Will it is that man participate in this mystery of love. For if passion is only realized in self-gratification, in love as man understands it, without being linked to the love of God, it will be nothing more than an "evil love," a "wasted love," a "love of the shell," and not a "lasting love," leading to the love of God. Man must consider all desire that is born within him in the light of his yearning to fulfil the Will of God, as manifested in the Torah and the mitzvot. Nachmanides teaches that "all love that is awakened in us must be invested in a subject or an object of a mitzvah" prescribed by the Torah. Thus, too, the Ba'al Shem Tov taught, in order that human love may have stability and value, it must lead to the love of God.

Inevitably, man acquires a knowledge of pure, beneficent joy, such as is offered him by God — who, having made him, knows and loves him.

Accordingly, man succeeds in transforming what may be a *nega*, a harmful "wound" resulting from the wrong use of pleasure, into what ought to be the aim of enjoyment, namely, *oneg*, "pleasure" in the highest degree of delight, of bliss, which the Creator wishes for man. These two words, *oneg* and *nega*, are formed with the same Hebrew letters. However, their rearrangement and transformation depend on the merit and aspirations of each individual man. For while "He created the world to do good to His creatures," "to give them joy," at the same time He entrusts man with the task of transmuting any *nega* into permanent *oneg*.

Understood and fulfilled in this way, *oneg* is not the momentary "pleasure" that "flies away like a dream" (Job 20:8), passes like a shadow or "dies out" like a flame. It is luminous and shining, reflecting the *oneg* that surrounds and fills the higher worlds. It is a lasting pleasure in a joy without end, for this joy is a *simḥah shel mitzvah*, a "joy of a mitzvah," a joy that the believing Jew feels and experiences when he fulfils a mitzvah. Thus, a physical act, and especially the physical, "vital" "act of love," fulfilled "in sanctity" as commanded by God, is called, quite simply, "mitzvah." Equally, the act of *zedakah*, of "justice-charity," performed for love of one's fellowman in the light of God's love, is called quite simply a "mitzvah." Now "one mitzvah gives birth to another mitzvah" (Avot 4:2) and so on, until it reaches and nourishes its "root" in the higher worlds; from above, it "will give radiance" and be a source of continual blessing to the one who fulfils it.

> The Joy engendered by the fulfilling of a mitzvah is always new.
> The "joy before God," as it intensifies, becomes "joy in God."

"To rejoice before God" (Deut. 12:18) has nothing in common with the exciting pleasures aroused by the senses, for these are instantaneous yet fleeting, long coveted yet quickly exhausted. Nor has the "Joy before God" (cf. Deut. 12:18; 16:11) anything in common with the "satiety" that pleasures of that kind procure; such pleasures engender boredom as they multiply, they follow, repeat and resemble one another, losing on the way their novelty and freshness through the effects of habit, and, eventually, they arouse disgust. Ecclesiastes (2:2) asks about this kind of pleasure, "What good does it do?"

"To live in joy before God" is the reflection of a "nostalgia" for God, experienced even while reacting to a physical or material pleasure. It is developed in a past reaching towards an ardently awaited present, it blossoms in the present, and it continues into the future by a growing, renewed desire, ripening into the "thirst for God, for the living God" (Ps. 42:3). The Sages of Israel say of such a joy that it is a *simḥah shel mitzvah*, a joy attained by fulfilling a mitzvah.

"Joy before God" is sustained by the *Ein-Sof*, the "Infinite," who in His goodness "each and every day renews the Primal Works" in the world which He created. This joy is nourished by Him who each and every day radiates from the Torah which He revealed. Thus this joy is constant and always new. In fact, writes the Gaon of Vilna, *simḥah*, "joy," is a continually renewed reality. As it develops, it is transformed from a joy manifested "before God," sustained and fed by the *Ein-Sof*, into a joy felt "in God." "Israel rejoices *in* Him who made him"* (Ps. 149:2) and "the Lord rejoices *in* His works" (Ps. 104:31).

Thus, their joy becomes their rendezvous. Israel becomes an "abode" for the Shekhinah, for the Divine Presence, and the Shekhinah becomes a "dwelling" for Israel. This joy awakens in Israel their innate, "hidden" love for God and transforms it into a true and active love. In God, the joy is bound up with a true and active love for Israel, reconfirming the love He promised them when he chose them to be His people. These two converging loves, the human and the divine, the one ascending, the other descending, seek to embrace in perfect harmony. They aspire to become one. The "Congregation of Israel" can now proclaim the *Yihud ha-Shem*, the "unity of the Name" of God, and can bring about a twofold *Yihud*, the union of God with Israel who, as it were, "makes Him God," and the union of Israel with God, who "makes them His people." God's love now descends to confirm to Israel that He loves them "with an everlasting love" (Jer. 31:2) and that he "has chosen" His people "with love" (cf. Deut. 7:7-8). From below, Israel's love for God replies, "And thou shalt love the Lord thy God with all thy soul" (Deut. 6:5) (the word "And" shows that this is the response that Israel is making to God's love).

Prayer illuminates every daily action.

Israel's love for God is expressed first of all by prayer; it is the primary "service" to God, for it is the "service of the

---

* *Be-Osav*, lit: "in *those* who made him" "*those*" refers to the "double heart" of man — *levavkha* (Deut. 6:5), spelled with double *bet* — in which the good and evil impulses are contained, both of which he must use in the service of God.

heart," a heart that feels, understands, desires and thinks. Israel joyfully prepares to perform this service of prayer, prays with joy and joyfully accepts the consequences of this service. The very preparation for prayer is in itself a prayer, and the time that follows praying is, again, a prayer; thus, the "whole of the day" is permeated with prayer. Prayer becomes a permanent, concrete reality, for it is the basis and the source of all daily actions; it illuminates them and gives them their real value, their true sense. He who truly prays is therefore continually in a state of prayer; he is engrossed and carried along by its intrinsic power.

The true joy experienced before, during, and after prayer comes from a humility that is "joyful but trembling" (cf. Ps. 2:11) and leads to total peace of mind. He who truly prays lacks for nothing. He "rejoices in his portion" and savours the privilege of "standing upright before God." And if he does ask God to satisfy his spiritual or even his material wishes, he does so in order to demonstrate that he has not forgotten that "all that is in heaven and on earth is Thine" (I Chron. 29:11), that all existence depends on Him alone. He does so to be able to use, in God's service, the kindnesses which He so abundantly heaped upon him. Indeed, the joy yielded by the spiritual and physical purification, by the preparation for prayer, could not exist without humility, for he who prays says to himself, "Who am I, poor, insignificant, wretched, transient creature that I am, to dare to address the Lord my Creator? Therefore, with David's royal prayer (Ps. 51:17) I ask Him, above all else: 'Open my lips that my mouth may declare Thy praise.' " When his lips have been opened, when they have been empowered to pray, then will his "trembling" humility allow him to rejoice in himself as he is. His humility will enable him to comprehend in whose presence he is standing upright and praying. It will give him the joy of knowing himself to be rich in the "gift of prayer," thanks to which he is able to pour out his soul before Him, the Source of Life, and thus keep his soul eternally alive. Furthermore, to know that along with the gift of prayer he has received not only the permission but also the command, the mitzvah, to address God through prayer, is the culmination of his joy.

> **The value of every mitzvah depends on the** *kavvanah,* **the pure "devotion" that accompanies it. The Reflective and Affective Character of** *kavvanah.*
> **Every mitzvah breathes its "vitality" into the one who fulfils it.**

Humility and joy contribute to the creation of *kavvanah,* the pure, disinterested devotion that resides within a Jew when he fulfils the mitzvah of *tefillah,* "prayer," and which must necessarily accompany every prayer.

The value, the quality, of every mitzvah depends on the *kavvanah* that permeates it. Though the mitzvah be of a physical, material nature, it yet needs a *kavvanah* to be entirely fulfilled. The *ma'aseh,* "the act of doing" a mitzvah, constitutes its "body," and the *kavvanah* that goes with it is its *neshamah,* its "soul." Deprived of *kavvanah,* the purely mechanical performance of a mitzvah is like a body without a soul, says the Ari ha-Kadosh in his teaching. The mitzvah is complete, "alive," only when it includes *kavvanah* as well as *ma'aseh.*

When an "upright" man, a *zaddik,* performs a mitzvah, he succeeds — thanks to the *kavvanah* — in reaching the spiritual element concealed within the object needed for fulfilling that mitzvah. He can elevate that object towards its root in the "world above," since everything that seems material to us is spiritual in essence. *Kavvanah* thus transforms the physical act of the mitzvah into a spiritual reality. In addition, its spiritual root is nourished and strengthened in the "world above," just as, conversely, it can be weakened by imperfect devotion. The *kavvanah* of the one who performs a physical mitzvah here below "inscribes" indelible "signs" into its root, which are a "pledge" of the purity of his intention. These signs will witness to his *kavvanah* when his soul has returned to its origin, and his body, having completed its task on earth, has been interred in the ground.

As for *tefillah,* "prayer," which is a spiritual mitzvah expressed in "thought" and "word," its underlying *kavvanah* is of prime importance, especially in connection with certain essential prayers.

It is indispensable that *kavvanah* should direct the recitation of the Shema (Deut. 6:4-9), especially of the first verse, "Hear, O Israel: the Lord our God; the Lord is One." Repeated without *kavvanah,* the Shema is worthless, devoid of meaning and life. For him who declaims it, as for those who hear him, the recital of the Shema (in particular of this opening verse) is an act of total and innermost "concentration." Equally for those present as for those absent, it is an act of all-embracing and extensive externalization. The believing Jew recites this first verse with eyes closed, descending into the depths of his soul. Then he recites the rest of the Shema with his eyes wide open, as if gathering together in his gaze all of Israel and even the whole wide world, in all its dimensions. He calls upon the whole world to proclaim the Unity of God, and then he leads it towards the higher worlds, bidding it to praise the Creator with a "Hymn" to His Glory, in harmony with all the worlds. So the universe is raised up to its Creator. Thus, to him who recites the Shema in this manner can apply that which King David said of himself: "as for me, I am all Prayer" (Ps. 109.4); he has transformed himself into a mitzvah.

In fact, every mitzvah breathes its "vitality" into the one who fulfils it. Due to this, man lives a full life: he "*lives* in it."

The Torah says: "Observe My laws and My commandments: he who practises them shall live by them [literally, "*in* them"]: I am the Lord" (Lev. 18:5). When the *kavvanah* permeates the body of the mitzvah, the latter itself becomes a *kavvanah*. As a result, it acquires the value of a concrete act, which directs the whole being of a believing Jew towards God. It assumes the characteristic of *hitbonenenut* and *regesh*, an act which is at the same time reflexive, contemplative and intuitive, emotive. Such an act spiritualizes the body, drawing it as close as possible to its Creator, whom we call the Spirit, the Being, but who, in truth, is infinitely more than that: He is One, with no relation to any number; He is Unique, without there being anything that could be compared to Him; He is All, without being composite.

When a Jew recites the Shema, through his *kavvanah* he assimilates all his being to his God, who desires that man, too, shall become one whole entity.

A Jew who prays in this manner acquires the certainty that his inmost thoughts, protected from all the contingencies of this world and returned to their original purity of essence in the "sphere of thought," are pleasing and acceptable to God.

Indeed, the *kavvanah* is a "concentration" of thought that a Jew attains when his wish to worship and serve God and to act rightly has become unshakeable, when he himself has overcome all the hesitations provoked by external circumstances and internal weaknesses. Thus, his spirit is protected from every *mahashavah zarah*, from every "alien thought" that might disturb the purity of his own thought, which strives to unite with divine Thought itself.

So that a true *kavvanah* can be born in him, the
Jew must banish from his mind every *maḥashavah
zarah*, every "alien thought."
Without the "thought of the Torah," the Jew's
thinking is likely to go astray.
The Struggle of Man When Fighting His Own
Thinking.
"Alien Thoughts" and "Alien Service."

Before reciting the Shema and beginning the daily prayer,
a Jew is required to proclaim the "blessing of the Torah," by
which he promises to "devote himself to the Torah," that is,
to respect it by studying and applying its teachings. By this
"blessing of the Torah" he lays a solid foundation to his
thinking; he passes on to it the stability and clarity of the
"higher thought," the higher wisdom that belongs to the
Torah. Without the light of the Torah, that "higher thought,"
the origin of which lies in a "supernatural," "supraterrestrial"
world, man's thinking, even if it seems transparently correct,
is likely to go astray. Thus strengthened by the "thinking of
the Torah," a Jew elevates his mind and binds it to the root of
Thought. He binds it to Him who "gives the Torah" and
makes man the gift of thought, of "knowledge," thus allowing man to "know" Him, that is, to worship and serve Him.

Now it is that the Jew can bring the offering of his human
— that is, relative — holiness to Him who alone is Holy, yet
whose absolute and utterly different holiness is "reinforced,"
as it were, by this offering of human holiness. In fact, the
Zohar says, "There is no holiness above without holiness
below." God expects man to "reinforce," "confirm" and proclaim His own Holiness. In return, the Holy One, blessed be
He, "sanctifies" the Jew by His mitzvot, which purify him
who performs them and help him to know God more profoundly and to serve Him with an ever-purer *kavvanah*.

To enable a true *kavvanah* to be born in him, a Jew must
banish from his mind every *maḥashavah zarah*, every "alien

thought" awakened by the "vanities of this world." Should he allow even one of them to intrude, he would be tolerating the presence of an "alien divinity," an *el zar*. He must remove all obscure "alien" thoughts that are opposed to his dawning, clear "conscience" — thoughts accumulated and deeply buried, yet which may spring up like a bad dream from the very depths of his subconscious, thus demonstrating a split in his personality. Indeed, to tolerate a *mahashavah zarah* during *Avodat ha-Shem*, the "service of God," would mean to replace *Avodat ha-Shem* with *avodah zarah*, an "alien service"* by which man, deifying himself, serves none but himself. Now, when man, under pressure from fantasies and alienations, distances himself from the essence of his being, he is serving an "alien" interest, for his own true interest is to worship and serve God.

So *kavvanah* is the process that thought undergoes in order to reach God purified and faultless, by a road without turnings and in pure faith. The *kavvanah* is the effort of thought to remain whole and constant.

Now, since thought, by its very nature, strives to extend itself, the Jew who wishes to remain master over his *kavvanah* must always be on guard and attentive to each of its thought processes. His thought must be ready to counter every distraction that might cause it to deviate, disturb its limpidity or dissipate its concentration.

This struggle of the man who is at grips with his own thought process that could incite him to sin, is, in truth, the most difficult and the longest of the battles man wages in the moral domain. That is why "the thought of sin is deemed to be more difficult to conquer than sin itself"; the duration of sin, in its realization, is not as long as the duration of the thought which conceived it.

---

* It is characteristic that idolatry should be described in Hebrew by the words *avodah zarah*, "alien service": service of an alien divinity, but equally, service alien to the truly Jewish soul.

Zaddikim, "upright men," have no need to wage this sort of struggle against the "alien thoughts" that may present themelves at the gates of their minds or even invade them, especially during prayer. They are able not only to master these mischievous, impure thoughts, but also to direct them into beneficent, righteous paths; they offer them a *tikkun*, they "repair" and reinstate them by leading them restored and luminous to the original, pure "roots," so as to place themselves at the service of God. In any case, the *kavvanah*, however right and pure it may be, cannot by itself become what it should fully be; it needs "God's help," the grace that He bestows upon the man who seeks to be master of his *kavvanah*.

> **The Shema, the Jewish Confession of Faith.**
> **Proclamation of the Unity of God.**
> *Yihud ha-Shem*, **the "Unification of the Name."**
> **Through the *Yihud*, a Jew attains the highest degree of the love of God; he "unifies" his being in the being of the one God; he "offers his soul" to God.**
> **"Acceptance of the Yoke of the Kingdom of Heaven" and "Acceptance of the Yoke of the Mitzvot."**

When the *Keri'at Shema*, the "recital of the Shema," is done with true *kavvanah*, it is called *Yihud ha-Shem*, "unification of the Name." This *Yihud*, as we have seen, has a dual character and is fulfilled in a dual sense. It is the *Yihud* of the worshipper who, in being united with God, finds he is "unified" in his own invisible being and its visible manifestations. It is likewise the *Yihud* of Him to whom the prayer is being directed and who, being "united" with man, is perceived by him in the invisible Unity of His being and its invisible manifestations. These are merciful and exacting; merciful while seeming to be severe, and severe while being intrinsically merciful:

it is thanks to the *Yihud* that the believer discovers the gentleness at the roots of the severity.

However, in the very depths of this double *Yihud* — human and divine — God remains God, exercising His Sovereignty which man acknowledges, and man still remains man, exercising the prerogatives that God has given him.

Such a *Yihud*, as that which the Shema achieves, allows a Jew to reach the highest degree of love for God, the crown of the "service in the Name" of God. Henceforth, he is capable of *mesirut nefesh*, he is ready to "offer his soul," to devote his life, to Him whom he worships. By the *hitpashetut ha-gashmiyyut*, the "casting off of his materiality," and by the *bittul ha-yesh*, the "obliteration of his physical existence," such a Jew attains to *Ayin*, to "Nothingness." Yet it is precisely from having touched for an instant this ethereal *Ayin* that the physical *yesh* of the Jew is strengthened so that he may be truly Man, a servant of God.*

The Shema consists of two principal and complementary acts: the *kabbalat ol malkhut shamayim*, the "acceptance of the yoke of the Kingdom of Heaven," which guides the thinking process that is called upon to bear witness to man's love for God (Deut. 6:4-9), and the *kabbalat ol ha-mitzvot*, the "acceptance of the yoke of the mitzvot," which directs the actions that are called upon to bear witness to that same love (Deut. 11:13-21).

The *mesirut nefesh*, to which a Jew may attain by virtue of the *kabbalat ol malkhut shamayim*, does not allow him to bury himself in the *Ayin*, thus fleeing from the life of this world and the demands of his earthly existence. On the contrary, the *mesirut nefesh* is achieved — with the *yesh* operating as the intermediary — in the concrete acts of the mitzvot, which a Jew performs "on earth."

---

* Cf. Alexandre SAFRAN, *The Kabbalah*, op. cit., p. 233f and 250ff; cf. E. STAROBINSKI-SAFRAN, "L'Existence, le Néant et l'Affirmation de soi dans l'expérience hassidique," in *Nova et Vetera, Fribourg*, 1985, 2nd edition, p. 129.

Rabbi Israel Ba'al Shem Tov declared that when he "recited" the Shema, he lived the *mesirut nefesh* so intensely —
renouncing his own life and offering it with joy to his Creator,
thus "committing his soul" to his Master — that it seemed to
him he was "no longer alive," "having put an end" to his life,
having offered himself as a sacrifice to God. Then, astounded
to be still alive and to have come back to "this world" from
the "other world," he had the sensation of being resurrected,
and would recite the blessing of *Sheheheyanu*, in which a Jew
thanks God for having "kept him alive." In fact, as he had
found himself suspended — by the *kabbalat ol malkhut shamayim*
— over the edge of non-being, he had to make an effort to
return from that "other world," where he yearned to contemplate the Shekhinah at close range, to "this world," where he
yearned to serve God in the most perfect way by the *kabbalat
ol ha-mitzvot*. Furthermore, said the Ba'al Shem Tov, every
Jew, whilst reciting the Shema, ought to think of himself as
being in heaven, so as to preserve the purity of his *kavvanah*.

> *Devekut*, the "adherence" of the soul to God, is a
> specifically Jewish mystical experience.
> In the performance of the mitzvah, the believer
> attains to *Devekut*.
> "Adherence" to God is at its very highest point
> when the believer reaches the heart of the mitzvah
> he is fulfilling.

It is *kavvanah* that gives life to *tefillah*, "prayer," and "directs"
it towards Him who receives it. But the essence of *tefillah* is
Devekut, the "devotion" of the soul to God, the intimate
"adherence" to God.

Like *kavvanah*, *Devekut*, too, is necessary for every *mitzvah*
and not just for *tefillah*. But whereas *kavvanah*, in permeating
it, accompanies the mitzvah that is being fulfilled, *Devekut* —
when it is complete, profound, and dynamic — extends the

mitzvah from which it arose, enhances the value of the present mitzvah and paves the way for the mitzvah that is to follow. Thus it is by means of a mitzvah that the true believer attains to *Devekut* and remains there.

All *Avodat ha-Shem* is founded on *Devekut*, which gives it depth and truth. A Jew enters the world to be an *oved ha-Shem*, a "servant of God," and this *Avodat ha-Shem* should embrace his whole life. And so it is that *Devekut* should give to that life — which is constantly being renewed — the meaning and content desired by the Torah, the very *Torah* which "appears as new to us every day as if it had been revealed this very day."

Devekut is thus (particularly for the *zaddik*) a permanent reality, which pervades his whole life. Each day afresh, it is the *Devekut* of today that one must live in today. Indeed, this is what the *Torah* requires, in a verse of the Book of Deuteronomy (4:4): "But you that did cleave — *ha-devekim* — unto the Lord your God are alive, every one of you, this day." Other verses (Deut. 11:22 and 13:5) call attention to the importance of the *davok*, the act that consists of "cleaving" to God, and the benefits that arise from it. These led the Ramban, the famous mystical exegete, to describe the man of *Devekut* as he who "remembers continuously the Name [of God] and his love for Him; His Name and his love for Him never leave his thoughts. When he is up and about, when he is lying down, when he rises and even when he is speaking, his heart is before Him. These very worthy men, while yet in their own lifetime, can have their souls linked to the bond of [eternal] life, for they are an abode for the Shekhinah."

Devekut is the goal towards which the soul that is "thirsty for God, for the living God" (Ps. 42:3), the soul that "longs and languishes for the courts of the Lord" (Ps. 84:3) is striving. It is the summit to which the love of God leads and it is precisely this summit which is desired by the believing Jew, above all by the man of the Kabbalah, the man of true Wisdom, the *zaddik*, the *hasid*.

There are different degrees of *Devekut*, depending upon its intensity, the nature of the mitzvah that produces it, and the time and place where that mitzvah is performed. *Devekut* is at its highest when the believer reaches the heart of the mitzvah that he is performing.

Through *Devekut* we keep "our hearts before Him," we feel drawn towards Him to whom we offer the whole of our self.

The little flame of the "candle that is our soul" (cf. Prov. 20:27), which is placed before the great Flame of the Divine, strives to be united with it and to lose itself within it. *Devekut* reminds the soul of its divine origin and enables it to sense the immediate Presence of God. It ardently desires, like a candle very close to a flame, to be rejoined to the Flame at its source. However, our soul does not dare cross the "boundary," the apparently short distance separating it from the Flame. Due to the nature given it by the Creator, it is constrained to remain what it is — a little candle — and, above all, that is what it should be. Now, according to the words of the wise King Solomon of Israel and the interpretation given by the Sages of Israel, the soul must remain the "candle-mitzvah," which, by the "light of the Torah" (cf. Prov. 6:23) that it radiates, and by the fire of faith (cf. Deut. 33:2) that it contains, should illuminate the path and infuse with warmth the one who is performing the mitzvah.

Man cannot identify himself with God; the frontier separating the created being from his Creator cannot be abolished. Even *Devekut* cannot do away with that distance between man and God. All it can do is give the man of faith the consciousness and the feeling of the "nearness" of God — for "the Lord is near to all who call upon Him in truth" (Ps. 145:18). Only occasionally can it reduce the tension that rises up within man's spirit from the concept and the reality of God. Man's perception of God "who encompasses all the worlds," being transcendent, impersonal, absolute, and above all rational comprehension — that perception, thanks to his *Devekut*, is in perfect harmony with his perception of God who is immanent and personal, who "fills all the worlds," yet whom man can envisage within himself.

God is King of the man who lives in *Devekut*; He is *Nora*, "formidable"; He inspires in man an "exalted," "reverential" fear, which demands to be translated into precise deeds. At the same time, man feels God as an understanding Father who inspires confidence. Yet again he feels Him, intuitively, as *Yedid Nefesh*, a "friend of his soul," who trusts him and for whom he has a "reverential" love, which desires to express itself in deeds. He who is so profoundly absorbed in *Devekut* lives it in *Emunah*, in "Faith."

> **Devekut is never perceived as a *unio mystica*, as a state of perfect union of the soul with God. Devekut is expressed by deeds, accomplished by mitzvot.**

This is why *Devekut* is always conceived and lived as a rich intellectual and intuitive experience of the Jewish soul that proclaims its God. But it is an experience expressed by deeds, carried out by the mitzvot that a believing Jew, obedient to his God, fulfils through "thought, word, and deed." This manner of conceiving and living *Devekut* is the same in essence, even if it differs in form, throughout all the currents of thought and every historical circumstance, from the Bible down to Hasidism, taking in on the way rabbinical literature, ethical philosophy, and, above all, the different schools of the Kabbalah.

Devekut is never perceived as a *unio mystica*, a state of perfect union with God, the union of the soul with the infinite

Being. The *unio mystica* is experienced as an almost inconceivable happiness, an unfailing joy; it is the greatest desire of non-Jewish, Far Eastern, Plotinian, Christian, and Islamic mystics. As for *Devekut*, in addition to the phase of inward contemplation, meditation, and speculation, it includes a phase of outwardness that leads to action.

The Torah itself revealed to us this need for action, which is proper to *Devekut* and is regarded as the highest concrete expression of the love of God.

The Torah recommends to the Israelites that they "cleave to God" and to this end, it uses various forms of the verb *davok*, which means "to cling to." In order for them to cling to God, the Torah exhorts the Israelites to "love God" by "observing His mitzvot," to "serve Him" by obeying Him, by "listening to His voice" (Deut. 13:5; 30:20), and to "walk in all His ways" (Deut. 11:22).* The verb *la-asot*, "to do," sums up all those exhortations that aim to lead a Jew to *Devekut*. It is this "clinging to God" which is the "condition of life" — a true life, unfolding in the light of the Torah of Life, revealed by Him who is the Life of Life. Now, for man, movement is vital to life; the Sages of Israel and the masters of the Kabbalah teach that this movement utilizes and conducts life here below to the true life above (the Hebrew term *ḥayyim*, "life," is in the plural). This power of movement allows the *anshei ma'alah*, the "spiritually exalted men," to live their lives on earth as a prelude to the true life, which they will live to its fullness, in a life-giving "rest," in the "world to come," in the "world of truth."

The masters of Jewish mystical thought and experience deeply examine the teaching on "cleaving to God" provided by the basic biblical, talmudic and zoharic texts; they discern its principles and determine its means of application. They

---

* "To walk in all His ways" means, according to the Talmud and the Zohar, to follow the example of His Goodness. The *Imitatio Dei* in Judaism has an ethical meaning, God being the principle, the source of morality.

agree in viewing and experiencing *Devekut* as a profoundly religious act, a synthesis of concentration and movement, rest and progression.

The Zohar is not hesitant in describing the state of the "union" between man and God, between the created being and his Creator. But "union" is, in truth, only an approximate, not an absolute description. At certain rare and favoured times, the *benei aliyah*, the "spiritually exalted men," can know a sort of fusion of *ehad be-Ehad*, of "one in One," the fusion of man, "unified" in his being, with the Being who is One in His essence. Likewise, over the centuries, some kabbalists have taught us that at "certain hours of grace," of *hitbodedut*, of "solitude" with God, when their deeply concentrated thought joins the root of Thought, certain *yode'ei hen*, "those who have penetrated the mystery of grace," of the "hidden wisdom," are able to arrive at a *Devekut* that is very close to the union of the soul with the Soul of Souls. They can then achieve the *bittul ha-yesh*, the "annihilation of self." This means that by an extreme intellectual and emotional effort, they are able to feel a "suppression of their physical being," especially during prayer.

That is an exceptional, sublime state of immediate communion with the Deity. (Rabbi Abraham Abulafia (13th century), Rabbi Hayyim Vital (16th century), and Rabbi Dov Baer of Lubavitch (18th-19th centuries), among others, have written about this state.) But even then, *Devekut* remains a specifically Jewish mystical experience, which cannot be disassociated from action. Having reached this state of intimate communion with God, the Jewish mystic will continue to observe the Torah and the mitzvot, to look for the *penimiyyut*, the "profundity" of the Torah through its study, and to seek the depths of the mitzvot through action.

Rabbi Shneur Zalman of Lyady, the founder of Habad Hasidism, cried out in a moment of deep *Devekut*, "Master of the World! I desire neither Your works, nor Your paradise, nor Your world to come! What I desire is You alone!" (His exclamation recalls that of the psalmist: "Whom have I in heaven but Thee? And there is none upon earth that I desire beside Thee!" (Ps. 73:25).) But the author of the *Tanya*, the magnum opus of Habad Hasidism, tells us that even when his soul is soaring thus towards God, he is not in search of rest, of salvation; he does not remain suspended in an ecstatic emptiness, but passes through the ethereal sphere, which might be regarded as a void, to return to the ground of action, action essentially composed of thorough study of the Torah and strict observance of the mitzvot.

The *Devekut* to which the author of the *Tanya* aspires is an adherence to God, Who identifies Himself with the essence of the Torah, the content of which is formed of the divine Names, and with the mitzvot, which constitute His "garments" as it were, "the garments of the King." He who has attained this *Devekut* encounters God in the letters of the Torah and establishes His Reign in this world by observing the mitzvot. The mitzvot are the path by which the Torah, which is above nature, reaches out to nature and transforms it into Torah. In fact, every action of the man of *Devekut* is a mitzvah that "draws" towards itself the Shekhinah and is clothed in the light emanating from the Author of the Torah, the *Ein-Sof*, the "Infinite."

This is the *Devekut* ardently desired by the author of the *Tanya*; and he himself clearly showed the way that leads to it. This great man of faith was also a scholar of the Law. He was the author of the code of religious law called the *Shulhan Arukh ha-Rav*,* "The Rav's *Shulhan Arukh*," in which he gives rules of conduct for the Jew who is a "servant of God," and especially, those rules that, thanks to *talmud Torah*, "study of the Torah," lead to *Devekut*, as experienced in the true fear and love of God.

---

* This title, *Shulhan Arukh*, "The Laid Table," is borrowed from Rabbi Joseph Caro's great religious Code (16th century).

> The Jew of *Devekut* "sets aside his own will" so
> that it may totally dissolve within the Will of
> God, which requires him to exist and to act.

To attain a state of *Devekut*, a man athirst for God must
make a double journey — from man to God and from God to
man. Loving God, he runs towards Him; fearing God, he
returns to himself. And again he runs towards Him and
comes back to himself.... Like Abraham, he moves "journey-
ing and camping," *halokh ve'naso'a* (cf. Gen. 12:9).

The author of the *Sefer Yezirah* knew the dilemma that
traps the man who ardently desires his God, wanting to
remain close to Him, and who, nevertheless, scrupulously
obeys His commands and walks "before," "with," and "after"
Him. He understands the inner wavering of such a man, so
he consoles him with the advice, "If your heart runs towards
Him, turn back at once." In the same vein, Rabbi Shneur Zalman
says, "Return by studying and applying the practical mitzvot."

All the authors of kabbalistic literature have brooded over
this march, begun over and over again, of the man hungry for
God, searching for *Devekut*. Kabbalistic literature describes the
impetus towards God, the return, and the interval which permit
this man, nonetheless, to make greater advances. They dwell on
the exploits, the often heroic efforts to reach his goal, namely, to
surrender himself fully to God so that God Himself will turn to
Him, will possess him, taking him entirely to Himself, sheltering
him all over with "the wings of the Shekhinah."

Kabbalistic literature also describes the difficulties that
such a man confronts in this "race" of his, the end of which
is total integration and dissolution within God. The literature
emphasizes the constraints he must accept in order to live this
kind of life as a man totally in accordance with his Creator's
Will, but it also defines all the benefits that result from this
for himself and for the world at large.

The man of *Devekut* is thus a man with a will, not one of

renunciation. In other words, he is a man who "renounces his *own* will" to no longer exist or act, in order to adhere to the Will which commands him to continue to do so.

Now, he cannot be a man in his dual and unitary constitution — spiritual and corporal — except on earth; he cannot act as a man except on earth.

But it is from here, on this earth, that he must "lift up his eyes to the heights" (Isa. 40:26), to the heavens, and it is here on earth that he must act so that "all his actions may be [done] for the sake of Heaven." His material acts will be spiritualized, so that the *ma'aseh*, the concrete "deed," is united with the *mahashavah*, the pure "thought" that preceded its realization. Thus the *mahashavah* becomes *ma'aseh* and the *ma'aseh* becomes *mahashavah*.

> **To Run and to Return.**
> **To Go towards God and Return to Oneself.**
> **"To Rise" towards God through the Torah and,**
> **for Its Sake, to Descend to the Level of Man.**

To describe the "race" run by one aspiring to lose himself in the Deity, the kabbalists use two terms that were employed by the prophet Ezekiel (1:14) to describe his great mystical vision: *razo va-shov*, "to run and to return," "coming and going." In a symbolic summary, these two verbs epitomize what a Jew must do to attain *Devekut*.

To the Jew who "runs," *razo*, to be freed of himself and to throw himself into Godliness; to him who "runs" and prepares to break out of his physical envelope to lose himself in Godliness; to him who runs to "escape from himself" in order to remain in ecstasy (*ek-stasis*), thus uniting "his spirit with the Spirit" — to this man it is said, "Halt! You cannot stay here, for as long as you live 'here below,' your place is not here; so 'go back,' *shov*, to yourself; do not delay to 'descend' to 'the earth God has given to men' (Ps. 115:16); and take with you the lights you have gathered at that instant in which, 'unified' in your being and physically spiritualized, you have believed that your wish would be granted. As King David wrote in moving terms in the Psalms, 'When shall I come and present myself before the face of God?' (Ps. 42:3). You have thought to see the One who declares, 'No man may see Me and live (Ex. 33:20).' "

Razo and *shov* are brought together, condensed into a single, very significant word, "Torah." Man must "rise," *razo*, to God through the Torah "and descend," *va-shov*, to men for the Torah's sake. ("*Razo va-shov*" has the same numerical value as *Torah*: 611.)

At the very moment when man, having arrived at the highest summit of spirituality, hopes to be freed from his burden, from his physical, material weight, he is charged with a mission: to return to earth, the place of his earthly life, there to prepare a "dwelling" for the Shekhinah. For God "desires to live below," among men, and there to establish His "Kingdom."

Israel's mission is therefore to "draw" the Shekhinah down to earth by obeying the Torah and the mitzvot. In this way, he will prepare the "dwelling" of God here below and proceed to extend the Kingdom of God on earth. God desires to be "King over all the earth" (Zech. 14:9), that is, to see how Man, Israel, by his *Avodat ha-Shem*, transforms what is earthly and material into a "vessel" that may serve the goal of Creation: to spread the Glory of God over all things.

Certainly the "whole earth has been filled with His Glory" (Isa. 6:3) and "there is no place where He is not present." But in the *olam*, in this "world," His Glory is still "hidden"; in the *olam* (cf. Ex. 3:15), in a "world" that "hides" the Glory of Him who is *Ne'elam*, "hidden," His Glory and His "Name" have not yet been disclosed. It is the man of *Devekut* who must unveil and reveal them through the Torah and the mitzvot, who must labour day after day for their complete "discovery," their final "revelation" in the messianic age. For in this world, His Name exists in an incomplete, elliptical form: "it is not pronounced as it is written." It is not yet proclaimed in its fullness; it is not "entirely" acknowledged in the respect due to His Will.

When His Glory has been fully revealed and His Kingship truly established in this world, thanks to Man's, Israel's, reverence for the Torah and the mitzvot, they will radiate from here below to the heights above, and will embrace all the worlds. The higher worlds will be perfected only when the world below will be perfected, for its role is decisive in this matter, and it is the Torah and the mitzvot which will bring about the perfecting of this world. They come from the higher world to be fulfilled in the here below, in "the world of action," the world where man, by the free will granted him by the Creator, can hasten or delay this perfecting. It will signal the end of the *tikkunim*, the "repairing" of the ontological-cosmic and moral-historical "ruptures" that have affected the worlds. (The first were caused by the "fall of the kings"; the second, by man's sin.) Again, it is by the "Torah that he keeps" and the "mitzvot that he observes" that Man, Israel, puts into effect these *tikkunim*, designed to return the worlds to their original "wholeness."

Such is the delicate, privileged task of Man. It is both a noble vocation and a heavy responsibility for Israel, to whom God has granted the Torah and the mitzvot as a means of perfecting the worlds and elevating them to their original wholeness.*

---

* In creating the world, God put into effect a Zimzum, a "reduction," a "restriction" of the original, purely spiritual, power of His Creation. Thus "diminished," "reduced," "weakened," this power was able to descend into the physical, material world. Man's presence makes this world the "world of action." It is Israel, the trustee of the "gift of the Torah" and the "grace of the mitzvot," which were conceived before the world's creation, who can and must lead this world (and all the worlds with it) back to its purely spiritual source.

> *Devekut* does not mean a "dissolving" of man in God in another world; on the contrary, it reinforces man's calling in this world, "in the presence of God and men."

As a loyal servant of God, the man who loves God does not dally in the temporary dwelling that his perfect *Devekut* allowed him to find in the world above. He comes down to his own people again. He is busy with the task assigned to him, namely, to serve God here below with all his being, body and soul, and to help his fellowmen to do so. He does not hesitate to "eliminate his will before His Will," while at the same time uniting his will with God's Will, so that it may be obeyed "in the world He created according to His Will."

Thus, *Devekut* does not consist in man's "dissolving" in God in another world; on the contrary, it reinforces man's vocation in this world, "in the presence of God and men." It is this world that the Jew, by observing the mitzvot, must transform into Torah, that is, lead it back to its origins inscribed in the Torah. Similarly, he must lead the worlds beyond and away from their present state, back to their Torah "origins." On account of this work of "restoration," Man, Israel, is much higher than the angels. The latter asked God to leave the Torah on high, so that it might "spread His Majesty in the heavens." But it is Israel to whom God made the gift of the Torah, this instrument of the world's creation, and the mitzvot, the instruments for transforming the world into Torah. He decided to give them to men who, being made of two contrary elements — body and soul — would have to "contend and prevail," like "Isra-el," against themselves and within themselves, "against men and against God" (cf. Gen. 32:29), so as to make the Torah and the mitzvot respected everywhere at all times.

As for the angels, they are not subject to temptations, to inner contradictions, or to the waverings of free will; they are "upright" and endowed with a special, distinct intelligence.

By their very nature, being incomplex, they are ready to fulfil the missions God entrusts to them in given places and at given times. That is why Israel is called not only God's "servant," but also God's "elder son." The Israelites are called "children of God" and have a genuine person-to-Person relationship with their heavenly Father, who favours them above the "heavenly angels."

"God has enough angels in heaven," exclaims Rabbi Menahem Mendel of Kotsk. He does not want men to be angels on earth. He wants them to be "holy men for Me" and not angels; men who eat, but not "any meat that is torn of beasts in the field" (Ex. 22:30). He wants "to be their God" to these men, who "eat and drink" according to the Torah's precepts; and who are clothed, but in clean "garments."

Men must seek within each object the "divine vitality" that allows it to exist, the "divine spark" that gives it life, so that each thing may be "a holy thing for them." Their physical being too must be holy. Let them strive for an ever-greater holiness, without, however, believing that they are able to attain absolute holiness (even in human terms), for there are no limits to holiness. Let them beware of thinking that their holiness might be compared, however distantly, with that of God, the Holy One, blessed be He, whose "holiness is above all holiness"; God's holiness alone is pure, absolute, for unlike human holiness, it is not conceived in opposition to impurity or non-holiness. Let them exclaim, like Hannah, "There is none so holy as the Lord, for there is none beside Thee" (I Sam. 2:2), and like David, "Thou art the Holy One, Thou who dwellest amid the praises of Israel" (Ps. 22:4).

> To him who performs his tasks with *Devekut*,
> God allows — even in this world — a taste of the
> joy of the world above.

The Torah is heavenly in origin: Torah *min ha-shamayim*; nevertheless, for him who seeks to fulfil the mitzvot, none of them is "in heaven" (Deut. 30:12). Each mitzvah "is very close to thee"; it is "in thy mouth and in thy heart, that thou mayst *do it (la- asoto)*" (Deut. 30:14), that you are able to do it. God desires that man, by fervent observance of the heavenly Torah and its mitzvot, make his earthly Labours a heavenly task.

All things in this world are physical "symbols" of spiritual realities in the higher world, with which there is contact through the mitzvot. Each mitzvah, in turn, by its practical fulfilment, is able to reach its source in the higher world and there leave its imprint on its "symbol."

The man who succeeds in experiencing *Devekut*, however imperfectly, knows no rest; he cannot enjoy perfect tranquility, for the physical, material life in "this world" weighs on him. So he aspires to live in "another," completely spiritualized world; he pines for the *olam ha-Ba*, "the world to come." But this same man who performs his task in *Devekut*, who lives closely attached to God, is allowed, even in the "here and now," to taste the joy of the world above, to experience the eternity of the world to come. For such a man, the *Olam*, the true "world," is *ha-Ba*, is "already coming" towards him, wherever he may be. The deeper such a man penetrates into the inner meaning of the Torah and the mitzvot, and the more he lets himself be permeated by their light, the closer "the world of truth" comes to him. His desire for the *Or Ein-Sof*, the "Light of the Infinite," permits him to receive even now its first glimmerings. He lives in close proximity to God, which is why God is for him the *Olam ha-Ba*. He is almost living within God, while God has His dwelling in him: the Shekhinah is present in him.

So it is that *Time*, detached from *Eternity* where it rightly belongs, can be hallowed by the Torah and the mitzvot, thus reverting to its source: it returns to lose itself in, and to become one with, *Eternity*.

Nadab and Abihu, sons of Aaron, "died before God."

A man of *Devekut* should be content with this foretaste of the heavenly *Olam ha-Ba*, with this nearness to God. The source and the goal of his meditations and, indeed, of all his actions, should be *li-khvod shamayim*, "for the honour of God." He should live uprightly in this world, while awaiting the abundance of the higher world, where the righteous sit crowned with their deeds, enjoying the radiance of the Shekhinah, the splendour of God's Presence. Through this nearness of God, he will receive whatever good he merits here below. King David celebrates this *Devekut* in exclaiming: "But as for me, the nearness of God is my good!" (Ps. 73:28).

However, for one who hungers after Godliness, even such a *Devekut* is too limited and inadequate. His soul aspires to be set free from the body in which it feels imprisoned; it ardently wishes to dissolve in the Deity. But that is not allowed him here below.

According to the kabbalists, Nadab and Abihu, the sons of Aaron, were not able to enter into Godliness: "They died before the Lord" (Lev. 10:2). Their souls burned with love for God, and yet they were punished for having tried to exceed the limits imposed on them concerning the manifestation of their love for God here on earth. They "offered strange fire, *esh zarah*, before the Lord, which He commanded them not. And a fire went out from the Lord and devoured them..." (Lev. 10: 1-2). The *esh zarah* that the sons of Aaron offered before the Lord was deemed to be "strange fire" because what they sought to gain by it was their personal salvation, "strange," "alien" to the order given by God. But God took account of the intrinsic value of their deed; "they died, [but] before the Lord." And God said, "I will be sanctified through them that come near me, and before all the people I will be honoured" (Lev. 10:3).

God is "sanctified" that is, "honoured" here below by men who "come near Him" but "before all the people." The man who tries to come nearer to God than is permitted him, and with a view to his own salvation, will die. Certainly, there have been exceptions: men whose souls thirsted for the "living God" to such an extent that they no longer thought of their own physical and spiritual needs, or of those of their fellows. These souls "ascended" to God, but it was God Himself who brought about these "ascents." Thus Enoch "walked with God [alone and not with men], then he was not, for God took him" (Gen. 5:24). Thus Elijah, whom "God would take up by a whirlwind into heaven" (II Kings 2:1), but only after the prophet had completed his task on earth; it was thanks to Elijah that "all the people...fell on their faces: and they said, The Lord, He is God; the Lord, He is God" (I Kings 18:39).

> The soul is sent to earth against its wishes, to observe the Torah and the mitzvot in union with the body.
> Its task accomplished, it will rise again to the world above, enriched by its "humanizing" activities.

We have seen that when man has in due course reached the peak of contemplative *Devekut* in God and has entered the higher world, his Master orders him to "return" home to men, to "go back" without delay to the "world of action," to act there in accordance with the Will of the Creator, as revealed in the Torah and the mitzvot.

"Four" great masters of the talmudic period "have entered paradise," the orchard of mystical contemplation and speculation, to live there in total *Devekut*. Of them all, only Rabbi Akiba "entered in peace and left in peace." He, the man of mystical faith and stern law, entered in peace because he was endowed with the Torah, for which he had hazarded his life to teach, and with the mitzvot, which he had very faithfully performed. However, he was not slow to return in peace, in order to continue his work and to serve as an example to his many pupils.

As for his companions, this subtle experience of *Devekut* was destructive to them. It cost one of them his life (he died), another his reason (he lost his spiritual mind), and a third his faith (he became a heretic). This was because they "entered into paradise" only to "contemplate the Shekhinah," to surfeit their eyes with the splendour of the Divine Presence and to "speculate" on the mysteries of the origins of the world, the mystery of God's actions, thus trying to satisfy their intellectual curiosity. They gave no thought to what they owed, in the world of action, to themselves and, above all, to their disciples, their loyal followers who had remained in this world. Believing that their souls were filled with divine light and their eyes with divine radiance, they considered themselves to be already emancipated from the "yoke of the mitzvot," the constraint of the law, from which only "the dead are free."

Now, the soul is sent to earth against its own will to observe the Torah and the mitzvot in union with the body. Exiled from the place of its felicity, it "descends" to this world. Once its task is done, it will be able to "rise once again" to the world above, enriched by the "humanizing" activities it carried out here below in the light of the Torah and with the help of the body. Loaded with "merit," the soul will occupy a higher place in the world above than it had before its "descent" to this world. It will be "rewarded" for having fulfilled the mitzvot — mostly of a physical nature — in guiding and "purifying" the body. That bliss that it will then know in the Presence of its Creator, will be a gift, of course, but also the reward of its efforts to fulfil the Will of God during its stay on earth. Before that stay here below, the happiness it knew was an entirely free gift, due to the Creator's magnanimity alone. Thus, the soul felt a certain unease in this happiness, not having "worked" to prove itself worthy of it. But of this new bliss that the Creator offers, the soul does feel worthy.

This "descent" therefore took place with an "ascent" in view.

The Zaddik, the "Upright Man."
His soul's "descent" to earth requires from him a more intense "labour."

The case of the zaddik, the "upright man," is not essentially different from that of every believing Jew as regards the "descent" and "ascent" of his soul — even if the zaddik is successful — however imperfectly — in experiencing the *aliyat neshamah,* the "ascent of the soul," many times during his earthly life.

Here below, the zaddik abases himself before God; he worships Him fervently and serves Him faithfully; by the example of his own behavior, his performance of the mitzvot, his study of the Torah — which without hesitation he makes his vocation — he makes God known among men, he helps his fellowmen to "love His Name."

But because of the special importance of his mission and the unusual purity of his soul and body, the "descent" of his soul to earth — its *yeridah* — requires of him a "labour," a more intense *avodat ha-Shem.* His soul's *aliyah,* its rising again, its final "ascent," will therefore be particularly "costly"; it can only take place once the zaddik's task has been completed. Among the *benei aliyah*, "the spiritually exalted," this definitive *aliyah* can happen earlier than among other believers, that is, after a relatively short life here on earth (this was the case, for example, with Rabbi Bon and with Rabbi Isaac Luria): this means that they will have fulfilled their *avodat ha-Shem*, their "service of the Name," their *avodat ha-kodesh*, their "labour of holiness," to the greatest depth and with the utmost intensity, without loss of time.

> **The zaddik arouses the souls of his followers and leads them to their roots.**
> **He lifts the "veil" woven by men's sins, which separates them from their Creator.**
> **The Differences between the Jews'** *Devekut* **and the** *unio mystica* **of non-Jews.**

Rabbi Akiba "left" the splendid "paradise" of supreme *Devekut* "in peace" to bring into this world a message of peace, to lead men to act in this material world according to the demands of the Torah and the mitzvot.

Like Rabbi Akiba, the zaddik, too, returns here below, after having successfully reached the top of the ladder of the *razo*, of the "race" that leads him to supreme *Devekut*, and he "lowers himself" down to the level of his followers, the better to understand and guide them. During the *razo*, during his "race," his body has been filled and made transparent by the divine light; it has been transfigured by having experienced his supreme contemplative and meditative *Devekut*. Therefore, at the time of the *shov*, of his "return," the zaddik will, in spite of his "abasement," undertake to "enlighten" and to "purify" his followers, to spiritualize them by *He'arah*, a labour of "illumination." He will waken their "divine souls" (which will purify their "animal souls"), raise them, and lead them back to their higher roots, placing each soul where it originally belonged.

The zaddik thus removes the "veil" which the sins of men have woven and which "separates" them from their Creator. The zaddik helps his followers to progress along the *darkhei teshuvah*, the "roads of the return" to God; he helps each according to his merits and abilities to "come close to their heavenly Father." He leads them towards a higher world, where he himself was merely a transient guest before God thrust him back into this world to fulfil his task here below "for the sake of God and men," according to the requirements of the Torah. To do this task well, the zaddik must remain very close to the higher world where he sojourned; like Adam, who, before sinning, linked earth to heaven; like Jacob, who in his dream saw a ladder linking earth to heaven; the zaddik too links the lower world to the higher world.

It is proper, therefore, once again to underline the difference between the Jews' *Devekut* and the *unio mystica* of non-Jews. In Jewish *Devekut*, brief, contemplative, meditative, even speculative phases are only preparatory stages, looking forward to the long road of action that continues the *Devekut* indefinitely. *Unio mystica*, on the other hand, is generally marked by a state of immobility, almost of unconsciousness, which he who feels it has produced in himself and for himself. For the sake of his own happiness, he seeks in it his own salvation; it is an ecstasy which cuts man off from the external world and finds its completion within itself. *Devekut*, unlike *unio mystica*, is not a state; it is a process that in a practical way seeks the spiritual and material good of others, and not the personal happiness of him who experiences it. Nevertheless, this good, which is sought for others, will rebound upon the man of *Devekut* himself.

> The "appearance" of this world is not to be
> understood as an illusion giving rise to pessimism.
> The Torah does not ask man to despise his natural
> life, but wishes him to give it a meaning that will
> raise it above simple nature.
> The Jew "sanctifies himself by what is permitted."

At the time of the *shov*, the man of *Devekut* does not regard this world and all it contains as pure "illusions"; neither does he despise the human body as being irremediably corrupt. In fact, it is precisely in this world of "illusion" that the Jew is called upon to fulfil the *mitzvot*, using for this purpose that which God has created. It is this world of "illusory appearance" that the Jew must traverse to arrive at its innermost recesses, where its "divine vitality" is hidden. Equally, the Jew must respect and spiritualize his human body, allowing it, therefore, a share in his *avodat ha-Shem*.

If this world is labelled "the world of illusion," "the world of lies," this is because such it is in relation to God, who created it, and because it exists only through God, who alone Is, who alone is True. It is in this sense that the world can be regarded as a *zel*, as a "shadow" (though a shadow silhouetted against a luminous background) by the Jewish philosophers from Philo, Maimonides, and the Jewish mystics, down to the Gaon of Vilna and his contemporary, Rabbi Shneur Zalman of Lyady. The "appearance" of this world is not to be understood — as in the teaching of Buddha or the philosophy of Schopenhauer — as an illusion that gives rise to pessimism. In the eyes of the Jew, the world is an apparent reality; it is the "divine raiment," shining and transparent, which King David celebrated in his psalms; it is completely permeated by a "divine reality," by which both the cosmos and man are nourished.

As for the human body, it contains no evil in itself, even though it does incline towards evil. The physical, material enjoyments brought by his deepest cravings can become a source of good or evil, depending on whether or not man experiences them in accord with the Torah and the mitzvot. The body itself is also summoned to *avodat ha-Shem*, its participation being indeed indispensable, for it is the body which strengthens the vitality and mobility of *avodat ha-Shem*.

The human body is the most wonderful creation of God, and He has created it fit to serve Him. The wonderful structure of the body must be respected, for it is a microcosm that symbolically condenses the entire macrocosm. It must be specially valued for its marvellous "appearance," for it is the *zelem Elohim*, the "image of God" (author of the *zel*, of the "shadow" of the world), which the body hides within itself. In order that this "image of God" may be made manifest, man must be conscious of, and prove himself worthy, of carrying it within him. When it has fulfilled its task, returned to dust and become completely purified, God authorizes its resurrection.

That is why what one may be tempted to call the rules of Jewish asceticism are only norms of temperate conduct, which are based on the Torah and the mitzvot, and aim to elevate the Jew to a certain degree of "sanctification." But the Jewish believer has been told, "Sanctify yourself by what is permitted to you!" And the Torah permits, even demands, that life may be sanctified also by means which might violate it. Life itself, as the Creator gave it to man, is intrinsically good, and his responsibility and his merit, if he remains faithful to it, is to keep that life pure and never to cause it harm.

The Torah does not ask man to despise his natural life. It does not ignore the needs of the body, nor does it command man to suppress them. What it wants is to give these needs direction and meaning, a goal which will raise them above simple nature. It is, in fact, to a higher spiritual nature that the Torah wishes to raise man's physical nature, by means of his obedience to the mitzvot. Far from requiring man to renounce the needs of his physical life, it asks him to satisfy them, yet to do so in accordance with the "Torah of Life" — which pays attention to everything that concerns man's daily life — and by the "shining mitzvot," which enlighten man on the use of things here below. Satisfying the needs of physical life is therefore itself a mitzvah, and the fulfilling of that mitzvah leads to holiness, to *kedushah.* It is in this way that the Jew "sanctifies himself by what is permitted."

Those Jewish mystics who are the most inclined towards asceticism have always strictly followed the percepts of Halakhah, Jewish religious law, which governs both the material and the spiritual aspects of the daily life of the believing, observing Jew.

That is why Jewish asceticism has never given birth to monastic orders. Though the kabbalists have sometimes formed "fellowships," they did not found institutions. They have always lived and acted "in the midst of their people," among men, even though they were distinguished from them by their spiritual elevation.*

> The *zaddik* is concerned with the relationship of
> his followers to God, His Torah and His mitzvot.
> He strives to carry out his tasks and thereby to
> "give his Creator cause to rejoice."
> God delights in doing good to His creatures.

In general, a devotee of the *unio mystica* aspires to salvation; he "liberates himself" from all earthly contingencies and therefore might consider himself released from all duty towards himself or others; his ultimate objective is to be released from existence. There are examples, nonetheless, of

---

* When Rabbi Simeon bar Yoḥai, the great second century mystic, left the cave where he had been living for several years, he saw men busy with the affairs of "temporal life," attending to ephemeral needs and neglecting the things of "eternal life," and he cast on them a fiery look, a devouring eye. At once, a celestial voice ordered him to "go back to his cave" so as "not to destroy God's world...."

mystics who, having achieved the *unio mystica*, have proved to have a great devotion towards their fellowmen.

As for the ẓaddik, most often the deeper his *Devekut*, the more closely does he feel bound to his followers. By his *Devekut* he "liberates" himself from his "individuality," from his personal characteristics; he is not yet trying to obtain his own salvation; moreover, he can never be sure of his salvation as long as he lives here below, for he might yet sin in the last moments of his life, as was the case of Yoḥanan Kohen Gadol. "For there is not a ẓaddik upon earth who does good and sins not" (Eccles. 7:20). Concerning this verse, the exegetes have observed that, nevertheless, a selfish thought can creep into the spirit of the ẓaddik who does good.

The first preoccupation of the ẓaddik, who devotes himself to *Devekut*, concerns the relations of his followers with God, His Torah, and His mitzvot. He leaves his restricted "individuality" here below to turn to the limitless universality above, embracing the Whole. He is therefore bearing the cares of the whole of Israel, and even of the whole world. He feels the duty to "labour" for their deliverance from the material or spiritual exile that they are experiencing and to facilitate the road of their Return to God, their Creator.

Thus the ẓaddik, returning to the world of action by the *shov*, endeavours to "draw down" upon this world, by the *hamshakhah*, the blessings that he has gathered in the higher spheres of supreme *Devekut*. He toils to cause them to descend in abundance upon Israel and upon humanity and, indeed, upon all of God's creatures.

Intimately united with God, living continuously in *Devekut* to the highest degree of concentration, the ẓaddik does not desire any reward, neither here below nor yet in the world to come. Moreover, as no recompense of God could possibly be imagined or comprehended by our senses, God gives us none here below, and this He does to leave our free will intact; "Oh how great is Thy goodness, which Thou has *laid up* for those who fear Thee" (Ps. 31:20). The z̲addik seeks only to carry out his task and thereby — as through each mitzvah he fulfils — to give his Creator cause to rejoice. Now, God delights in doing good, in gratifying His creatures with the "fruits" of His Goodness. In order to do so, he expects men to desire to understand the signs of His Goodness; He "needs," as it were, the desires of the z̲addik to rise to the heights. Knowing this, the z̲addik attempts to "help" God and above all, he prays that God's Will be realized. God expects the z̲addik to prepare the hearts of his followers so as to make of them "vessels" worthy to receive His Blessing. This is what the Torah reveals to us in the Book of Genesis: "...for the Lord God had not caused it to rain upon the earth, [for] there was no man to till the ground. But [then] there went up a mist [a prayer] from the earth and [it] watered the whole face of the ground" (Gen. 2:5-6). When man's prayer rises, the rain of blessing is ready to come down to "water the ground."

"The Holy One, blessed be He, desires the prayers of the z̲addikim," state the Talmud and the Zohar.

Just as He gave the *kohanim*, the "priests," the mitzvah "to bless the children of Israel" (cf. Num. 6: 23-27) so that, summoned by their blessings, "He would bless them," so God bids the z̲addik to bless the people.

> **In the days of the Messiah, the creation of the world will finally be complete: the material will become spiritual.**

The z̲addik is working to hasten the coming of the *Gillui*, the "revelation," the "manifestation" of God's Goodness, in its fullness and splendour.

The total *Gillui* will take place in the messianic age. It is then that men "will bless," "recognize" and "offer thanks" to

God, who is "Good and does Good." It is then that the "Face" of His Goodness, no longer "hidden," will be "open," "visible" to the eyes of His creatures. It will appear in its original light, as at the Creation. Since man's eyes cannot bear the brightness of this original light, the Holy One, blessed be He, concealed it for the sake of the z̲addikim, for the times to come. "Until the messianic age comes, only its glimmerings shine, in the souls of the z̲addikim of each generation and in the letters of the Torah, which they study day and night." "In the days to come," when His people Israel will consist only of z̲addikim, God will bring that light out from where He had kept it hidden and will illuminate the whole world with it. Once again, the world below will shine spiritually as in the first hours of the universe, and the human body — the "flesh" — now "purified" and transparent, will once again be clothed in "garments of light." "And the glory of the Lord shall be revealed, and all flesh — *basar* — shall see it together" (Isa. 40:5), "for they shall see with their own eyes the Lord returning to Zion..." (Isa. 52:8). "The sun shall no more be thy light by day; neither for brightness shall the moon give light unto thee: but the Lord shall be to thee an everlasting light, and thy God thy glory" (Isa. 60:19).

Having sinned and thereby having corrupted the world, Man vaguely hears "the voice of the Lord God walking in the garden" (Gen. 3:8) of the world. To "atone" for his sin and "restore" the ruined world, man, aided by his "spiritual hearing," will have to listen attentively to God and "obey His voice," that is, observe His commandments. Only then will he be able to grasp God with total clarity, by his spiritual vision.

"He will see what he hears and he will hear what he sees" as at the time of the revelation on Sinai, when "all the people saw the voices" (Ex. 20:15). (They saw, says the *Zohar H̲adash*, "the letters of the Decalogue which appeared out of those voices.")

The revelation on Sinai is directly connected with the eschatological age. The Decalogue opens with the evocation of the Exodus "out of the Land of Egypt, out of the house of bondage" (Ex. 20:2), and that exodus prefigures the exodus from the "exile" of the future. The revelation on Sinai is linked with the messianic age. The "giving of the Torah" indicates that the harmful effects of the "stain of sin" ceased for the time being, having been redressed by a *tikkun*. The material creation of the world should have been completed at the time of the revelation on Sinai, since thenceforth it is based spiritually on the Decalogue. It was on Sinai that the Torah and the mitzvot were revealed and promulgated as vital instruments for the world's salvation, and it was then that the preparation for the messianic age began.

In the "days of the Messiah," the creation of the world will have attained its goal, good will be distinct from evil, and evil things will be transformed into good. What is material will become spiritual; what is external and obscure will fade away; and that which is internal and luminous will reappear.

God desired *le-zakkot*, "to favour," "to confer a right on" Israel with the Torah and its numerous mitzvot. In the days of the Messiah, Israel will have succeeded, by its esteem and observance of this gift, in reaching a *hizdakkut*, a "purification," a *hizdakekhut*, a "clarification" (drawing their strength from their common root *le-zakkot*), a total "sanctification."* In those days, Man who has been enriched by his *zekhut*, "merit," made *zakh*, clear (because of his *zekhut*) — "pure," "clear," "far seeing" — "will see the voice" of God.

---

* When a Jew is about to fulfil a mitzvah, he recites the following blessing: "Praise be to Thee, O Lord our God, King of the Universe, who has sanctified us by Thy mitzvot." The sincere performance of the mitzvot purifies, spiritualizes and hallows believing Jews; it enables them to penetrate the meaning of each mitzvah and to draw near to Him who has "sent" His mitzvot here below.

God is indebted to Israel.

Is it only the *zaddik* who can lead mankind, the world, to apprehend God by sight, to recognize His goodness with his eyes? Is it only the *zaddik* who can hasten the divine manifestation, the *Gillui*, in the messianic age?*

Of course, in a barren world, which refuses to listen to His voice, the Creator must be content with the presence of one single *zaddik* to keep the world alive, looking towards its future "restoration," as it is written: "And the *zaddik* is the foundation of the world" (Prov. 10:25).

However, the Creator of the world, Author of both Torah and Mitzvot, wishes His Kingship to be established and accepted here below. Now, it is not proper that a kingship be recognized by one man alone, however "upright" he might be. In fact, "there is no king without a people" and "In the multitude of people is the king's glory" (Prov. 14:28). "He whose Name has spread His Majesty throughout the heavens should also be glorified on earth" by the whole people. It should be glorified on earth even more so than in the heavens.

This "*zaddik*-nation," which is destined to serve God, to "sing" the Glory of God, *Shir El*, is *Isra-el*. God "has formed this people" for Himself so that it may celebrate His Glory, so that it may be "His servant" (cf. Isa. 43:21; 44:21).

It is to Israel as a people that God has made the "gift of the Torah and the mitzvot," and not to some "persons," to some "elect," not even to the "Fathers" of the Hebrews, who nevertheless revealed Him to the world. On "this day" (of the promulgation of the Torah on Sinai), Israel became "the

---

* We read in the Psalms of David, "The heavens are the heavens of the Lord, but He has given the earth to the sons of man" (Ps. 115:16). Rabbi Menahem Mendel of Kotsk wondered, "Why has He given it to the sons of man?" And he gave this answer: "So that men should raise the earth to the height of the heavens. He who succeeds in doing this is truly a *zaddik*!"

people of the Lord their God" (cf. Deut. 27:9). It was then that God made the children of Israel a people and gave them their mission to be, for His sake, "a kingdom of priests — servants — and a holy nation" (Ex. 19:6) by keeping the Torah, by spreading it abroad in the world and fulfilling its mitzvot. (Moses himself "received the Torah on Sinai" for the sake of Israel and in order to "transmit" it to them.)

God must be "King on the earth" as He is "King in the heavens." It is Israel, "the kingdom of priests," of "servants," who, by serving God, extend "His Kingdom on earth." God has "singled out" this "holy nation" to make it a model of a "servant" people, so that all peoples may recognize at last that the Lord is "King over all the earth" (Zech. 14:9). It is only when Israel has established the "divine Kingship on earth" that the "divine Kingship in the heavens" will be perfect. (The angels themselves cannot "serve" God in heaven if Israel does not "serve" Him here below.) God thanks Israel, as it were, for the "love and charity which it shows Him." In fact, "if Israel had not accepted my Torah, where would My Kingship exist?" — how could it have been established on earth? Thus God is indebted to Israel....

> The people of Israel is not only the sum total of all its members, each having his own personality; the people of Israel has its own personality.

For the Reign of God to be established on earth, God must reign over individual men as well as over the community. He reigns insofar as His Torah and his mitzvot are respected. In fact, any individual Jew cannot by himself study the whole Torah to its depths; he cannot exhaust its riches, fulfil all its mitzvot and penetrate the hidden mysteries of each one. Certain passages of the Torah (as well as certain prayers) ought only to be read "in community"; certain mitzvot can only be discharged by the community (especially by the community as a nation, as a State), although the community must then appeal to its individual members.

There is, therefore, a close bond between the Israelites as individual members of the people of Israel and the people of Israel which embraces them. It is not enough to say that there is a common identity of existence and of name in that the individual and the people are called Israel. Each Jew is linked by his soul, and the whole people by its soul, to a spiritual "root" in the world above. The people of Israel here below corresponds to the *Keneset Yisrael,* the spiritual "community of Israel" in the world above. The roots of the Israelites and those of Israel are "united" in the higher world.

Thus the people of Israel is not only the sum total of all its members, the Israelites, each of whom has his own personality; for the people, too, has its own personality, and all of its members are interdependent for the fulfilment of their respective personalities.

Thus it is that if any one of the six hundred thousand Israelites — who constituted the people of Israel prepared to receive the Torah — had not been present at Mount Sinai, the Torah could not have been revealed.

Similarly, if a single letter is missing from the Scroll of the Torah, from the *Sefer Torah,* the latter is not fit for the appointed public reading during a religious service. Each Israelite soul possesses one letter of the Torah, which was given to the whole people of Israel. It thus follows that if one letter, personifying one Jewish soul, is missing, the *Sefer Torah* is *pasul,* "defective" (though this defect can be amended). There exists between the Torah and the people of Israel a fundamental, even an ontological identity, for both were present in the Creator's Thought before the creation of the world.

> In all circumstances, the Israelite must rely on
> *Kelal Yisrael.* He cannot observe a single mitzvah
> without referring to the "Community of Israel,"
> for he could not fulfil it on his own.

As exemplified previously, the people and the individual Jew are dependent on each other because of their respective relationship to God. The Torah and the mitzvot are the bond that unites them, and the Israelite is only he who cherishes the Torah and the mitzvot, of which Israel is the only unimpeachable trustee and guardian, according to the immutable Will of God. Consequently, if a Jew "departs from the community" of Israel, he is to be regarded as having denied the divine Principle, for, according to the Zohar, the *Keneset Yisrael,* the "spiritual community of Israel," is identified with *emunah,* "faith." *Kelal Yisrael,* Israel as a whole, is without sin, as it is written, "As for Thy People, they are all *zaddikim* (upright)" (Isa. 60:21), even though some Israelites sin individually.

In all circumstances, the Israelite must rely on *kelal Yisrael.* He cannot observe a single mitzvah without reference to the "community of Israel," for he could not fulfil it alone. The Maggid of Mezeritch emphasizes the affinity between the Hebrew term *"mitzvah"* and the Aramaic word *"zavta,"* which means "company." The Jew must fulfil each mitzvah *be-zavta,* "in company," "together with," "while cleaving to." He must cleave to God on the one hand, and to Israel on the other, in order to be helped in fulfilling the mitzvah. The *yahid* — the individual Israelite — is called upon to live by the Torah and the mitzvot *yahad,* "together" with the "tribes of Israel," with the community of Israel (cf. Deut. 33:5). Even his prayers are formulated in the plural; God accepts them in particular when the Jew recites them "in community" with his co-religionists. A Jew could not alone fulfil all the mitzvot, for some of them concern Jews placed in particular situations. To fulfil a mitzvah, a Jew will therefore be led to "unite" with his co-religionists, for "whatever he lacks to fulfil the mitzvah, he may find in another" and "whatever another may lack, perhaps he himself may possess"; he therefore places himself in solidarity with, and at the disposal of, his fellow Jews in observing the mitzvot. For this reason, the kabbalists recommend that in getting ready to fulfil a mitzvah, a Jew should recite a preparatory prayer, in which he declares that he does so "in the name of all Israel." It is not out of pride that he makes this declaration. On the contrary, in his humility he feels unable to fulfil the religious duty demanded by the mitzvah fully on his own; therefore, he is relying on "all Israel." It is precisely his inability that permits him to do this, and he knows he can call on *"kelal Yisrael"* for spiritual support. In turn, he will be able to let "all Israel" benefit from the mitzvot he has himself fulfilled and which will be added to the sum of the mitzvot prescribed for "all Israel."

In this "preparatory" prayer, a Jew further declares that the mitzvah he is getting ready to fulfil "contains (potentially) all the other mitzvot, which depend upon it." He is acknowledging that he is powerless to fulfil them in their totality, for the mitzvot themselves constitute a living, unitary organism, embracing all aspects of life, which are diversified but unified. It must be remarked again that in their origin, the mitzvot formed a perfect unity, for they were proclaimed in a single *utterance* by Him who gave them on Sinai. And, states the MaHaRShA, (Rabbi Samuel Eliezer Edels, 1560-1631), they only appear in their plurality in the eyes of those who receive them, namely the children of Israel.

"Each Jew is present in every other Jew."
"That other Jew is himself."
The Jews and Israel constitute one inner, organic
unity, for they are bound to the Unity of God, the
source of their unity.

Between the Israelite as an individual and Israel as a people, therefore, there exists an active interdependence, and, even more, an existential interpenetration. In fact, the kabbalists teach us that the soul of the Jewish people is reflected in the soul of each Jew, and that the souls of all Jews are reflected in the soul of the Jewish people. "Each Jew is present in every other Jew."

This is how the kabbalists explain the suffering one Jew feels when any other Jew suffers because he is Jewish: "that other Jew is himself." And God Himself "suffers all their suffering." "I will be with him in trouble" (cf. Ps 91:15). "And the people believed: they understood that the Lord had visited — *pakad* — the children of Israel, that He had looked upon their affliction" (Ex. 4:31). *Pakad*, "He had visited them," can also mean "He gave Himself to them as a *pikkadon*, a 'pledge.' " "The Shekhinah, the Divine Presence, weeps when the *Keneset Yisrael* is oppressed" on account of its faithfulness to God and because it remains Jewish in spite of the vicissitudes that sweep down on it.

The Israelites and Israel form an inner, organic unity, for they are bound to the Unity of God, source of their unity. "Thou, Thou art one and Thy Name is One" (cf. Zech. 14:9); "For there is none like Thee...and who is like Thy people, Israel, one upon the earth!" (II Sam. 7:22-23). The Shekhinah is identified with the *Keneset Yisrael*, "the spiritual community of Israel," which means that the Presence of God never leaves the people of Israel, and that this Presence dwells in the Jew when he devotes himself to studying the Torah and seeking the deepest meaning of the mitzvot.

Therefore, a Jew begins the "preparatory prayer," which

he recites before fulfilling a mitzvah, by testifying that it will be recited for the sake of the "Name of the *Yihud*," the "Unification" of the Powers of God — reflecting the inner spiritual unification of the Jew and the people of Israel through the Torah and the mitzvot.

> **The people of Israel is called to live in close communion with God — *Devekut* — in the same way as each single Israelite.**

Devekut, a close communion with God, is by its very nature a personal experience, which can be experienced not only by each single Jew, but also by the whole people of Israel.

"Israel" knew a supreme, extraordinary form of *Devekut* when "it camped there before the mount [of Sinai]" (Ex. 19:2). "*It* camped — like a single man, with a single heart." It was there that they accepted their calling to be a "kingdom of priests" (Ex. 19:6), of "servants" — and, the Ramban adds, "in order to cleave (by *Devekut*) to the holy God, as God said (Lev. 19:2), 'speak to all the congregation of the children of Israel: You shall be holy; for I the Lord your God, am Holy.' "

In speaking about *Devekut*, Moses addressed both the people of Israel and every single Jew, alternately using the singular and the plural. He said to them, "Now, therefore, hearken [singular], O Israel, to the statutes and to the judgments that I teach you [singular] to do them, that ye [plural] may live...." "But ye [plural] that did cleave — *ha-devekim* — unto the Lord your God are alive everyone of you this day. Behold, I have taught you [plural] statutes and judgments, even as the Lord my God commanded me..." (Deut. 4: 1, 4-5).

Holiness, *Devekut*, thus concerns "the people of Israel," "the whole congregation of the children of Israel." The people of Israel is called to live in *Devekut*, as each Israelite does: the *Devekut* of Israel (the people), too, must be personal; it also is attained and expanded by respect for the mitzvot and leads to an ever-more faithful observance of them.

In the Decalogue, God addresses the whole people of Israel and, at the same time, each of the children of Israel individually.

Israel, the people of the Torah, and the Israelite, the man of the mitzvot, cleave to their God collectively and individually; they help one another to carry out, in a worthwhile manner, the task God has assigned them, namely, to remain faithful to the Torah and the mitzvot and, thanks to their fidelity, to lead the world towards salvation.

In the Decalogue, the quintessence of the Torah and the mitzvot, God addresses Israel; however, it was in the "desert," a land not possessed by any nation, nor inhabited by any people, that He proclaimed His Ten Utterances, thereby showing that these were intended for all peoples, for mankind throughout the world.

In the Decalogue, God addresses the whole people of Israel and, at the same time, each of the children of Israel individually. The Voice of God speaks to all; however, each perceives it on a personal level, according to his own capacity to interpret it and to act in accordance with it.

The people of Israel responds to God's call, but it is also each of its children who agrees to fulfil, personally, what God requires. "And all the people answered [singular] with one voice and said: All that the Lord has spoken will we do" (Ex. 24:3).*

Each of the Israelites present at the foot of Mount Sinai made the demands of the Torah his own, "as if the Torah had been given to him alone," "was only for him," as if the mitzvot had been ordained for him alone.

The time of the revelation on Sinai, the proclamation of

---

* See also Ex. 19:8 and 24:7 for the plural used in place of the singular.

the Torah and the mitzvot, was a messianic time: a time of *Gillui Shekhinah*, of the "manifestation of the Divine Presence" among men. In order that this effusion of divine "grace" upon men might take place — "grace" that was concentrated in the Torah — the whole of the people of Israel and each of the children of Israel had to be present, filled with a joy compounded of the fear and love of God.

The teachings that were given in that revelation of messianic consequence have been, since that day, sometimes rejected, sometimes loyally accepted. The world falls and rises again, but in spite of its zigzag progress, in spite of its painful vicissitudes, it moves towards total messianic salvation, for this must inevitably come to pass: it is inscribed in the very act of the first Creation.* The time of salvation was foreseen by the Creator and cannot fail to happen, but through his free will, man can influence the progress of history and so can "hasten" the coming of the salvation that the world so urgently requires. If man is truly "worthy," he will be able to "make the days of the Messiah come." Then Israel and humanity will come out of exile, they will be "set free from their distressing imprisonment," and, with a joy compounded of the love and fear of God, they will celebrate the *Gillui*, the "revelation" of the Goodness of God and the advent of His Reign.

> **Every man must regard himself as if he were alone in the world; he will then take upon himself responsibility for the world's salvation.**

God calls Man to labour with Him, his Creator, in the

---

* *Reshit*, the "beginning" of the world, will reappear in its pure form in *She'erit*, the "remainder" of the world, which will experience the messianic age. *Reshit* and *She'erit* will meet (these two words are formed with the same letters differently arranged). Similarly, the Adam who sinned is destined to be transfigured and become the Adam of Redemption. ADaM: Adam, David, *Mashi'ah* (Messiah).

spiritual "consolidation" and salvation of the world. This call was not addressed solely to Israel and the Israelites gathered at Mount Sinai; it is addressed to each Jew personally. According to the Sages, "Each Jew, each man, must say to himself, 'it is for love of me that the world was created.' " He is therefore responsible for this salvation and must work towards it, keeping faith with the Torah and the mitzvot of God. Each must regard himself as if he were alone in the world; then he will take upon himself the responsibility for the world's salvation. Each must remember that it is said of him, "There is no man other than you in the place where you are; try then to be a Man"; it is upon you that the future of this place rests. Emotionally affected, man can then say to himself, "Yes, the Holy One, blessed be He, has only me in this world; and as for me, I have only Him to whom I can turn...."

Hillel (1st century), known for his goodness and humility, once expressed this audacious thought: "If I — *ani* — am here, everything is here!" If he was able to say this, it was because he relied, to fulfil the task incumbent upon him, upon Him whom the Zohar called *Ani*, "I am," upon His Presence "here." Because he was ingrained with, and established in, the "I am" of God, who Alone is the true "I," the "I" of Hillel was truly great.

> One single man can "destroy" the world "in a single hour," but he can also "in a single hour" "gain the world" and prepare himself for the world above.
> "The 'return to God' of the whole world begins with the 'return to God' of a single man."

"Adam (Man) was created alone" so that men might know that one man can bring about the "fall" of the world, the "world's loss," but also that one man can work for its restoration, can "build" it up anew; one man can "destroy" the world "in a single hour," but he can also, "in a single hour," "gain the world," prepare himself for the world above.*

However, it can happen that "sitting solitary," in silence, and meditating on his precarious circumstances, man would ask, "Who am I and what is my life? How is it that the weight of the world has been put on my shoulders and that I am required to carry out this immense task of saving the world?"

If that man, who is "sitting solitary," devotes himself to the study of the Torah and the fulfilment of its mitzvot, the instruments needed for the world's salvation, he will become aware of a comforting voice which says to him, "Have confidence in *yourself*! God, who made you, knows you; He does not require of you anything you cannot do. Do not consider yourself 'evil' in your own eyes."** He will hear a voice urging him: "Be a *zaddik* (an upright man), and not a *rasha* (a wicked man)! *You* can become a *zaddik*, and although 'there is no perfect *zaddik* on earth,' you can be a *zaddik* who might be 'the foundation of the world' " (cf. Prov. 10:25).

---

* The sages of Israel affirm that "Adam was created alone" so that none of his descendants might claim to have more noble ancestors than others, as well as to show the unique worth of each human being and the respect due to him: each human being "is worth the whole world."

** "Do not look upon yourself as 'evil' in your own eyes." This saying of the Mishnah (Avot 2:13) requires man not to despise himself, not to undervalue the powers that are always in him to help him do good.

   To give greater force to this advice of the Mishnah, the Zohar takes King David as an example. He, the humble man of prayer, said to God in his psalms (86:2), "Preserve my soul, for I am a devout man — a *hasid*." However, this claim did not detract from his humility.

   Some commentators have pointed out that in this saying of the Mishnah, the phrase *bifnei azmekha*, "in your own eyes," can also mean "for yourself." The meaning of this saying would then be: the man who lives solely for himself, with no concern for others, can truly be considered a *rasha*, a "wicked person." To such a man, the Sages advise, "Do not be a *rasha*, a 'wicked person' living solely for yourself!"

It is to such a Jew, who as we have seen, does not think himself capable of fulfilling a mitzvah without relying on *kelal Yisrael*, on the "whole of Israel," that the immense work of the world's salvation is entrusted. In fact, the Talmud and the *Zohar Hadash* teach that the sins of the world can be pardoned by the "return" to God of a *yahid*, one single man. The Ba'al Shem Tov says, "The 'return' of the world begins with the 'return' of a *yahid*, of one man alone." ("In the world," says Rabbi Nahman of Bratslav, great grandson of the Ba'al Shem Tov, "man is a symbol of separation and union alike:" he is at the same time separate from, and united to, other men.) "Every human being can, by his deeds, tip the scales of the whole world to the side of merit," towards good and salvation, state the Sages of Israel.

Taking fresh confidence in himself, accepting the task entrusted to him, the *yahid* will understand that the *avodat ha-kodesh*, the "holy work" he is undertaking, can truly be the harbinger of salvation. His confidence will be so great that he will ask himself, "When, then, will my 'labour' equal that of my Fathers?" His Fathers — Abraham, Isaac, and Jacob — were truly "alone" in a corrupt world: they were "alone" in revealing the existence of the one God, in making His Will known, to "make souls" (cf. Gen. 12:5) — that is, to form consciences that would search for Him and root themselves in Him. The Fathers celebrated His reign on earth ahead of time; therefore they were able to achieve the spreading of the first "messianic lights" in this world. Now, their example must stimulate and sustain the "children of Abraham, Isaac, and Jacob," the "believing sons of believers"!

The messianic era is the "sum," the fulfilment, of
all the preceding ages that prepared the way for
it.
Today, the way is being prepared for the reunion
of past and future by the daily observance of the
Torah and the mitzvot.

The question, "When will my 'labour' equal that of my
Fathers?", which is asked by the faithful Jew who is deter-
mined to fulfil his task of salvation, demonstrates that he is,
nevertheless, uncertain of being able to do so. He tells himself,
" 'The ancients were like the sons of angels.' Who among the
descendants of our Fathers — Abraham, Isaac, and Jacob —
could compare with them?" Should such a man therefore give
up working for the world's salvation? Certainly not. It is true
that "the task is immense," but "you are not expected to finish
the work alone, even though you have no right to refuse to
take part." You ought to realize that your contribution is
necessary, and possibly even decisive.

The messianic era is the "sum," the fulfilment of all the ages
that preceded it and prepared the way for it. If one single day,
even one hour, were lacking from these preparatory times, the
perfecting and advent of the messianic age could not take place.
So it is that the history of the world, from its creation to its
completion, constitutes a painful messianic process, every instant having its place in the unfolding of this process.

The coming of the Messiah will signal the true and full
realization of the messianic era. Moreover, the person of
the Messiah had been designated, through his "name"
before the world's creation, and through his "spirit" at the
moment of creation; and yet he will attain his "full stature"
only when Jewish participation is consummated. All Jews
of all times must contribute personally to the coming of the
Messiah: they are called upon to "sanctify" the times in
which they live through Torah and mitzvot, thus, by their
"merits," bringing forward the fullness of messianic time,

a condition vital to the coming of the Messiah.

Man has a particular affinity with the times in which he lives. As the Gaon of Vilna says, man is the only creature whose creative existence is in close relationship with time, with his time: "time is the friend of man"; "a human being and time constitute a couple — man and wife." A man and his time are so close that they identify with one another. *Zeman*, "time," *mezammen*, "invites" man to make it fruitful, to give it a meaning and a content by fulfilling a mitzvah. Each of the three hundred and sixty-five days of the year entreats him not to commit an *averah*, a "transgression" of the Torah's law, which includes "three hundred and sixty-five prohibitions." In turn, man invites time to leave its "sterile," futile immobility in order to labour with him. So man will be what he does with his time, and time will be what man makes of it. Man will see that not a moment of his time is wasted, and time will make of him a man who is fully alive. Together, they will transfigure one another to enter — "full of days" (Gen. 24:1) like Abraham — into living Eternity.

Of all creatures, man alone is conscious of the presence of time, which appears to him not only as cyclical and recurring, but above all as linear, inasmuch as he recognizes that time has a direction, a movement towards a goal.

Linear time implies not only progress towards an end, but also continuous contact with its starting point. From this arises the importance of the mitzvah that commands the Jew: "*Zakhor*," "Remember...." The starting point moves along a linear trajectory towards the moment when it will coincide with the finishing point.

Throughout and during each of his days, a Jew must sense the presence of the starting point without losing sight of the "hoped for" and "expected" goal. The "today," *ha-yom*, must be for him the potential meeting place of these two points that he aims to bring as close together as possible. The "today" thus marks the granting of the prayer in which a Jew asks God to "renew our days as of old" (Lam. 5:21), to "revive our days as they were in the past."

For a Jew, "thinking in retrospect" and "having in prospect" join in the "today," where they nurture one another. Retrospection means bringing into the present an event that happened in the past; having in prospect means anticipation of the event that will take place and which a Jew evokes and wishes to see happen "soon, in our days."

The reuniting of past and future is being prepared in the present by the observance, on this very day, of the Torah and the *mitzvot*: "Let these words — these commandments — which I command thee *ha-yom* (this day), be graven in thy heart" (Deut. 6:6). "This day" means: "Each day let them be like new in your eyes." Each day they will be new again, not only because they will find afresh their original, "past" newness, but also because they will be renewed by the *hiddushei Torah*, the "new," "original" interpretations of the texts of the Torah, and by the discoveries that faithful Jews joyfully make of the as-yet-unexpected depths of the mitzvot.

> Every morning, a man should regard himself as having been created anew and put into a world that itself is also "a new Creation."

Thus the time by which the Jew links the past and the future, the time that he lives according to the Torah, God's Charter of Creation, becomes a time of uninterrupted creation. This time "emulates" its Creator, He who "in His Goodness, each day, without end, renews the Primal Works" of Creation. In truth, each day God breathes into the world abundant new life: He "gives it life."

Man, to whom God has given responsibility for this world, must also, like his Creator, act each day with a care for perpetual renewal; he must strive continually to renew and to refashion himself and his achievements.

In fact, writes the author of the *Kedushat Levi* (Rabbi Levi Isaac of Berdichev, 1740-1809), God invites man "to contemplate that which He is giving him today. Each day He presents him with a bright new world, one rich in new blessings. And to man, whom He has put into this world to serve Him, He makes the gift of an intelligence that each day is newly enlightened so that he may receive a fresh abundance of blessings." In an earlier century, the author of the *Roke'ah* (Rabbi Eliezer of Worms, 1165-1230) had bid the Jew acknowledge that "every morning, after a night's sleep prefiguring death, the Holy One, blessed be He, restores the soul to its place in his body, which before his reawakening, could be regarded as dead...."

Every morning, man should therefore regard himself as a "new creation" in a newly created world, says the author of the *Degel Mahaneh Efrayim* (Rabbi Moses Ephraim of Sudylkow, 1740-1800). Man really *is* different every day from what he *was* the previous day and from what he *will be* tomorrow. Each day he is seeking his own identity; he is trying to be what he ought to be: himself.

> **As each man is unique, so his mission is also unique. In the world, everyone has a particular "task" to perform.**

"God created [the world] in order to perfect — *la-asot* — what He had created," says the Ba'al Shem Tov. Man is called upon to emulate his Creator by "creating in order to perfect," *la-asot*, what He has created; in order to add what is "lacking," to restore what is broken or "spoiled," to reunite what has become severed. These "missing things," these "breakages," these "spoilings," these "separations" were preconceived by the Creator so that man could "restore" them by using his creative faculties, so that he should have the "merit" of bringing them a *tikkun*.

Man always has a mission to perform, whose assignment is new every day, for every day he himself is a new man acting in a new world.*

The *He'arah*, the "illumination" that God sends down upon each day, is always unique. Ever since God created the world, states the Ari ha-Kadosh, there have never been two identical days. Each day has its own *behinah*, its particular personality and identity. Facing this *behinah* of each day, there appears the individual *behinah* of each man, each Jew, serving God. "Man was created individually" for "each man has his own thoughts, his own way of judging and acting, his own faculties." Therefore, it is said: "Offend no man," for each has virtually the qualities that others do not have. Each man is a unique, new creation; before he was born there was no one in the world like him, and that is why he was born: his unique, irreplaceable being was needed.

The identity of each man, each Jew, is revealed in his "efforts," destined to complete the tasks which will bring about the messianic times, to contribute to the completion of the "stature" of the Messiah, to hasten the *Gillui Kevodo Yitbarakh*, the "manifestation of His Glory, blessed be He."

The task required of man today is different from that which will fall to him tomorrow; if it is today's "task" that he must continue tomorrow, then the manner of doing it will be different.**

---

* The *yezer ha-ra*, the "evil tendency," is also "renewed each day" in man, and each day man must invent new means to combat this "old and foolish king."

** Even in regard to prayer, the prayer that the Jew offers today is different from that offered on any previous day. "There have never been two identical prayers in this world," stated the Ari Ha-Kadosh. "And there never will be, until the coming of the Messiah," added the Or haHayyim haKadosh (Rabbi Hayyim ben Attar, 1696-1743).

Today's "task" cannot be done tomorrow, for tomorrow
the man responsible for that "task" will be a new man, and
his "task" will also be new. So if "I do not finish my task today,
when shall I do it?"

Man must not leave today's "task" unfinished, for this
"today" is irreversible, irreplaceable. If he does not finish it, the
empty space that will result in the sequence of days leading to
the days of the Messiah will break the whole order of days.*

> The man of the Kabbalah attempts every day to
> discover his exact assignment, which means for
> him to discover the scattered "divine sparks,"
> which he himself is called upon to "gather up"
> and to lead back to their original "roots."
> All the "liberated" "sparks" will form the roots
> of the total "messianic liberation."

Thus a Jew is born to accomplish a mission which he alone
is able to do this very day, thereby hastening the advent of
the days of the Messiah.

But how shall he recognize the mission assigned to him,
which he must integrate into the economy of Israel's mission?

This is what preoccupies the man of the Kabbalah.

Every day he attempts to discover his exact assignment,
namely, to discover the particular "sacred sparks," scattered
and exiled, which he himself is called upon to "reveal," to
"select," to "gather up" in order to "elevate" and to lead back
to their "roots" and to reintegrate into their place of origin.

Thus he will labour to restore peace in the world, and
between this world and the world above, and to create harmony between all the worlds.

---

* *Avar zemano...* "He who recites the Shema morning and evening and fails
to do so one occasion, is compared to one who has never recited the
Shema!"

Every day new "sparks," proper for that day, await that particular Jew who is able to release them, states the author of *The Toledot* (Rabbi Jacob Joseph of Polonnoye, 1704-84). The *berurim*, the "clarifications," must be performed on a particular day by one particular man and no other; that man must set free the "sparks" that are waiting for *him*, those with which *he* has affinities.

All the "sparks" set free, will form the roots of the *Ge'ullah Shelemah*, the total "messianic deliverance."

Great is the "merit" of one who succeeds in discovering the "sparks" which it is incumbent upon him to set free.

This man is truly a *zaddik*.

He is carrying out the *tikkunim*, the "restorations" that have been assigned to him, and for him alone; he is making up the sum of the particular *tikkunim*, which must be integrated into the general *Tikkun* of the world, and which are essential for the world to regain its original state of enlightenment.

Through his "labours," he is fulfilling the requisite conditions for the advent of the messianic age. Through his indispensable contributions to the fulfilment of the "stature" of the Messiah, he is paving the way for his coming.

"To complete" the work of salvation — that is the mission of the *zaddik*.

"To contribute" to the work of salvation — that is the mission of the individual Jew, of every man.

It is in being faithful to this daily process of "renovation," of *hithadshut*, that the *zaddik* and the Jew can successfully complete their missions.

This human "renovation" will be crowned and rewarded in the grand, thorough "renewal" of the messianic times.

Being satisfied with the work of "renewal" fulfilled by Man, by the *zaddik*, by Israel, God "reveals" Himself in a shining *Gillui Shekhinah*, in an extraordinary "manifestation of His Presence," and declares, "Here am I; I am creating new heavens and a new earth" (Isa. 65:17).

Once again, the heavens and the earth are new; new as in the moment of their first appearance, the moment in which they were created, when "In the beginning God created the heavens and the earth"; creation then (*bara*, in the past tense) — creation now (*bore*, in the present tense). The starting point and the finishing point are united in one single point. The new creation meets the old one, for the old has become new and the new, old. It is thus that the Creator, the "Ancient of Days," willed it from their first creation; it is thus that He sees them in this moment; and we, Israel, we human beings, we shall see "our days renewed as of old" (cf. Lam. 5:21).

The *Keter*, the divine, royal "Crown," which preceded the creation of the world, and which is the first of the *Sefirot*, the divine creative manifestations, is at last accepted within the *Malkhut*, the divine, terrestrial "Kingdom," the "foundation" of the *Sefirot*. And in the vision of the kabbalist poet, Man, Israel, "places the Crown on the King's head...."

So God is enthroned as "King over all the earth" (Zech. 14:9), and man sees his difficult and awe-inspiring mission finally accomplished. The Reign of God is established here below and "confirmed" in the world above and throughout all the worlds, which become one under the Sovereignty of the One, the only God.

"May the pleasant grace of the Lord our God be upon us. and the work of our hands confirm unto us..." (Ps. 90:17).

Glossary

Aggadah, name given to those sections of Talmud and Midrash containing homiletic expositions of the Bible, stories, legends, folklore, anecdotes, or maxims. In contradistinction to *Halakhah.*

Berakhah (pl. *berakhot*), blessing; formula of praise and thanksgiving.

Devekut, "devotion"; attachment or adherence to God; communion with God.

Erez Israel, Land of Israel.

Galut, "exile"; the condition of the Jewish people in dispersion.

Gaon (pl. *geonim*), head of academy in post-talmudic period, especially in Babylonia; Jewish religious scholar.

Habad, initials of *hokhmah, binah, da'at*: "wisdom, understanding , knowledge"; Hasidic movement founded in White Russia by Rabbi Shneur Zalman of Lyady (18th century).

Haggadah, ritual recited in the home on Passover eve at *seder* table.

Ha-Kadosh Barukh Hu: "The Holy One, blessed be He"; a cognomen of God.

Halakhah (pl. *Halakhot*), an accepted decision in rabbinic law. Also refers to those parts of the Talmud concerned with legal matters. In contradistinction to *Aggadah.*

Hallel, term referring to Psalms 113-118 in liturgical use.

Hanukkah, eight-day celebration commemorating the victory of Judas Maccabaeus over the Syrian king Antiochus Epiphanes and the subsequent rededication of the Temple (circa 165 B.C.E.).

Hasid, adherent of Hasidism.

Hasidei Ashkenaz, medieval pietist movement among the Jews of Germany.

Hasidism: (1) religious revivalist movement of popular mysticism among Jews of Western Germany in the Middle Ages; (2) religious movement founded by Rabbi Israel Ba'al Shem Tov in the first half of the 18th century in Poland and Russia.

"Holy One blessed be He", see *Ha-Kadosh.*

Kabbalah (Cabala, Cabbala), the Jewish mystical tradition.

Kaddish, liturgical doxology.

Kavvanah, "intention"; term denoting the spiritual concentration accompanying prayer and the performance of ritual or of a commandment.

Kiddush, prayer of sanctification, recited over wine or bread on eve of Sabbaths and festivals.

Kiddush ha-Shem, term connoting martyrdom or act of strict integrity in support of Judaic principles.

Mazzah (pl. *Mazzot):* unleavened bread replacing bread during the week of the Passover.

Midrash, method of interpreting Scripture to elucidate legal points (*Midrash Halakhah*), or to bring out lessons by stories or homiletics (*Midrash Aggadah*). Also the name for a collection of such rabbinic interpretations.

Mikveh, ritual bath.

Mishnah, earliest codification of Jewish Oral Law.

Mitzvah, biblical or rabbinic injunction; applied also to good or charitable deeds.

Nizozot, "sparks"; mystical term for sparks of the divine light imprisoned in all matter.

Omer, first sheaf cut during the barley harvest, offered in the Temple on the second day of Passover.

Omer, Counting of (Heb. *Sefirat ha-Omer*), 49 days counted from the day on which the *omer* was first offered in the Temple (according to the Rabbis, the 16th of Nisan, i.e., the second day of Passover) until the festival of *Shavuot;* a period of semi-mourning, for historical reasons.

Pesah, Passover.

Purim, festival held on Adar 14 or 15 in commemoration of the delivery of the Jews of Persia in the time of Esther (4th century B.C.E.).

Rosh Ha-Shanah, two-day holiday (one day in biblical and early Mishnaic times) at the beginning of the month of Tishri (September-October), traditionally the Jewish New Year.

Seder, ceremony observed in the Jewish home on the first night of Passover (outside Erez Israel first two nights), when the *Haggadah* is recited.

Sefer ha-Bahir, one of the most ancient books of the Kabbalah.

Sefer Torah, manuscript scroll of the Pentateuch for public reading in synagogue.

Sefer Yezirah, "Book of Creation," one of the basic books of the Kabbalah.

Sefirot, the ten creative powers emanating from God.

Shaddai, name of God found frequently in the Bible and commonly translated "Almighty."

Shavuot, Pentecost; festival of Weeks; second of the three annual pilgrim festivals; commemorates the receiving of the Torah at Mount Sinai.

Shekhinah, Divine Presence.

Shema (Yisrael), "Hear O Israel" (Deut. 6:4). Judaism's confession of faith, proclaiming the absolute unity of God.

Shulhan Arukh, Jewish Law as codified by R. Joseph Caro (1488-1575).

Siddur, among Ashkenazim, the volume containing the daily prayers (in distinction to the *Mahzor,* containing those for the festivals).

Simhat Torah, holiday marking the completion in the synagogue of the annual cycle of reading the Pentateuch; in Erez Israel observed on *Shemini Azeret* (outside Erez Israel a separate celebration on the following day).

Sparks, see *Nizozot.*

Sukkah, booth or tabernacle erected for *Sukkot* when, for seven days, religious Jews "dwell" or at least eat in the *sukkah* (Lev. 23:42).

Sukkot, festival of Tabernacles; last of the three pilgrim festivals, beginning on the 15th of Tishri (see *Sukkah*).

Tallit (gadol), four-cornered prayer shawl with fringes (*zizit*) at each corner.

Talmud, "teaching"; compendium of discussions on the Mishnah by generations of scholars and jurists in many academies over a period of several centuries (200-500 C.E.). The Jerusalem (or Palestinian) Talmud mainly contained the discussions of the Palestinian Sages. The Babylonian Talmud incorporates the parallel discussions in the Babylonian academies (see *Mishnah*).

Talmud Torah, term generally applied to Jewish religious (and ultimately to talmudic) study; also to traditional Jewish religious public schools.

Tanna (pl. *tanna'im*), rabbinic teacher of mishnaic period.

Tefillin, phylacteries, small leather cases containing passages from Scripture and affixed on the forehead and arm by male Jews during the recital of morning prayers.

Torah, (1) Pentateuch or the Pentateuchal scroll for reading in synagogue; (2) entire body of traditional Jewish teaching and literature.

Yom Kippur, or *Yom ha-Kippurim,* Day of Atonement, solemn fast day observed on the 10th of Tishri.

Zaddik, the Just: person outstanding for his faith and piety; especially a Hasidic rabbi or leader.

Zimzum, "contraction"; mystical term denoting the process whereby God withdraws or contracts within Himself, thus leaving a primordial vacuum in which creation can take place; primordial exile or self-limitation of God.

Zizit, fringes attached to the *tallit* and *tallit katan.*

Zohar, Sefer ha-Zohar, the "Book of Splendour"; mystical commentary on the Pentateuch; main textbook of Kabbalah.